"*Language for God in Patristic Tradition* has the distinction of being both a marvelously clear introduction and a sophisticated exploration of the intellectual world and work of early Christianity in relation to one of the thorniest problems in Scripture: the use of human language—often violent language—to describe God. The book is suitable for students, scholars and thoughtful inquirers alike. It is lucid, interesting and instructive—illuminating a clear description of the history of the problem with fascinating examples of ancient, learned interpreters at work in a conversation that continues today."

Robin Darling Young, associate professor of spirituality, The Catholic University of America

"One major obstacle modern people face in comprehending patristic literature is the ideas and language ancient Christian writers employed as they read the Bible and interpreted the Bible's statements and stories about God. In *Language for God in Patristic Tradition,* Mark Sheridan explains clearly and cogently both the 'why' and the 'how' of the church fathers' language of biblical anthropomorphism. He employs plenty of primary source material as he does so. Sheridan's immense learning is expressed in lively, accessible prose that will encourage and educate readers new to patristic exegesis while refreshing—and likely deepening—the perspectives of those more familiar with the world of the church fathers. Highly recommended."

Christopher A. Hall, Distinguished Professor of Theology, Eastern University

"At its core this masterful introduction to the patristic language about God by Mark Sheridan is about interpreting Scripture in a manner worthy of God. This was the primary concern and challenge of the ancient Christian interpreters who interpreted Scripture primarily in a theological sense—which is what language about God should do. Our modern concern has always had more to do with a historical consciousness of the text of Scripture and so we find much of the ancient approach to Scripture unintelligible and enigmatic. This text brings us into the mindset of the Fathers' approach to interpretation in order to help us read with them the mind of the divine author of Scripture. This text should be required reading for anyone interested in the history of interpretation in the early church."

Joel C. Elowsky, associate professor of historical theology, director of the Center for the Study of Early Christian Texts, Concordia Seminary

LANGUAGE FOR GOD IN PATRISTIC TRADITION

WRESTLING WITH BIBLICAL ANTHROPOMORPHISM

MARK SHERIDAN

FOREWORD BY THOMAS C. ODEN

An imprint of InterVarsity Press
Downers Grove, Illinois

InterVarsity Press
P.O. Box 1400, Downers Grove, IL 60515-1426
World Wide Web: www.ivpress.com
Email: email@ivpress.com

InterVarsity Press® is the book-publishing division of InterVarsity Christian Fellowship/USA®, a movement of students and faculty active on campus at hundreds of universities, colleges and schools of nursing in the United States of America, and a member movement of the International Fellowship of Evangelical Students. For information about local and regional activities, write Public Relations Dept., InterVarsity Christian Fellowship/USA, 6400 Schroeder Rd., P.O. Box 7895, Madison, WI 53707-7895, or visit the IVCF website at www.intervarsity.org.

Cover design: Cindy Kiple
Interior design: Beth McGill
Image: 'Origin Teaching the Saints' by Eileen McGuckin, www.sgtt.org

ISBN 978-0-8308-4064-9 (print)
ISBN 978-0-8308-9700-1 (digital)
Printed in the United States of America ∞

Library of Congress Cataloging-in-Publication Data
Sheridan, Mark.
  Language for God in patristic tradition : wrestling with biblical
anthropomorphism / Mark Sheridan.
      pages cm
  Includes index.
  ISBN 978-0-8308-4064-9 (pbk. : alk. paper)
  1. God--Biblical teaching. 2. Anthropomorphism. 3. God
(Christianity) 4. Bible—Hermeneutics. 5. Bible—Criticism,
interpretation, etc. I. Title.
  BS544.S54 2014
  220.609'015--dc23

                                                                    2014033350

P   25   24   23   22   21   20   19   18   17   16   15   14   13   12   11   10   9   8   7   6   5   4   3   2   1

Y   36   35   34   33   32   31   30   29   28   27   26   25   24   23   22   21   20   19   18   17   16   15

Contents

Foreword

THIS BOOK WILL KEEP THE PREACHING PASTOR out of a whole lot of trouble. Constantly in biblical teaching we use human language to speak of God, knowing very well that God transcends human speech. We may stumble over the Bible's words if we are unaware of how profoundly the classic Christian tradition has examined this question. This book gives the ordinary reader access to that wisdom.

I first met Mark Sheridan in one of the most beautiful places in Rome, the University of Sant Anselmo where he was rector. I had handpicked him for a very difficult job: editing the Genesis 12–50 volume of the Ancient Christian Commentary on Scripture. That volume encompasses the biblical narrative from Abraham to the burial of Jacob in the Promised Land.

As a biblical scholar with a pastoral heart who was thoroughly immersed in the ancient Christian writers, he took the reader on a remarkable journey, introducing the thoughts of Hippolytus, Clement, Origen, Augustine, and all the major biblical interpreters who first interpreted the biblical authors' intention in using human language for God. These were the first biblical exegetes to work out the plain sense and spiritual meaning of the Bible's language of, from, and about God in a sophisticated way for all subsequent generations.

Thomas C. Oden

Note of Gratitude

My happy experience with the preparation of the second volume of the Ancient Christian Commentary on Scripture (*Genesis 12–50*), published by InterVarsity Press, prompted me to propose this book as an additional source for the same audience. I wish to thank first of all the editorial staff at InterVarsity Press, especially James Hoover, who approved the proposal, and David Congdon, who oversaw the process of editing. My thanks are due also to the anonymous reader of the Press and to several friends who read portions of the manuscript and offered helpful suggestions: J. Brian Butler, Michael W. Oborne, Miloš Vojár and Ignatius Bartsch.

Mark Sheridan

Abbreviations

ABBREVIATIONS OF THE WORKS OF ORIGEN

The abbreviations used for the works of Origen are those found in *Origeniana Quinta*, ed. Robert J. Daly (Leuven: Leuven University Press, 1992).

CCels	*Contra Celsum*
ComCt	*Commentary on the Canticle of Canticles*
ComJn	*Commentary on John*
ComMt	*Commentary on Matthew*
ComRm	*Commentary on Romans*
Hom 1R(1S)	*Homilies on 1 Kings (1 Samuel)*
HomGn	*Homilies on Genesis*
HomEx	*Homilies on Exodus*
HomEz	*Homilies on Ezekiel*
HomJos	*Homilies on Joshua*
HomJd	*Homilies on Judges*
HomJr	*Homilies on Jeremiah*
HomLev	*Homilies on Leviticus*
HomNum	*Homilies on Numbers*
PArch	*Peri Archon—De Principiis*
Philoc	*Philocalia*

ABBREVIATIONS USED FOR PHILONIC TREATISES

The abbreviations used for the works of Philo are those used in David T. Runia, *Philo in Early Christian Literature: A Survey*, Compendium Rerum Iudaicarum ad Novum Testamentum (Minneapolis: Fortress; Assen: Van Gorcum, 1993), p. xv.

Abr.	*De Abrahamo*
Congr.	*De congressu eruditionis gratia*
Deus	*Quod Deus sit immutabilis*
Leg.	*Legum allegoriae*
Migr.	*De migratione Abrahami*
Mos.	*De vita Moysis*
Opif.	*De opificio mundi*
Plant.	*De plantatione*
Post.	*De posteritate Caini*
QG	*Questiones et solutiones in Genesim*
Sacr.	*De sacrificiis Abelis et Caini*
Sobr.	*De sobrietate*
Somn.	*De somniis*

ABBREVIATIONS OF GREEK AND LATIN WORKS

Augustine

Doctr. chr.	*De doctrina christiana*
Enarrat. Ps.	*Enarrationes in Psalmos*

Clement of Alexandria

Paed.	*Paedagogus*
Prot.	*Protrepticus*
Strom.	*Stromata*

Cicero

Tusc.	*Tusculanae disputationes*

Eusebius of Caesarea

Hist. eccl.	*Historia Ecclesiastica*
Praep. evang.	*Praeparatio evangelica*
Dem. evang.	*Demonstratio evangelica*
Comm. Ps.	*Commentarius in Psalmos*

Irenaeus

Adv. haer.	*Adversus haereses*

John Cassian
>   *Inst.*   *Institutiones (Institutes)*

Seneca
>   *Ira*   *De Ira*

Sextus Empiricus
>   *Pyrrh.*   *Pyrrhoniae hypotyposes*

Tertullian
>   *Marc.*   *Adversus Marcionem*

ABBREVIATIONS OF SERIES AND JOURNALS

AB   Anchor Bible

ACCS   Ancient Christian Commentary on Scripture

ACT   Ancient Christian Texts. Downers Grove, IL: IVP Academic, 2009–.

ANF   Alexander Roberts and James Donaldson, eds. Ante-Nicene Fathers. 10 vols. Buffalo, NY: Christian Literature, 1885–1887. Reprint, Grand Rapids: Eerdmans, 1951–1956; Reprint, Peabody, MA: Hendrickson, 1994.

ACW   Ancient Christian Writers: The Works of the Fathers in Translation. Mahwah, NJ: Paulist, 1946–.

CSEL   Corpus Scriptorum Ecclesiasticorum Latinorum. Vienna, 1866–.

CCL   Corpus Christianorum. Series Latinorum. Turnhout, Belgium: Brepols, 1953–.

CPG   M. Geerard, ed. *Clavis Patrum Graecorum*. Turnhout, Belgium: Brepols, 1974–1987.

EHA   Marco Conti, trans. *Commentary on the Epistle to the Hebrews*. Works of Ephrem in Armenian. ACCS translation project.

FC   Fathers of the Church: A New Translation. Washington, DC: Catholic University of America Press, 1946–.

GCS   Die griechischen christlichen Schriftsteller der ersten drei Jahrhunderte. Berlin: Akademie-Verlag, 1897–.

HOP   Ephrem the Syrian. *Hymns on Paradise*. Edited by S. Brock.
        New York: St. Vladimir's Seminary Press, 1990.

ICC   International Critical Commentary

IOEP   John Chrysostom. *Interpretatio omnium epistularum Pauli-
        narum*. Edited by F. Field. Oxford: Clarendon, 1849–1862.

JECS   *Journal of Early Christian Studies*

JTS   *Journal of Theological Studies*

LCL   Loeb Classical Library. Cambridge, MA: Harvard University
        Press; London: Heinemann, 1912–.

MKGK   *Matthäus-Kommentare aus der griechischen Kirche*. Edited by
        Joseph Reuss. Berlin: Akademie-Verlag, 1957.

NPNF   Philip Schaff et al., eds. A Select Library of the Nicene and
        Post-Nicene Fathers of the Christian Church. 2 series (14 vols.
        each). Buffalo, NY: Christian Literature, 1887–1894; Reprint,
        Grand Rapids: Eerdmans, 1952–1956; Reprint, Peabody, MA:
        Hendrickson, 1994.

NETS   New English Translation of the Septuagint

NTA   K. Staab, ed. *Pauluskommentare aus der griechischen Kirche:
        Aus Katenenhandschriften gesammelt und herausgegeben*
        (Pauline Commentary from the Greek Church: Collected and
        edited by Catena Writings). NT Abhandlungen 15. Munster in
        Westfalen: Aschendorff, 1933. (Commentators: Didymus the
        Blind of Alexandria, pp. 6-44; Severian of Gabala, pp. 225-98;
        Theodore of Mopsuestia, pp. 172-200; Theodoret of Cyr, pp.
        226-460; Gennadius of Constantinople, pp. 118-19; Oecu-
        menius of Tricca, pp. 432-46.)

PL   J. P. Migne, ed. Patrologia Cursus Completus, Series Latina.
        221 vols. Paris: Migne, 1844–1864.

PG   J. P. Migne, ed. Patrologia Cursus Completus, Series Graeca.
        166 vols. Paris: Migne, 1857–1886.

PO   Patrologia Orientalis. Paris, 1903–.

SCh H. de Lubac, J. Daniélou et al., eds. Sources Chrétiennes. Paris: Editions du Cerf, 1941–.

SA Studia anselmiana

TEM Theodore of Mopsuestia. *Epistolas b. Pauli commentarii.* Edited by H. B. Swete. Cambridge: Cambridge University Press, 1880–1882.

TU Texte und Untersuchungen

WBC Word Biblical Commentary

All uncited translations of ancient texts are the author's.

A single asterisk (*) in a footnote indicates that a previous English translation has been updated to modern English or amended for easier reading. The double asterisk (**) indicates either that a new translation has been provided or that some extant translation has been significantly amended.

Introduction

ANCIENT PHILOSOPHERS AND THEOLOGIANS, Greek, Jewish and
Christian, were critical of certain presentations of God that attributed to
the divinity human characteristics and emotions. For them these were not
merely questions for speculation or theorizing, but concepts or misunderstandings that could influence human behavior adversely. This is a perennial problem, not just a premodern one. The goal of this book is to show
how ancient writers perceived the problem and how they dealt with it.

Ancient Christian writers accepted the Scriptures of both the Old and
New Testaments as inspired, or as "divine writings," and they were concerned that these writings should be interpreted in a way that is "fitting to"
or "worthy of God." They were also quite sensitive to the charge that many
passages in these Scriptures posed a challenge to such an understanding.
However, they were not the first to confront the problem. Many Greek and
Jewish authors had already faced the challenge. One of the earliest, if not
the earliest, to formulate the problem was the Greek philosopher Xenophanes of Colophon, who lived in the late sixth century B.C. He has been
called an "intellectual revolutionary" for whom "the problem of God" was
central.[1] He is famous for stating, "If cattle and horses had hands, and were
able to paint with their hands, and to fashion such pictures as men do, then
horses would pattern the forms of the gods after horses, and cows after

---

[1]See Werner Jaeger, *The Theology of the Early Greek Philosophers: The Gifford Lectures 1936* (Oxford: Clarendon, 1948), pp. 41-42.

cattle, giving them just such a shape as those which they find in themselves."[2] This was generally understood as a criticism of the highly anthropomorphic depiction of the gods in Greek mythology. The surviving fragments of Xenophanes's writings were preserved because they were cited with approval by the late second-century Christian writer Clement of Alexandria, and through him they exerted influence on later Christian writers. The influence of the Greek philosophical tradition on Christian interpretation will be explained more fully later on.

Hellenistic Jewish writers experienced a similar difficulty with a literal reading of the Pentateuch, the Scriptures attributed to Moses. As the pseudonymous second-century-B.C. Jewish author of the *Letter of Aristeas* explains: "For you must not fall into the degrading idea that it was out of regard to mice and weasels and other such things that Moses drew up his laws with such exceeding care. All these ordinances were made for the sake of righteousness to aid the quest for virtue and the perfecting of character."[3] This kind of interpretation was developed extensively by later Greek-speaking Jewish writers such as Aristobulus (second century B.C.) and especially Philo of Alexandria (a contemporary of St. Paul), who greatly influenced later Christian authors.

The most influential of these Christian authors in developing the tradition of interpretation both in the East and in the West was Origen of Alexandria. One of his greatest concerns was the misinterpretation of the Scriptures on the part of the ordinary, simple people. As he stated in his basic work *On First Principles* (4.2): "[The simple] think of Him [God] things such that they would not attribute to the most cruel and unjust human being. The reason why all those we have mentioned have mistaken, impious, and vulgar conceptions about the divinity derives from the incapacity of interpreting spiritually the Scriptures, which are accepted only according to the literal sense." Origen's solution to the problem was both theoretical and practical, as will be explained at length.

---

[2] The Greek text is preserved by Clement of Alexandria, *Strom.* 5.110 (Xenophanes B 15). See Jaeger, p. 213.
[3] *Letter of Aristeas* 144, in R. H. Charles, ed., *The Apocrypha and the Pseudepigrapha of the Old Testament* (Oxford: Clarendon, 1913).

Misinterpreting the Scriptures—that is, reading them literally without an interpretation "worthy of God"—could also have a disastrous effect on the spiritual life of the Christian, as the early fifth-century Latin writer John Cassian explained: "We have heard that some people try to excuse this most destructive disease of the soul [anger] by attempting to extenuate it by a rather detestable interpretation of Scripture. They say that it is not harmful if we are angry with wrongdoing brothers, because God himself is said to be enraged and angered with those who do not want to know him or who, knowing him, disdain him."[4] For Cassian, interpreting the Scriptures in a manner "worthy of God" was a major part of the contemplative life, but it also had direct influence on the daily life of the Christian.

Modern commentators in what is usually called the "historical-critical" tradition, which dates from the late seventeenth century, tend to be focused on recovering the original meaning of the biblical texts as far as possible. That means trying to reconstruct the historical situation in which they were written, identifying the author or authors and following the development of various layers of redaction of the texts where that is pertinent. To engage in such reconstruction, it is not necessary to be a believing Christian. Ancient Christian commentators had a quite different orientation. They sought to find a meaning that was useful or relevant "for us," to use the Pauline phrase (1 Cor 9:10), in other words, a Christian meaning. The ancient commentators did not have the critical tools at their disposition to trace the Scriptures' complex historical growth, but they did engage in "theological" interpretation; that is, they interpreted the Scriptures in the light of their understanding of the nature of God. As we shall see, they found a way to neutralize the older or problematic texts by interpreting them in the light of other or later ones.

The notion of "theological interpretation" may need further explanation. First, a word about "theological." The word is being used here in the original sense of the word *theology*, which is composed from the Greek words *theos* ("God") and *logos* ("discourse"), that is, a discussion of the

---

[4]John Cassian, *The Institutes*, ACW 58, trans. and anno. Boniface Ramsey, O.P. (New York: The Newman Press, 2000), p. 193.

nature of God or of divinity. This Greek word (*theologia* and related forms) had a long history, especially in philosophical discourse, before it entered into the Judeo-Christian vocabulary.[5] Later Philo of Alexandria would call Moses the "theologian" (*theologos*), because he was intimate with God and was able to speak about the divine nature.[6] For similar reasons the Evangelist John came to be known as "the theologian." The goal here is to set in relief one aspect of ancient Christian interpretation, that of reading and interpreting from the point of view of a certain understanding of God.

The notion of "theological interpretation" should be understood here then as the search for the correct understanding of the biblical texts by the major early Christian writers, especially those in the Greek and Latin traditions. The principal tool used in this search was an understanding of God, of the divine nature, derived in part from the Greek philosophical tradition, particularly the exclusion from the divine nature of anthropomorphic (in human form) and anthropopathic (with human passions) traits, but also informed by the understanding of God as revealed by Jesus Christ, a chief aspect of which was the divine love for humankind (*philanthrōpia*). What did not conform to these essential traits had to be excluded from (or distinguished from) the "true" meaning of Scripture, and the text had to be interpreted so as to provide a meaning that both conformed to or was fitting to the divine nature and was useful. This latter criterion of usefulness derives from the statement found in 2 Timothy 3:16, that "all scripture is inspired by God and is useful for teaching, for reproof, for correction, and for training in righteousness."[7]

Perhaps it should be emphasized that this book is chiefly about specifically "Christian" interpretation. There were other kinds of interpretation of biblical texts in the ancient world, including Jewish and what the Chris-

---

[5]For a brief sketch of this history, see G. Ebeling, "Theologie," in *Die Religion in Geschichte und Gegenwart; Handwörterbuch für Theologie und Religionswissenschaft*, ed. K. Galling, 3rd ed. (Tübingen: Mohr, 1962), pp. 754-69.

[6]Philo, *Mos.* 2.115.

[7]For the notion of and the role of the "useful" in ancient interpretation, see Mark Sheridan, "The Concept of the 'Useful' as an Exegetical Tool in Patristic Exegesis," in *From the Nile to the Rhone and Beyond: Studies in Early Monastic Literature and Scriptural Interpretation* (Roma: Pontificio Ateneo Sant'Anselmo, 2012), pp. 177-82.

tians regarded as "heretical" interpretations such as those of Marcion or the various "Gnostic" interpretations of Valentinus, the *Letter of Ptolemy to Flora*, and those found in the Nag Hammadi manuscripts. Most of these, with the exception of Marcion, did not have direct influence on the development of Christian interpretation and lie outside the scope of this book. The Hellenistic Jewish interpretations, however, were to have a strong influence on Christian exegesis, as will be explained in chapter three. Many modern interpreters of different religious traditions or even secular ones can often agree on what might have been the original historical setting and meaning of particular texts, because modern interpreters seek to establish the original meaning of the biblical texts. Ancient Christian interpreters were not primarily interested in the original meaning, but rather in finding a meaning that is suitable for us—in other words, a Christian meaning.

The first chapter of this book explains how the phrase, "God is not like humans," found in Numbers 23:19, was used by both Philo of Alexandria and Origen of Alexandria to introduce important distinctions for the understanding of Scripture. These included the distinction between theology (concerning the divine nature = *theologia*) and the divine plan (*oikonomia*). Using phrases from Numbers and Deuteronomy, both authors drew an analogy between the way a father speaks to children and the way God is often portrayed in the Scriptures. This was perhaps the most comprehensive solution ever developed for dealing with problematic texts, and it was a specifically theological solution, because it was based on an understanding of what God is like considered in himself. Other Christian writers such as John Chrysostom, although they did not use these texts, developed a similar approach based on the notion of the divine condescension (*synkatabasis*) in dealing with humans. The chapter also notes the three principal adversaries or publics to which these explanations were directed by Origen: the philosophers exemplified by Celsus, the heretics represented by Marcion and the simple faithful, the majority in the church.

The second chapter describes the development of the philosophers' theological critique of the Greek mythology found in the epic poetry ascribed to Homer and the defense of Homer developed through allegorical exegesis. The first in this line of critical philosophers was Xenophanes, who states: "One god is the highest among gods and men; In neither his form nor his thought is he like mortals."[8] The theological critique of the poets begun by Xenophanes was continued by the later philosophers, especially Plato, who banned the poets from his Republic. The earlier Stoics also made use of Xenophanes's concepts in order to justify the procedure of allegorizing Homer. Later manuals of Homeric interpretation (Pseudo-Heraclitus and Pseudo-Plutarch) make extensive use of the notions of what is fitting for God or worthy of God. Both Philo of Alexandria and all the major Greek-speaking church fathers had studied Homer and Homeric interpretation as part of their basic education.

The third chapter is devoted to Hellenistic Jewish interpretation and Philo of Alexandria. Already in the second century B.C. the unknown author of the *Letter of Aristeas*, mentioned earlier, certainly regarded the laws of the Pentateuch as the divinely inspired work of Moses, but he could not imagine that God would be interested in making laws about mice and weasels and so on. Such laws must be interpreted to contain ethical teaching for humans. However, it is chiefly in the exegetical writings of Philo that the criterion of what is worthy of or fitting for God comes to be widely applied to the interpretation of the Scriptures. For example, with reference to Genesis 2:7: "the Lord God formed man of dust from the ground, and breathed into his nostrils the breath of life," he writes, "for God forbid that we should be infected with such monstrous folly [*atopia*] as to think that God employs for inbreathing organs such as mouth or nostrils; for God is not only not in the form of man, but belongs to no class or kind."[9] He then explains that the expression "breathe into" must be understood to mean that God sent his spirit into the human intellect so that humans could have knowledge of God. The expression also has an ethical sense, because, just as the face is the dominant part of the body, so is the intellect the dominant part of the soul and God gives his spirit to this part.

---

[8]Quoted in Jaeger, *Theology of the Early Greek Philosophers*, p. 42, where it is quoted from Clement of Alexandria, *Strom.* 5.109 (Xenophanes B 23).
[9]Philo, *Leg.* 1.36-39; LCL 226:171.

For Philo Moses was above all a theologian (*theologos*): he spoke about the divine nature.[10]

The fourth chapter seeks to show how later Christian interpreters understood and used some of the texts in the New Testament that seemed to interpret Old Testament texts in a new way. At the center of the New Testament interpretations of Old Testament was the figure of Jesus. The texts were used to interpret him, and he was used to interpret the texts, as he seemed to have done during his lifetime. Jesus is portrayed in the New Testament as criticizing the law and even seeming to contradict it: "It was also said, 'Whoever divorces his wife, let him give her a certificate of divorce.' But I say to you that every one who divorces his wife, except on the ground of unchastity, causes her to commit adultery; and whoever marries a divorced woman commits adultery" (Mt 5:31-32; cf. 19:3-9; Deut 24:1). In the second occurrence of this teaching (Mt 19:3-9), Jesus is presented using the principle of interpreting Scripture by means of Scripture. He cites Genesis against Deuteronomy.

The relationship of Paul to the Law, the Prophets and the Writings (later called Tanak) was complex. He was raised as a Pharisee, but came to regard legal observance as an obstacle to the preaching of the gospel among the Gentiles. His polemic against imposing the law on the Gentiles in Galatians and Romans is well-known. His arguments go beyond expediency and assert that the law of Moses as a code of observances is no longer valid. Paul also alludes to the principle of what is fitting to God: what is considered unfitting to or unworthy of God must be interpreted allegorically, as he interprets the law regarding muzzling the ox that treads the grain in 1 Corinthians 9:8-9.

New Testament authors showed a variety of approaches toward the Jewish Scriptures and made selective, even if extensive, use of them. By the end of the second century and probably as a result of the Marcionite controversy, the Law, the Prophets and the Writings had been included in the Christian canon. At the same time, a change in the concept of Scripture itself was becoming apparent, especially in writers such as Clement of Al-

---

[10]See Philo, *Mos.* 2.115.

exandria and Origen, who had great influence on subsequent commentators who followed. Scripture was no longer regarded as a source of proof by selective quotation from texts, but rather as a coherent body to be interpreted in its entirety. Running commentaries on the entire text of the biblical books beginning with Origen became common and required confronting many previously ignored texts.

The fifth chapter presents the principal early Christian interpreters, both Greek and Latin, beginning with the Alexandrians, Clement and Origen. Although Clement did not write commentaries on the Scriptures, he did make extensive use of them and developed the concept of what is fitting to God or worthy of God as a key to interpretation. Origen thought of himself as following the example of Paul in interpreting the Scriptures, and he frequently invoked Pauline texts to justify his procedures. However, as might be expected from one strongly influenced by the Greek philosophical tradition and by Philo, the concept of what is worthy of God plays a significant role in his exegetical work. In treating the question of the unity of the Testaments, Origen discusses the statements of the Old Testament where God is said to be angry and points out that similar things can be found also in the New Testament. This leads to the general conclusion: "whenever we read of the anger of God, whether in the Old or the New Testament, we do not take such statements literally, but look for the spiritual meaning in them, endeavoring to understand them in a way that is worthy of God" (*deo dignum*).[11] It is worth underlining the double criterion for meaning: it must be "useful to men" and "worthy of God." Similar terminology and criteria are found in the works of the later Greek interpreters: Eusebius, Didymus and Chrysostom.

Among Latin Christian writers Tertullian is the first to use the criterion of "worthy of God" extensively, particularly in his work *Against Marcion*. It may reasonably be inferred that Marcion had also appealed to this norm in his own works. Arguing against Marcion's doctrine of a dual divinity— the Old Testament creator God and the New Testament Savior God, Ter-

---

[11]Origen, *PArch* 2.4.4; translation from Origen, *On First Principles*, trans. and ed. G. W. Butterworth (New York: Harper and Row, 1966), p. 100.

tullian states: "But the Christian truth has distinctly declared this principle, 'God, if he is not one, is not,' because we more properly [*dignius*] believe that that has no existence which is not as it ought to be."[12] The same terminology can be found occasionally in the writings of Hilary, Ambrose and Jerome, but it abounds in Augustine, who was of course well acquainted with philosophic criticism of the classical or poetic portrait of the gods found in Cicero and other Latin writers.

The sixth chapter examines three different texts or sets of texts that posed a particular challenge in terms of the concept of God: the story of the creation in Genesis, which abounds in anthropomorphisms; the story of Abraham, Sarah and Hagar in Genesis 15, which seemed to condone adultery; and the story of the conquest of the land in the book of Joshua. In Deuteronomy 7:1-2 the Israelites are commanded to annihilate seven nations in the land into which they are to enter, a command to engage in ethnic cleansing dutifully carried out in the book of Joshua. But this command was very difficult to reconcile with the divine *philanthrōpia* ("love of humankind") revealed by Jesus Christ. The solutions early Christian interpreters proposed to these theological questions were chiefly in terms of allegorical interpretations.

The seventh chapter is dedicated to the special problem of the book of Psalms, which by the time of Jesus was thought to have been written by David, who was a prophet. But this book is filled with anthropomorphisms and "anthropopathisms" (to coin a word), especially the anger of God, as well as with imprecations directed against enemies and cries for vengeance. By the fourth century, if not before, this most heterogeneous of all the books of the Old Testament had become the Christian prayer book. It was used extensively in the liturgy and recited in its entirety by monks and nuns. However, the psalms, produced over hundreds of years and inspired by different theologies, often contained sentiments difficult to reconcile with the teaching of Jesus Christ. It was necessary to give them a Christian meaning. The early Christian interpreters employed a variety of techniques to do this, including the determination of the speaker in the passage, inter-

---

[12]Tertullian, *Marc.* 1.3; ANF 3:273.

preting passages as prophecy fulfilled already or to come about in the future, and of course allegory. But the leading criterion was theological, what was fitting to the nature of God.

The final chapter offers a comparison of ancient and some modern or recent approaches to dealing with these texts. Although many of the presuppositions of ancient interpretation are no longer tenable in the light of our historical knowledge and many of the rules used by ancient Christian interpreters may no longer be viable, their theological interpretation of the texts still has value for us today. Finding a Christian meaning for the Scriptures is still a challenge. This chapter seeks to compare how ancient and modern interpreters meet this challenge, especially with reference to some texts already examined in chapters six and seven.

Those unacquainted with ancient methods of interpretation may find it useful to begin with the appendix on ancient Christian hermeneutics (p. 217).

1

God Is Not Like Humans

God is not as man to be deceived nor as the
son of man to be threatened.

NUMBERS 23:19[1]

As a man he takes on the manners of his son.

DEUTERONOMY 1:31[2]

ANCIENT CHRISTIAN INTERPRETERS USED THE TWO quotations cited above in order to explain how biblical texts should be read, as will be explained in this chapter. These two texts were understood to refer to the distinction between *theologia* (who God is) and *oikonomia* (what God does). Origen of Alexandria used the word *theologia* ("theology") to refer to the nature of God as he is in himself in distinction from his plan for human salvation (*oikonomia*). In his *Homilies on Jeremiah* he distinguishes between when "the Scriptures speak theologically about God in relation

---

[1]These verses have been cited as they are cited by Origen. The ancient versions differed from one another. The RSV (translated from the Hebrew text) has: "God is not man, that he should lie, / or a son of man, that he should repent." The Greek version of the Septuagint in a modern translation (NETS) gives: "God is not to be put upon like man, / nor is he to be threatened like a son of man."

[2]RSV: "you have seen how the LORD your God bore you, as a man bears his son." LXX (NETS): "You saw, how the Lord God nursed you, as some person would nurse his son."

to himself" and when they "involve his plan for human matters."[3] In his work refuting the pagan philosopher Celsus, referring to the seraphim and the cherubim in the prophets Isaiah and Ezekiel, he says, "But, as these things are expressed in a very obscure form because of the unworthy and irreligious who are not able to understand the deep meaning and sacredness of the doctrine of God [theologia], I have not thought it right to discuss these matters in this book."[4] Origen is referring here obliquely to the triune nature of God, which was revealed explicitly only with the coming of Jesus Christ; but in his understanding of Scripture, it lies hidden also beneath the letter of the Old Testament writings and can be discovered there by those who know how to interpret them correctly.[5] The triune nature of God is a matter of "theology" (in the sense in which Origen uses this word), even though it is only revealed in the course of the development of the divine plan (oikonomia). In his Commentary on John, he states: "And it may be that the prophetic testimonies not only proclaim the Christ who will come, nor teach us this and nothing else, but that they teach much theology. It may be possible to learn about the relationship of the Father to the Son and of the Son to the Father through the things which the prophets announce about him, no less than from the apostles who describe the greatness of the Son of God."[6] Here we see the distinction between proclaiming "the Christ who will come," which refers to "the plan for human matters," and "much theology" (theologia), which includes the doctrine of the Trinity.

Origen was not alone in making this distinction. In the next century, the first historian of the church, Eusebius, a great admirer of Origen, also used this distinction. At the beginning of his Ecclesiastical History, he states: "My work will begin, as I have said, with the dispensation [oikonomia] of the Savior Christ,—which is loftier and greater than human conception,—

---

[3]Origen, HomJr 18.6. All quotations of HomJr are from Origen, Homilies on Jeremiah, Homily on 1 Kings 28, trans. John Clark Smith, FC 97 (Washington, DC: Catholic University of America Press, 1998).
[4]Origen, CCels 6.18; in Origen, Contra Celsum, trans. Henry Chadwick (London: Cambridge University Press, 1953).
[5]For a discussion of Origen's understanding of the Old Testament, see The Westminster Handbook to Origen, ed. John Anthony McGuckin (Louisville: Westminster John Knox, 2004), pp. 159-62.
[6]Origen, ComJn 2.205; FC 80:150.

and with a discussion of his divinity [*theologia*]."[7] Many other early Christian writers made this distinction and used the word "theology" in a restricted sense (compared to later use) to refer to the nature of God.[8]

Rather than discussing this subject in the abstract, it is best to introduce some examples of how this was done. In the history of Christian biblical interpretation it is not an exaggeration to say that all roads lead to or from the figure of Origen of Alexandria, whose imposing corpus of biblical commentaries left an indelible mark on all later patristic exegesis. It is useful, therefore, to begin with a passage from Origen's homilies on the book of Jeremiah to illustrate the nature of this "theological" interpretation. After citing Jeremiah 18:7-10, a speech attributed to God, which ends with the phrase "I will repent about the good which I decreed to do to them," Origen observes that "to repent seems to be culpable and unworthy not only of God but also of the wise man" and he adds: "But God, a foreknower of what happens in the future, is unable not to have decided to be good and to repent for this."[9]

At this point Origen decides to broaden the discussion from a particular verse to a wider discussion of the divine nature. He states: "But see what we are generally taught about God. Where 'God is not as man to be deceived nor as the son of man to be threatened' (Num 23:19), we learn through this text that God is not as man, but through another text that God is as a man, when it says, 'For the Lord your God has taught you as a man teaches his son' (Deut 8:5), and again, 'As a man he takes on the manners of his son' (Deut 1:31)."[10] The two contrasting statements that God "is not as man" and that he "is as a man," drawn from Numbers 23:19 and Deuteronomy 1:31 serve to introduce a programmatic affirmation about the nature of Sacred Scripture: "whenever the Scriptures speak theologically [*theologōsi*] about God in relation to himself and do not involve his plan

---

[7]Eusebius, *Hist. eccl.* 1.1.7. See also *Dem. evang.* 3, proem. 2.

[8]E.g., see Basil, *Adversus Eunomium* (PG 29:577); Gregory of Nazianzus, *In theophania* (orat. 38); Gregory of Nyssa, *Contra Eunomium* 3.3.48-49, 59; G. H. Ettinger, *Theodoret of Cyrus: Eranistes* (Oxford: Clarendon Press, 1975), pp. 140, 143.

[9]Origen, *HomJr* 18.6.2.

[10]Ibid., 18.6.3.

for human matters [*oikonomia*], they say that he is not as a man."[11] On the other hand, "whenever the divine plan involves human matters, it carries the human intellect and manners and way of speaking." It is, says Origen, "just as we, if we are talking with a two-year-old child, speak inarticulately because of the child—for it is impossible, if we observe what is fitting for the age of a full-grown man, and when talking to children, to understand the children without condescending to their mode of speech—something of this sort also seems to me the case with God whenever he manages the race of men and especially those still infants (1 Cor 3:1)."[12] Origen describes how mature adults even change the names of things for small children. This does not mean that the adults are immature, but that in order to converse with children they speak in a childlike language. The Greek word translated here as "condescending" (*synkatabasis*) is used also by other early Christian authors, notably John Chrysostom, to describe what God is doing in Scripture.

The same holds true for God. He speaks to us as children, as it is said: "Behold, I and the children which God has given me" (Is 8:18; Heb 2:13). In other words, the Scriptures contain, from a theological point of view, infantile language, and Origen underscores this point, saying, "to speak more dramatically, as a baby."[13] This then is the meaning of the statement in Deuteronomy, when it says that "the Lord your God took on your manners as a man would take on the manners of his son" (Deut 1:31). The reader looking at a modern translation from the Hebrew text of Deuteronomy may be confused, for the Hebrew text is different. But Origen was reading the Greek version known as the Septuagint in which there are found two variant readings for this verse. One contains the Greek verb *trophophorein*, which allows the translation of the verse: "as someone would nurse [literally "provide food for"] his son"; and the other variant, the one in Origen's manuscript, has the Greek verb *tropophorein*, which can be translated: "as someone would take on the manners of his son." It

---

[11]Ibid., 18.6.3.
[12]Ibid., 18.6.4.
[13]Ibid., 18.6.5.

is a difference of one letter, but Origen's version allows him to develop a whole theory about the nature of the Old Testament Scriptures. To insist on this word (*tropophorein*), he suggests that "those who have translated from the Hebrew, failing to find a suitable Greek term, seem to have represented it as, 'The Lord your God took on your manners,' (that is, he has taken on your manners) as if some man would take on the manners of (in light of this example which I have mentioned) his son."[14] Origen may in fact be correct in saying that the translators coined the word, because it cannot be found in all of the Greek literature available to us prior to the time of the Septuagint.

Armed with this idea, that God like a father takes on the manners of a son, that is, adapts himself to the limited human perspective, Origen can explain the original question that was the point of departure; namely, how is it possible that God can be said to repent? "Since we really do repent, when he talks with us who repent, God says, 'I repent,' and when he threatens us, he does not pretend to be a foreknower, but he threatens us as one speaking to babes. He does not pretend that he foreknows all things before their generation (Dan 1(13):42), but as one who, so to speak, plays the part of a babe, he pretends not to know the future."[15] He also threatens the nation on account of its sins, just as a father might threaten a child.

Only children would read the text literally. In short, God is not really like a man, and according to Origen, one can find numerous other passages that correspond to this phrase: on the one hand, "whenever the Scriptures speak theologically about God in relation to himself and do not involve his plan for human matters, they say that he is not as a man."[16] On the other hand, when the divine plan involves human matters, it assumes a human mode (*tropos*) and accommodates itself to human language. The word "accommodate" corresponds (in a theological-etymological sense) to the Greek word *tropophoreo*. Thus, by means of a supposed etymology or play on words, Origen has created a general theory to explain (or neutralize) all

---

[14]Ibid.
[15]Ibid.
[16]Ibid., 18.6.3.

the scriptural texts that are not in accord with the true nature of God. They may be explained in virtue of the divine condescension (*synkatabasis*) and accommodation (*tropophorein*).

Origen observes that many similar anthropomorphisms (*anthropika*) are to be found in the Scriptures; for example, "Speak to the sons of Israel. Perhaps they will hear and repent (cf. Jer 33:2-3)."[17] He explains that God has said, "Perhaps they will hear" not as one who doubts; rather, "He pretends then that he does not see your future so that he may preserve your self-determination by not foretelling or foreknowing you will repent or not, and he says to the Prophet, 'Speak, perhaps they will repent.'"[18] This is an example of the numerous scriptural passages that talk about God's "taking on the manners of man" (*tropophorein*).[19] Origen then singles out an important case of this: "If you hear of the anger of God and his wrath (cf. Dt 29:23, 24-27), do not suppose that anger and wrath are passions of God." The Greek word translated as passion, *pathē*, always has a negative connotation and is not the equivalent of "emotion." That is why one must not imagine that anger and wrath are passions of God. These are ways of speaking (dispensations of language) that are useful for converting and bettering the children, "since we also use a fearful expression with children, not from an actual state of mind but because of a purpose to cause fear."[20] Likewise, "God is also said to be angry and wrathful in order that you can convert and become better."[21]

In homily 20 on Jeremiah Origen expands on the notion that in the Scriptures God acts as a father with children and offers some general principles concerning the interpretation of the Scriptures. A basic principle is that "everything recorded about God, even if it may be immediately unsuitable, must be understood worthy of a good God."[22] Origen then mentions as "unsuitable" on the part of God anger, wrath, regret, sleeping.

---

[17]Ibid., 18.6.6.
[18]Ibid., 18.6.6-7.
[19]Ibid., 18.6.7.
[20]Ibid.
[21]Ibid.
[22]Ibid., 20.1.1.

These things must be understood as "obscure" sayings in the sense of Proverbs 1:6, "to understand a proverb and a figure, the words of the wise and their riddles." The word "figure" here translates the word *ainigmata* in Greek (from which comes *enigma* in English), which could more literally be translated as: "dark or obscure sayings." In other words, talk about God's anger, regret and so on constitutes obscure sayings that need to be properly interpreted to give them a sense that is "worthy of God," that is, suitable to the divine dignity. Origen explains that the word of God is not like that of all others.

> For of no one else is the word a living being, of no one else is the word God, for of no one else was the word in the beginning with that one of whom it was the word, even if it was only . . . from a certain beginning. So indeed the anger of God is an anger . . . of no one else, an anger of none whatever, and just as the word of God has something of a nature alien beyond every word of anyone else—and what is God and what is a living being while being a word, what subsists in itself and what is subject to the Father, has an alien nature—so too, since once it was named as being of God, what is called anger has something alien and different from all the anger of him who is angry, so too his wrath has something individual. For it is the wrath of the purpose of the One who reproves by wrath, who wishes to convert the one reproved through the reproof.[23]

Having made clear that the word of God is not like human words nor to be interpreted in terms of human passions, Origen is able to speak of wrath, anger and regret as part of the "reproving work of God" and the "educative work of God."[24] All of this explanation has been, as Origen himself says, "a preface" to commenting on the saying of Jeremiah: "You deceived me, and I was deceived" (Jer 20:7). After offering many other examples of the "educative work of God," Origen returns to the image of a father correcting his son: "Perhaps then, as a father wishes to deceive a son in his own interest while he is still a boy, since he cannot be helped any other way unless the boy is deceived, as a healer makes it his business to deceive the patient

---

[23]Ibid.
[24]Ibid., 20.2.1.

who cannot be cured unless he receives words of deceit, so it is also for the God of the universe, since what is prescribed has to help the race of men."[25] With such remedies, Origen observes, "the whole divine Scripture is filled."[26] The comparison of God with a father and son and that of the physician and the patient allows him to formulate a general principle about what at first sight seem to be "unsuitable" passages in the Scriptures: "By analogy to the father and the healer, such is something of what God does."[27]

A few years later Origen returned to this subject in his works *Against Celsus* and his *Commentary on Matthew*. In *Against Celsus*, he responds in a detailed way to the derision of the pagan philosopher Celsus (an otherwise unknown second-century figure known chiefly through Origen's apologetic work against him) against the passages of Scripture that speak of the anger of God, that attribute human passions to the divinity, something that was considered unacceptable in educated philosophical circles. Origen answers with the comparison of the way adults speak when they talk to small children. Again he cites Deuteronomy 1:31, "The Lord your God took on your manners as a man would take on the manners of his son."[28] The Logos assumes human ways (manners) in the interests of men. He adds:

> There was no need for the multitude that the words put into God's mouth, which were intended to be addressed to them, should correspond to His real character. However, anyone interested in the exposition of the divine scriptures, "by comparing spiritual things with spiritual," as it is said, will discover from them the meaning of the sayings addressed to the weak and of those spoken to the intelligent, while often both meanings lie in the same text for him who knows how to understand it.[29]

Origen insists that the anger of God spoken of in the Scriptures is not an emotional reaction, but a method for correcting sinners. To illustrate this method, which, according to him, is the teaching of the Scriptures, he

---

[25]Ibid., 20.3.2.
[26]Ibid., 20.3.2.
[27]Ibid., 20.3.3.
[28]Origen's translation, *CCels* 4.71.15.
[29]Origen, *CCels* 4.71.16.

cites a number of texts: Psalm 6:2; Jeremiah 10:24; 2 Samuel 24:1; 1 Chronicles 21:1; Ephesians 2:3. By comparing these texts, says Origen, one arrives at the conclusion that it is a question of correction on the part of God. He pretends to be angry, as one does with children in order to make an impression. He notes that each one brings this wrath on himself because of his own sins, as Paul states in Romans 2:4-5. Furthermore he observes that the Logos (Word) teaches us not to be angry at all, as it says in Psalm 36:8: "Cease from anger and forsake wrath," and Paul also says: "You too must put aside these, wrath, anger, evil, blasphemy, shameful talk" (Col 3:8). He concludes that the Scripture would not have attributed to God that which it has commanded us to abandon completely. Obviously, he says, one must interpret all the references to God's anger in the same way that we interpret references to his sleep, citing Psalm 43:24 and Psalm 77:65.[30] He concludes his refutation of Celsus:

> Therefore we do not attribute human passions [*anthrōpopathos*] to God, nor do we hold impious opinions about Him, nor are we in error when we produce explanations concerning Him from the scriptures themselves by comparing them with one another. The task of those of us who give an intelligent account of Christianity is simply to deliver our hearts from stupidity as well as we can and to make them sensible.[31]

In his *Commentary on Matthew*, Origen takes up again the two texts of Numbers 23:19 ("God is not as man to be deceived") and Deuteronomy 1:31 ("The Lord your God took on your manners as a man would take on the manners of his son") in the context of the explanation of the parable of the wedding feast (Mt 22:2), where we find the phrase "The kingdom of heaven is like a man, a king." Using a technique of interpretation that assumes every word must have some significance, Origen takes as his starting point the word "man," which seems superfluous, because the comparison in the parable is with a king. But in this understanding there are no superfluous words in Scripture. Every word counts and is present for some reason. He explains: "It could certainly have said: 'the kingdom of heaven

---

[30]Ibid., 4.72.30.
[31]Ibid., 4.72.45.

is like a king' without the addition of 'man,' but since this term is present, it must also be explained."[32] Then Origen makes a direct allusion to Philo of Alexandria, saying: "Someone before us has written books on the allegories of the sacred laws and has presented texts both where it is narrated of God as if He had human passions as well as texts that set in relief His divinity."[33] Next Origen cites the two texts of Numbers and Deuteronomy. Actually Philo had also used these two texts to treat of the nature of God. To Philo we shall return later in chapter three.

Origen continues, saying that he will put forth the parables where God is called "man" as an answer to the "heterodox who put themselves in opposition to the God of the Law, of the Prophets and of the creation because of what is expressed in this manner in the ancient Scriptures."[34] The word "heterodox" is a clear allusion to Marcion, who, a hundred years earlier, had attributed "the ancient writings," that is, the Old Testament, to a different God from the Father of Jesus Christ. Origen asks rhetorically: "if God is compared to a man [in the parables of the Gospels], for what reason, in line with these parables, do you not accept that the anger, the wrath, the change of heart, of decisions, being seated or taking a walk by God are not also a parable?"[35] In short he is suggesting that there is a lack of theological consistency on the part of the followers of Marcion, who in the time of Origen were still quite active and seen as a threat to correct belief. He then poses a second rhetorical question: "if, as a consequence of God being called 'man' in the parable, you do not want to understand in a parabolic sense all the passages of Scripture that ascribe human passions to Him, then tell us why the God of the universe is called 'man' in the Gospel, since (as you suppose) he has nothing human in Him."[36] Origen's logic is that, since God is compared to a "man" (a king) in the parable (which the Marcionites accept) and there it must be interpreted in a symbolic sense, they ought to be willing to interpret all the other passages of the Scriptures that ascribe human charac-

---

[32]Origen, *ComMt* 17.17.
[33]Ibid.
[34]Ibid., 17.18.
[35]Ibid.
[36]Ibid.

teristics to God also in a figurative sense. The heart, then, of the theological problem is the attribution of human passions to God.

We will not pause here to follow all of Origen's argumentation, but it is important to note the introduction into this passage of the technical Greek term *anthrōpopathos* (with human passions), which is found for the first time in Greek literature in the works of Philo. In these two works (*Against Celsus* and the *Commentary on Matthew*) Origen was responding to the philosophical criticism of Celsus and to the heretical criticism of Marcion and his followers, but he was also concerned about the "simple" persons in the church and the danger for them of attributing human passions to God, as can be seen from the comparison with the small children in the *Homilies on Jeremiah* noted earlier. The problem of the "simple" was in fact a major concern of Origen and not only in the last period of his life when he was preaching at Caesarea. These people, who are actually the majority, are designated by many terms in his works: the many, the uneducated, unlettered, and so on. Already in his work *On First Principles*, written when he was still in Alexandria, he had observed in the fourth book, dedicated to the interpretation of Scripture, "Moreover, even the simpler of those who claim to belong to the Church, while believing indeed that there is none greater than the Creator, in which they are right, yet believe such things about him as would not be believed of the most savage and unjust of men."[37] According to Origen, the reason people "hold false opinions and make impious or ignorant assertions about God appears to be nothing else but this, that scripture is not understood in its spiritual sense, but is interpreted according to the bare letter."[38]

Origen was concerned, then, with three distinct categories of persons: the philosophers represented by Celsus, the heretics represented by Marcion and the simple believers. In the next chapter we will take a look at the philosophical tradition. In fact Christianity had presented itself almost from the beginning as a philosophy, the only true philosophy. Paul's speech in the Areopagus (Acts 17:22) is the first step in this direction. It

---

[37]Origen, *PArch* 4.2.1.
[38]Ibid., 4.2.2.

was therefore important to answer the philosophical objections to the Scriptures. Many other non-Christian writers were to raise objections against what appeared to be crude anthropomorphisms or mythological presentations in the Jewish and Christian Scriptures.[39]

Here it may be useful to say something about Marcion, to whom Origen was alluding in the passage cited above, and who had a profound impact on the development of Christian interpretation. His was a very different kind of reading of the Scriptures, and resulted in the rejection of most of them. We do not know how much Origen actually knew about Marcion or whether he had access to any of his writings. Most of our knowledge of Marcion comes from the Latin polemical writing *Against Marcion* by Tertullian, to which Origen did not have access, and the work by Irenaeus of Lyons *Against Heresies*, which Origen probably knew in Greek.

A native of Sinope in Pontus, Marcion arrived in Rome about A.D. 140. He was the son of a bishop and a prosperous ship owner who became a benefactor of the church in Rome. Marcion maintained that the church had been mistaken in keeping the Old Testament as its Scriptures, that the law, denounced by Paul as the cause of sin and the principle of injustice, could not be the work of the God of Jesus Christ. Consequently he attributed it to a Demiurge or Creator God different from the perfect God, the God of pure love and mercy, visibly embodied in Jesus Christ. He further concluded that the gospel must be dissociated from Judaism, and so he repudiated the Old Testament as containing no revelation of the Christian God. However, the New Testament writings contained numerous references and citations of the Old Testament writings. Marcion found the solution to this in the claim of Paul (Gal 1:11-12) that he had received his revelation not from man but directly from the Lord. He concluded that only Paul had correctly understood Jesus. This led him to produce his own edition of Paul's letters in order to remove what he saw as interpolations, among which were the allegorical interpretations of

---

[39]See John Granger Cook, *The Interpretation of the Old Testament in Greco-Roman Paganism* (Tübingen: Mohr Siebeck, 2004); and also Cook, *The Interpretation of the New Testament in Greco-Roman Paganism* (Tübingen: Mohr Siebeck, 2000).

Old Testament passages found in the Pauline letters, especially Galatians and 1–2 Corinthians. Among the Gospels only that of Luke was acceptable, since Luke had been the friend and companion of Paul. Marcion insisted on reading the texts of the Old Testament literally, rejecting any kind of spiritual interpretation, and so for him the only consistent solution was to reject it. Marcion's ideas were condemned by the Roman church in 144, after which he founded his own church.[40] Marcion's influence was widespread, as can be seen by the numerous denunciations of him for centuries to come. His teaching also led indirectly to the establishment of the canon of the New Testament, that is, of the list of officially recognized writings of the church. In reality Marcion had arrived too late on the scene to effect such a rejection of the Old Testament. Christian interpretations of these writings were already deeply embedded in the tradition, as can easily be seen by the numerous references to Old Testament writings in the New Testament.

The challenge articulated by Marcion was, however, taken seriously by early Christian writers, and much early Christian interpretation was developed to demonstrate that the real meaning of the Old Testament texts is not in contradiction with the teaching of Jesus Christ. Marcion had posed in a dramatic way the problem of reading the Old Testament with a Christian sense. However, his solution was, from a theological point of view, very poor, for it ended up producing another god besides the Father of Jesus Christ.

The theological interpretation of the Scriptures by the early Christian writers being described here did not involve a rejection of portions of Scripture as did that of Marcion. Rather it was an interpretation that often distinguished between the literal or obvious sense and what Christian writers understood to be the true or Christian meaning of the Scriptures. With regard to the Old Testament Scriptures, this meant a more profound or hidden meaning. Origen and many other early Christian interpreters viewed or valued the letter of the Scriptures in a way similar to that of

---

[40]For a summary of Marcion's doctrine and additional references, see A. A. Stephenson, "Marcion," in *New Catholic Encyclopedia*, ed. B. A. Marthaler (Detroit: Thomson Gale, 2003), 9:142-43.

Marcion, but they assumed that Scripture had to have a deeper or non-literal meaning. This assumption was not limited to the Alexandrian school, which included Clement, Origen, Eusebius, Didymus and Cyril, but extended also to Antiochene writers such as John Chrysostom and Theodoret of Cyrrhus.[41] Clement of Alexandria developed a theory that all sacred texts in all religions contained hidden meanings.

> Wherefore, in accordance with the method of concealment, the truly sacred Word, truly divine and most necessary for us, deposited in the shrine of truth, was by the Egyptians indicated by what were called among them *adyta*, and by the Hebrews by the veil. Only the consecrated—that is, those devoted to God, circumcised in the desire of the passions for the sake of love to that which is alone divine—were allowed access to them.[42]

After surveying also all the writings of the philosophers, he concludes:

> For only to those who often approach them, and have given them a trial by faith and in their whole life, will they supply the real philosophy and the true theology. They also wish us to require an interpreter and guide. For so they considered, that, receiving truth at the hands of those who knew it well, we would be more earnest and less liable to deception, and those worthy of them would profit. Besides, all things that shine through a veil show the truth grander and more imposing; as fruits shining through water, and figures through veils, which give added reflections to them.[43]

In addition it is interesting to note that one of the common ways of describing Sacred Scripture for Philo, Origen and many others in antiquity was as the "sacred oracles" (*theia logia, hieroi chrēsmoi*). Oracles by their nature are obscure and require an interpretation. This notion is reflected in the modern phrase "oracular" speech, meaning enigmatic or obscure.

The problems Origen confronted were still there 150 years later, when

---

[41]The term "Alexandrian School" is here used to designate a school of thought or interpretation in which allegory was used to find the deeper meaning of Scripture. It also designates the catechetical school of Alexandria, of which Origen was appointed head by the bishop. The term "Antiochene School" is also used to designate a school of thought, beginning with Diodore of Tarsus about 360. For more on this distinction, see chap. 5 below.

[42]Clement, *Strom.* 5.4; ANF 2:449.

[43]Ibid., 5.9; ANF 2:457. Clement devotes 5.4-10 to this subject and returns to it later in the same work.

John Chrysostom, famous for his preaching in the city of Antioch, also found it necessary to distinguish constantly between God as he appears in the economy of salvation and as he is in himself. Although he did not make use of the text of Numbers 23:19 as Philo and Origen had done, he did use the category of God's condescension (*synkatabasis*), or willingness to adapt himself to the level of human beings. In a homily on the story of Noah in Genesis, where the text says: "God was mindful of Noah, and of all the wild animals, all the cattle, all the birds, and all the reptiles that were with him in the ark" (Gen 8:1), Chrysostom observes: "Notice once again, I ask you, the considerateness of Sacred Scripture: 'God was mindful,' it says. Let us take what is said, dearly beloved, in a sense befitting God [*theoprepōs*], and not interpret the concreteness of the expressions from the viewpoint of the limitations of our human condition. I mean, as far as the ineffable essence is concerned, the word is improper; but as far as our limitations are concerned, the expression is made appropriately."[44] The important distinction here is between the "considerateness" of Sacred (divine) Scripture and "a sense befitting God." The Greek word (*synkatabasis*) translated here as "considerateness" is also often translated as "condescension."[45] The notion of God's "considerateness" is in direct relation with the "limitations of our human condition," which can be more literally translated: "the weakness of our human nature." The idea is similar to that of Origen when he speaks of God's acting like a parent toward children. For Chrysostom, God behaves with "considerateness," that is, in a human way, so that he can communicate with and be understood by humans. We must not take these expressions literally but interpret them "in a sense befitting God." The Greek word used here (*theoprepōs*) had long been used in the tradition of biblical interpretation as a kind of flag to avoid a literal reading of the texts or, as Chrysostom says, to avoid understanding "the concreteness of the expressions from the viewpoint of the limitations

---

[44]John Chrysostom, *Homilies on Genesis 18–45*, FC 82, trans. Robert C. Hill (Washington, DC: Catholic University of America Press, 1986), p. 149.

[45]In his introduction to John Chrysostom, *Homilies on Genesis 1–17*, FC 74 (Washington, DC: Catholic University of America Press, 1986), translator Robert C. Hill objects to the translation "condescension" because it suggests "patronizing" (p. 17).

of our human condition." Thus, when the text says that "God was mindful of Noah" and of all the animals, this is not to be understood in the same way that humans are "mindful" of something. The word is appropriate to us, not to God.

Chrysostom seems constantly to be concerned that his hearers will take the text too literally, and he frequently (several hundred times) introduces this distinction between God's "considerateness" in formulating things in a human way and what is "a sense befitting God." In Psalm 7 we find these words in reference to God: "If you do not turn back, he will make his sword gleam; his bow he bent and prepared it, and on it he prepared implements of death; he forged his arrows for those that are being burnt" (Ps 7:13-14 NETS). Chrysostom asks how "the one who merely by looking is capable of turning the world upside down" can be said to have sword and bow, implying that this is absurd. But then he offers a more extended reflection on the question of such language. He asks: "Why on earth, then, is such language used? For the reason of the materialism of the listeners, and for the purpose of startling their thinking through the familiar names of these weapons. What need has he of weapons, after all, in whose hand rests the spirit of us all and before whose gaze no one can stand their ground?"[46] He asks rhetorically: "would anyone with sense be bold enough to take these words in the way they are spoken?"[47] This of course is intended to be a reductio ad absurdum. The answer is that the psalmist "proceeds to employ materialistic expressions so that even those extremely dull may understand that one should not stop short at the expressions but derive from them ideas appropriate to God."[48] Chrysostom's real concern, however, is not that people will imagine God using human weapons literally, but that they will think of him as having human passions, and so he continues: "And so if anyone wonders why on earth anger and wrath are mentioned in connection with God, much more will they wonder in this case. If, however, these things are not to be taken in

---

[46]John Chrysostom, *Commentary on the Psalms*, trans. Robert C. Hill (Brookline, MA: Holy Cross Orthodox Press, 1998), 1:135.
[47]Ibid.
[48]Ibid.

the sense spoken but in a sense appropriate to God, it is clear that this is true also of anger and wrath."[49] To attribute anger to God is not appropriate (*theoprepōs*). Evidently Chrysostom had difficulty convincing his audience of this, for he continues by noting in regard to the expression "He has strung his bow and reared it": "why are you surprised if this expression is used in the Old Testament when even in the New ... John says something similar? 'But even now the axe is lying at the root of the trees.' So what is this? Is God imitating a woodcutter chopping wood with his axe?"[50] Obviously that too is an absurd idea, as is the idea that God is really angry. It appears that for Chrysostom, as for Origen, a major concern was with the "simple," those in his congregation who took the texts too literally and did not rise to a meaning "worthy of God."

One more text from Chrysostom is worth adding here because of its close resemblance to the father-child comparison employed by Origen. In commenting on the first line of Psalm 6: "Lord, in your anger do not censure me, nor in your rage correct me" he warns:

> When you hear of anything of anger and rage in God's case, do not get the idea of anything typical of human beings; the words, you see, arise from considerateness. The divine nature, after all, is free of all these passions. On the contrary, he speaks this way so as to make an impression on the minds of more materialistic people. For in our case, too, when we converse with foreigners, we use their language; if we speak with children, we babble away with them, and even if we are extremely gifted, we show considerateness for their undeveloped state. What is surprising in our doing this when we do it also in actions, like biting our nails and feigning anger, all for the sake of instructing the children? God likewise, wanting to make an impression on materialistic people, made use of such words. For in so speaking, you see, his concern was not for his own glory but for the benefit of his listeners.[51]

It is striking that, although the references to Numbers and Deuteronomy are missing, the same basic image of a father correcting children is

---

[49]Ibid.
[50]Ibid., 1:134-35.
[51]Ibid., 1:95.

used, as had been done earlier by Philo and Origen, to distance God as he is in himself from the presentation in the text.

To summarize what has been presented in this chapter: the overarching comparison between a human father's way of speaking to children and the way God is presented in Scripture serves to prevent the text of the Scriptures from being read too literally. To do so would be to read the sacred text in a way unworthy of God. God as he is in himself (*theologia*) must be distinguished from the way he is presented in the economy of salvation. In the Scriptures God adapts himself (shows "considerateness") to the human condition ("human weakness"). This fundamental distinction is developed through the introduction of a technical vocabulary, which includes the terms *anthropomorphic* and *anthropopathic*. To think of God with such traits or ascribe them to God was to think of God in terms not "worthy of God" (*axios tou theou*) or not fitting to God (*theoprepēs*), or not suitable/appropriate to God (*anoikeion*). We will encounter this terminology over and over again, for it provided the basic tools to the ancient Christian interpreters for finding a meaning useful to us.

2

The Philosophers' Critique of Myth and the Defense of Homer Through Allegorical Interpretation

It is the unanimous teaching of all philosophers that
God is never angry, nor does he injure anyone.

CICERO, *DE OFFICIIS*

THE TWO WORKS ATTRIBUTED TO THE GREEK POET HOMER, the *Iliad* and the *Odyssey*, had from time immemorial formed the basis for Greek culture and education. Originally transmitted orally perhaps before the standard system of Greek writing was developed, they told the story of the Trojan War (the *Iliad*) and the long wanderings of Odysseus after the war until he returned home (the *Odyssey*). The Greek historian Herodotus (fifth century B.C.) thought Homer had lived four hundred years before his time, that is, in the ninth century, but more recent studies place him in the period 750–650 B.C. In any case these poems are the oldest works of Greek literature and came to form the basis for Greek education already by the sixth century B.C., if not before. The myths contained in these works were developed in other ancient writings such as those of Hesiod and later in the Homeric Hymns and the works of the tragedians.

However, popular though they were, these works contained stories and portraits of the gods that were considered scandalous by later generations. Even before the development of the philosophical critique of mythology, a method seems to have emerged for interpreting them in such a way as to remove the scandal. Later on this practice came to be called "allegory." The word "allegory" is first found in the writing of the first-century-B.C. Latin orator Cicero, but before that other words had been employed for this interpretive practice. The basic idea is that the text says one thing, but the real meaning is something else.

The original terminology associated with the discovery of hidden, non-literal meanings, however, appears to be the word group associated with the root *ain-*: *ainos, ainigma, ainittesthai, ainigmatodes*. This terminology is found in the Derveni papyrus, the earliest example of extended allegorical interpretation, dated to the fourth century B.C. but whose text may be from the previous century. The text is a commentary on an Orphic poem. For this author the proper term for allegorical writing is *ainittesthai*, "to speak in hints" or "to speak enigmatically." His word for "allegorically" is *ainigmatodes*, "in the mode of an *ainos* or *ainigima*."[1] This terminology is mentioned here because it will be employed also by Christian writers many centuries later, such as John Chrysostom and others in the so-called Antiochene school, who were theoretically opposed to allegorical interpretation.

In the philosophical tradition the notion of what is fitting or appropriate in general was first used as an instrument for criticizing an anthropomorphic conception of the gods by Xenophanes, whose philosophical theology, according to Werner Jaeger, "has done more than anything else to smooth the way for accepting Judaeo-Christian monotheism."[2] In one

---

[1]See Andrew Ford, "Performing Interpretation: Early Allegorical Interpretation of Homer," in *Epic Traditions in the Contemporary World: The Poetics of Community*, ed. Margaret Beissinger, Jane Tylus and Susanne Wofford (Berkeley: University of California Press, 1999), p. 38; Andrew Ford, *The Origins of Criticism: Literary Culture and Poetic Theory in Classical Greece* (Princeton, NJ: Princeton University Press, 2002), pp. 72-76; Peter T. Struck, *Birth of the Symbol: Ancient Readers at the Limits of Their Texts* (Princeton, NJ: Princeton University Press, 2004), pp. 29-33. For the terms *ainos* and *ainigma*, see H. J. Scheuer, "Ainos," in *Historisches Wörterbuch der Rhetorik*, ed. Gert Ueding (Darmstadt: Wissenschaftliche Buchgesellschaft, 1992), 1:295-98; and J. König, "Aenigma," in *Historisches Wörterbuch der Rhetorik*, ed. Gert Ueding (Darmstadt: Wissenschaftliche Buchgesellschaft, 1992), 1:187-95.
[2]See Werner Jaeger, *The Theology of the Early Greek Philosophers: The Gifford Lectures 1936* (Oxford: Clarendon, 1948), pp. 38-51.

fragment Xenophanes states: "One god is the highest among gods and men; In neither his form nor his thought is he like mortals."[3] This God, says Xenophanes, "ever abides in the selfsame place without moving; nor is it fitting [*epiprepei*] for him to move hither and thither, changing his place."[4] Deity must also and above all be free from any moral weakness. In another fragment Xenophanes says, "Homer and Hesiod say that the gods do all manner of things which men would consider disgraceful: adultery, stealing, deceiving each other."[5] He also notes the tendency of each race to project its gods in its own image and likeness, observing, "The gods of the Ethiopians are black with snub noses, while those of the Thracians are blond, with blue eyes and red hair."[6] And in the same vein he remarks satirically that "if cattle and horses had hands, and were able to paint with their hands, and to fashion such pictures as men do, then horses would pattern the forms of the gods after horses, and cows after cattle, giving them just such a shape as those which they find in themselves."[7]

Jaeger concludes that Xenophanes can really be understood only as a theologian. The source of his theology is not really philosophical, nor does it rests on logical proof, but "springs from an immediate sense of awe at the sublimity of the Divine."[8] His criticism of the anthropomorphic conception of the gods is that all these human frailties, moral or otherwise, are out of keeping with God's essential nature. Neither human misdeeds nor speech nor human form nor generation are appropriate to the divine. The concept of God thus becomes a hermeneutical principle or tool.

PLATO

The theological critique of the poets begun by Xenophanes was continued by the later philosophers, especially Plato, who banned the poets from his Republic. In fact the critique of the traditional Greek myths by Plato was

---

[3]Ibid., p. 42. The fragment is found in Clement, *Strom.* 5.109 (Xenophanes B 23). The translations of Xenophanes are from Jaeger.
[4]Ibid., p. 45n28 (Xenophanes B 26).
[5]Ibid., p. 47 (Xenophanes B 11, B 12).
[6]Ibid., p. 47n42; Clement, *Strom.* 7.22 (Xenophanes B 16).
[7]Ibid., p. 47n41; Clement, *Strom.* 5.110 (Xenophanes B 15).
[8]Ibid., p. 49.

so sweeping and severe that he is regarded by later defenders of Homer as the chief enemy. Plato was very much interested in myth because he wished to substitute philosophical discourse for mythical discourse.[9] In the Republic, in the context of discussing the education of the guardians of the ideal city, Socrates raises the question of telling false stories to children and says of Hesiod and Homer: "They made up untrue stories, which they used to tell people—and still do tell them" (377d).[10] Asked for an example, he refers in particular to the story related by Hesiod of how Kronos castrated his father and swallowed the children borne to him by his consort Rhea. Without mentioning these events explicitly, he says: "As for what Kronos did, and what his son did to him, even if they were true I wouldn't think that in the normal course of events these stories should be told to those who are young and uncritical. The best thing would be to say nothing about them at all" (378a). Plato's argument is that such stories have a deleterious effect especially on the young and impressionable. Socrates continues with this generalization:

> Nor, in general, any of the stories—which are not true anyway—about gods making war on gods, plotting against them, or fighting with them. Not if we want the people who are going to protect our city to regard it as a crime to fall out with one another without a very good reason. The last thing they need is to have stories told them, and pictures made for them, of battles between giants, and all the many and varied enmities of gods and heroes towards their kinsmen and families. (378c)

Plato was fully aware that these stories had long been allegorized in an effort to make their objectionable features more acceptable, but he rejected this solution.

> As for the binding of Hera by her son, the hurling of Hephaestus out of heaven by his father, for trying to protect his mother when she was being beaten, and the battles of the gods which Homer tells us about, whether

---

[9]For the larger context of Plato's treatment of myth, see especially Luc Brisson, *How Philosophers Saved Myths: Allegorical Interpretation and Classical Mythology* (Chicago: University of Chicago Press, 2004).

[10]The quotations from Plato's *Republic* are taken from Plato, *The Republic*, trans. G. R. F. Ferrari and Tom Griffith (Cambridge; New York: Cambridge University Press, 2000).

these stories are told as allegories or not as allegories, we must not allow them into our city. The young are incapable of judging what is allegory and what is not, and the opinions they form at that age tend to be ineradicable and unchangeable. (378d–e)

The Greek word translated here as "allegory" is not in fact the Greek word "allegory" but the word *hyponoia*, which means the meaning beneath the letter. Plutarch says that this was the word commonly used earlier for this interpretive practice.[11] The basic problem for Plato is that these stories give a false view of the nature of divinity. It is simply impossible to imagine that gods worthy of the name would behave this way. So Plato lays down some basic principles concerning theology (the nature of divinity). One is that God (or god) is good and the source only of good, not of evil or what is harmful (379a–c). Another principle is that the gods do not change their form or undergo transformations, nor do they engage in deception. They are not like magicians. "God is simple and true in deed and word" (382a–383a). The conclusion is that the works of Homer cannot be used in the education of the young: "not if we want our guardians to become god-fearing and godlike, to the greatest extent possible for a human being" (383c). Plato's critique of Homer's depiction of the gods is thus a theological one, based on the nature of divinity; gods cannot be depicted as behaving like bad people. Plato was concerned above all with the deleterious influence these texts could have on the young, that is, that they would model their behavior on them. Socrates says:

"For, my dear Adeimantus, if our young should seriously hear such things and not laugh scornfully at them as unworthy speeches, it's not very likely that anyone of them would believe these things to be unworthy of himself, a human being, and would reproach himself for them, if it should enter into his head to say or do any such thing. Rather, with neither shame nor endurance, he would chant many dirges and laments at the slightest sufferings."
"What you say is very true," he said. (388d)

Unlike Plato the earlier Stoics also made use of Xenophanes's concepts

---

[11]*De aud. poet.* II 19e; LCL 197:100.

in order to justify the procedure of allegorizing Homer. Later manuals of Homeric interpretation (Pseudo-Heraclitus and Pseudo-Plutarch) make extensive use of the notions of what is "fitting for God" (*theoprepēs*) or "worthy of God" (*axios tou theou*). In fact the defenders of Homer were in basic agreement with the critics regarding the theological criteria.

One may well wonder why, given the severity of these critiques on the part of the philosophers, Homer was not simply abandoned in favor of more suitable material. The answer is similar to the question of why the Christians did not simply abandon the portions of the Old Testament that were incompatible with the teaching of Jesus. Although the works of Homer never acquired the status of sacred scripture and Greek religion was not a "religion of the book," the Homeric myths were deeply embedded in Greek culture. As the first-century interpreter and defender of Homer known as Pseudo-Heraclitus states it:

> From the very first age of life, the foolishness of infants just beginning to learn is nurtured on the teaching given in his [Homer's] school. One might almost say that his poems are our baby clothes, and we nourish our minds by draughts of his milk. He stands at our side as we each grow up and shares our youth as we gradually come to manhood; when we are mature, his presence within us is at its prime; and even in old age, we never weary of him. When we stop, we thirst to begin him again. In a word, the only end of Homer for human beings is the end of life.[12]

However, this author has no illusions about what is depicted in Homer's works and fundamentally agrees with the philosophers in criticizing him: "If he meant nothing allegorically, he was impious through and through, and sacrilegious fables, loaded with blasphemous folly, run riot through both epics." One could hardly ask for a more thorough indictment.

The solution for Pseudo-Heraclitus, however, is not to abandon Homer and his myths but to interpret him allegorically in a way that is in accord with fitting and appropriate notions of divinity. He accuses Homer's accusers of being ignorant and failing to recognize "Homeric allegory" be-

---

[12]Donald A. Russell and David Konstan, *Heraclitus: Homeric Problems*, Writings from the Greco-Roman World (Atlanta: Society of Biblical Literature, 2005), p. 3.

cause they "have not descended into the secret caverns of his wisdom" and "they seize hastily on what they take to be his mythical invention, because they do not know what is said in a philosophical sense."[13] Heraclitus the Grammarian goes on to accuse Plato and the other philosophers of actually borrowing what is true in their philosophy from Homer. Thus, when Homer is interpreted correctly, that is, allegorically, all valid philosophical content can be found already in his works. "As the originator of all wisdom, Homer has, by using allegory, passed down to his successors the power of drawing from him, piece by piece all the philosophy he was the first to discover."[14] This strategy of defense will be used later by Christian writers in order to find not only the teaching of Jesus in Old Testament texts but also to find there what is true in the teaching of the philosophers, because they borrowed from Moses, who like Homer had lived before all the philosophers.

Heraclitus interpreted Homer's poems in terms of what were in his time the traditional divisions of philosophy, logic, physics and ethics. In the *Iliad* it is said that "the other Olympians sought to bind in chains" the ruler of them all, Zeus:

> Hera and Poseidon, Pallas Athena too;
> but, goddess, you came and freed him from his bonds,
> swiftly summoning the hundred-handed to high Olympus,
> whom the gods call Biareus, and men Aegaeon,
> for he is stronger than his father is.[15]

Heraclitus exclaims that for these lines, if they are taken literally, Homer deserves to be banished not just from Plato's Republic but also "beyond the furthest pillars of Heracles and the inaccessible sea of Ocean." The reason is that "Zeus comes very near to being chained up, and the conspiracy against him is put together not by the Titans or the audacious giants at Pallene, but by Hera (who has two titles, one from her kinship with him, and one from her marriage) and by his brother Poseidon." For

---

[13]Ibid., p. 7.
[14]Ibid., p. 63.
[15]Ibid., pp. 39-41.

Heraclitus the Grammarian "there is only one remedy for this impiety: to show that the myth is an allegory."[16] He explains that in these lines we have "a theological account of the oldest natural substance, which is the origin of all things. Homer is the sole originator of the scientific doctrine of the elements, and taught all his successors the ideas which they were held to have discovered." By the word "theological" Heraclitus seems to mean the representation of nature in terms of gods. He continues at some length to explain that the philosophers such as Thales and Empedocles also spoke enigmatically and allegorically, when they discoursed about nature. The story of "the binding of Hera" is for him in reality an allegorical account of the system of the four elements and suggests that Homer is suggesting in these lines "some future disturbance in the universe." Thus the gods represent different elements: "Zeus, the most powerful element, is the object of a conspiracy by the others: by Hera, i.e., air; by Poseidon, i.e., water; and by Athena, i.e. the earth, since she, the Worker Goddess, is the creator of all things." After further explanation of how these elements were almost fused into one, Heraclitus exclaims triumphantly: "So the inescapable charge relating to the impious 'binding of Zeus' admits of a scientific explanation in allegorical terms."[17]

Other passages of Homer are to be interpreted in terms of ethics. The figure of Eris is described by Homer as "Small when she first arms, but later on her head hits heaven as she walks on earth."[18] Heraclitus insists that "it is not a goddess to which Homer has given shape—one so utterly monstrous, capable of incredible changes and reversals of form, one moment cast down upon the ground, and the next reaching up to the infinite grandeur of the aether." Instead this is an allegory of "what always happens to quarrelsome people: strife begins with a trivial cause, but once roused it swells up into what is indeed a great evil."[19]

Homer describes Ate as "powerful and strong of foot,"[20] and Heraclitus

---

[16]Ibid., p. 41.
[17]Ibid., p. 49.
[18]Homer, *Iliad* 4.442-43.; Russell and Konstan, *Homeric Problems*, p. 55.
[19]Russell and Konstan, *Homeric Problems*, p. 55.
[20]Homer, *Iliad* 9.505; Russell and Konstan, *Homeric Problems*, p. 67.

comments: "her foolishness is indeed strong, since she is full of irrational impulse and launches herself like a runner on every kind of injustice." He then generalizes: "So Homer is, as it were, a painter of human passions, attaching the names of gods allegorically to things that happen to us."[21] Thus the stories of the gods are not to be taken literally but as descriptions of human behavior, as indeed they are and as Xenophanes had remarked much earlier.

Pseudo-Heraclitus was neither the first nor the last to interpret the traditional Greek myths found in the poetry of Homer and Hesiod in an effort to make them acceptable to later readers with a more refined ethical and theological sensibility. Another work on the subject from antiquity later than Heraclitus was attributed to Plutarch (ca. A.D. 46–120). It is titled simply *Concerning Homer.*[22] This unknown author also notes, like Heraclitus, the role of Homer in Greek education: "It is appropriate that Homer, who in time was among the first of poets and in power was the very first, is the first we read. In doing so we reap a great harvest in terms of diction, understanding, and experience of the world."[23] This he sets out to demonstrate to his readers. For him it is clear that Homer in the *Iliad* "is presenting physical prowess, in the Odyssey the nobility of the soul."[24] Plutarch (or Pseudo-Plutarch) defends the mythical aspect of Homer: "he cultivates an extraordinary and mythical treatment of events to fill his audience with anxiety and wonder and make the listener's experience deeply moving."[25] He insists that "even in these mythical or fabulous passages, if one considers carefully and not superficially the specific things he has said, it becomes clear that he was adept at every kind of wisdom and skill and provides the starting points and so to speak the seeds of all kinds of discourse and action."[26] Likewise he asserts, contrary to Plato, that these works not only please, astound and enchant, "but also can have a per-

[21]Russell and Konstan, *Homeric Problems*, p. 67.

[22]Plutarch, *Essay on the Life and Poetry of Homer*, ed. John J. Keaney and Robert Lamberton (Atlanta: Scholars Press, 1996).

[23]Ibid., p. 67n1.

[24]Ibid., p. 69n4.

[25]Ibid., p. 69n6.

[26]Ibid., p. 71n6.

suasive or educative effect through those parts that are useful in the pursuit of virtue."[27]

This author devotes much time to analyzing the poetic and rhetorical forms to be found in Homer's writings, but he also insists that the various forms of human discourse, "the historical, the theoretical and the political," also have their origins in Homer.[28] Like Heraclitus, he asserts that Homer, if interpreted correctly, contains the whole of philosophy (theoretical discourse): "This is the road to understanding the nature of reality and of divine and human matters, to distinguishing on the ethical plane those things which are good and those which are bad, and to learning any rule of reasoning appropriate for reaching the truth." For him too philosophy includes the divisions of "physics, ethics, and dialectic." Homer provides the beginnings and seeds of all these and thus deserves our admiration. Pseudo-Plutarch admits that Homer did this through "enigmatic and mythic language" because that is the nature of poetry. But the fundamental reason for it was pedagogical (in plain contradiction to Plato): "They did this so that lovers of learning, delighted by a certain elegance, might more easily seek and find the truth, while the ignorant would not scorn what they could not understand. That which is signified through hidden meanings may be attractive where that which is said explicitly is of little value."[29] The same arguments will be used later by early Christian writers to explain why there is so much obscurity in the Scriptures and why they are in need of allegorical interpretation. In other words, narratives are more useful for teaching and likely to leave an impression than a presentation of abstract truths.

For example, Pseudo-Plutarch explains that Aphrodite has the same force as what Empedocles calls "love," and Ares corresponds to what the same philosopher called "strife." Sometimes they come together and sometimes they are separated. "Harmony comes from the mating of Ares and Aphrodite, that is, harmony of opposites: the ponderous and the swift

---

[27]Ibid., p. 71.
[28]Ibid., p. 141n74.
[29]Ibid., p. 157n92.

mixed proportionately together."[30] By dividing the gods into those who help the Greeks and those who help the Trojans, he says that Homer is hinting "at the manner in which things possessing opposite natures oppose one another, and he reveals their various powers allegorically." Then he gives a whole series of examples, which provide a kind of hermeneutical key for interpreting the myths: "He sets Apollo against Poseidon, hot and dry against wet and cold; Athena against Ares, rational against irrational (that is, good against evil)," and so on. With regard to the question of fate, Homer is "of the same opinion as the most respected of philosophers after him, Plato, Aristotle and Theophrastus, that everything does not come about through fate, but a certain amount falls under the control of men, who have freedom of will."[31]

Both Jewish Hellenistic writers such as Philo and the early Greek Christian writers such as Clement, Origen, Didymus of Alexandria, Basil of Caesarea and Gregory of Nazianzus had studied Homer as a normal part of their education and were also well acquainted with the interpretation of Homer using allegorical methods.

Latin Philosophical Writers

This concept of what is fitting, worthy or appropriate to divinity and a specific terminology for it enter into Latin literature with Cicero and Varro. Cicero, who had studied philosophy in Greece with Posidonius, is largely responsible for the creation of a Latin philosophical vocabulary. The speech of the Stoic Lucilius Balbus in Cicero's *De natura deorum* 2.28.70 refers to the passage of Xenophanes quoted above in Plato's *Republic*. Balbus remarks sarcastically:

> We know what the gods look like and how old they are, their dress . . . and all about them is distorted into the likeness of human frailty. They are actually represented as liable to passions and emotions—we hear of their being in love, sorrowful, angry; according to the myths they even engage in wars and battles, and that not only when as in Homer two armies are con-

---

[30]Ibid., pp. 166-67n102.
[31]Ibid., p. 191n120.

tending and the gods take sides. . . . These stories and these beliefs are utterly foolish; they are stuffed with nonsense and absurdity of all sorts.[32]

Arguing for intelligence and providence as attributes of the gods and
against ignorance on their part, Balbus observes, "But ignorance is foreign
to the divine nature, and weakness, with a consequent incapacity to
perform one's office, in no way suits with the divine majesty."[33] However,
other interlocutors in this dialogue also appeal to Xenophanes's criterion.
In refuting the Epicurean position, Cotta asks, "for who could form a
mental picture of such images? Who could adore them and deem them
worthy of worship or reverence?"[34] He goes on to say that Epicurus "does
away with that which is the most essential element of supreme goodness
and excellence."[35] The same Cotta, criticizing the Stoics' deified abstrac-
tions, states, "Fortune has a very strong claim to be counted in this list, and
nobody will dissociate fortune from inconstancy and haphazard action,
which are certainly unworthy of a deity."[36] Further on in the same critique
he observes, "So far did this sort of error go, that even harmful things were
not only given the names of gods but actually had forms of worship insti-
tuted in their honor. . . . Let us therefore banish from philosophy entirely
the error of making assertions in discussing the immortal gods that are
derogatory to their dignity."[37]

The same kind of terminology is employed by Cicero to argue against
the divine origin of dreams in De divinatione, where the interlocutor
(Marcus) states,

> Why does God, in planning for the good of the human race, convey his
> warnings by means of dreams which men consider unworthy [digna ducant]
> not only of worrying about, but even of remembering? . . . And hence, if
> most dreams are unnoticed and disregarded, either God is ignorant of that
> fact, or he does a vain thing in conveying information by means of dreams;

---

[32]Cicero, De natura deorum 2.28.70; LCL 268:191-193.
[33]Ibid., 2.20.77; LCL 268:199.
[34]Ibid., 1.43.21; LCL 268:117.
[35]Ibid.
[36]Ibid., 3.24.61; LCL 268:345.
[37]Ibid., 3.24.63-4; LCL 268:347.

but neither supposition accords with the nature of a god [*sed horum neutrum in deum cadit*].[38]

Quotations from Cicero could be multiplied, but this is sufficient to illustrate the Latin terminology. A similar terminology can be found in certain passages of Varro and later Seneca.

The Notion of Divine Anger and the Concept of *Apatheia*

In his work *De officiis*, Cicero states that "it is the unanimous teaching of all philosophers that God is never angry, nor does he injure anyone."[39] Cicero did not follow the teachings of a single philosophical school, but reports about various schools of thought.

The passions were understood by the Stoics as a movement contrary to reason and indeed to humanity's very nature. The idea of passion should not be equated with the modern concept of "emotion," for the passions had an exclusively negative connotation. They were understood as irrational impulses of the soul, which cause a state of disease. Just as there are sicknesses of the body, so also the effect of these passions clashing within a person is to rob the soul of health and bring on illness.[40]

Cicero reports that Dionysius of Heraclea had commented on Achilles's statement in Homer "My rage rekindles, and my soul's in flame" as follows:

Is the hand as it should be, when it is affected with a swelling? or is it possible for any other member of the body, when swollen or enlarged, to be in any other than a disordered state? Must not the mind, then, when it is puffed up, or distended, be out of order? But the mind of a wise man is always free from every kind of disorder: it never swells, never is puffed up; but the mind when in anger is in a different state. A wise man, therefore, is never angry; for when he is angry, he lusts after something; for whoever is angry naturally has a longing desire to give all the pain he can to the person who he thinks has injured him; and whoever has this earnest desire must necessarily be much pleased with the accomplishment of his wishes; hence

---

[38]Cicero, *De divinatione*, 2.125; LCL 154:511-13.
[39]Cicero, *De officiis* 3.28.102; LCL 30:378.
[40]Cicero, *Tusc.* 4.10.23.

he is delighted with his neighbor's misery; and as a wise man is not capable
of such feelings as these, he is therefore not capable of anger.[41]

If the passion of anger is a human disease, it could hardly be attributed
to divinity. Humans must do all in their power to combat this disease by
resisting it with reason. For the Stoics that meant seeking to eliminate the
passions of anger. As Seneca observes, "In the first place, it is easier to exclude harmful passions than to rule them, and to deny them admittance
than, after they have been admitted, to control them; for when they have
established themselves in possession, they are stronger than their ruler and
do not permit themselves to be restrained or reduced."[42] And later in the
same work, he insists: "Anger must by all means be removed. . . . Let it be
put away entirely, it can do us no good."[43] It is impossible that such a destructive force should exist among the gods.

> But there are certain agents that are unable to harm us and have no power
> that is not beneficent and salutary, as for example, the immortal gods, who
> neither wish nor are able to hurt; for they are by nature mild and gentle, as
> incapable of injuring others as of injuring themselves. Those, therefore, are
> mad and ignorant of truth who lay to the gods' charge the cruelty of the sea,
> excessive rains, and the stubbornness of winter, whereas all the while none
> of the phenomena which harm or help us are planned personally for us.[44]

Not only anger was foreign to God, but also all passions. He was thus
held to be *apathēs*, which could be considered the opposite of
anthrōpopathos (with human passions). It rules out human passions on the
part of the divinity, as it does all other human attributes. Aristotle states in
his *Metaphysics* that "there is some substance which is eternal and im-
movable and separate from sensible things . . . and moreover that it is im-
passive and unalterable; for all the other kinds of motion are posterior to
spatial motion."[45]

---

[41]Cicero, *Tusc.* 3.9; LCL 141:246-49.
[42]Seneca, *De ira* 1.7.2; LCL 214:125.
[43]Ibid., 2.27.1; LCL 214:222.
[44]Ibid.
[45]Aristotle, *Metaphysics* 1073a; LCL 287:150-55.

According to Sextus Empiricus the teaching that divinity is without passion (*apathēs to theion*) was the common doctrine of all Greek philosophers.[46] For example, later on Plotinus (a contemporary of Origen) taught that "what is not subject to death and to decay is without passion [*apathēs*]."[47]

To summarize the contents of this chapter: the role of the Homeric epics in the Greek educational tradition necessitated the development of a way of interpreting them in such a way as to neutralize their harmful influence on the young. This later came to be called allegory. Earlier it was referred to as *hyponoia*, indicating meaning beneath or underlying the text. The philosophers, beginning with Xenophanes and later even more forcefully with Plato, criticized the mythological presentation of the gods from a theological point of view. We find the term "anthropomorphic" introduced in philosophical discourse to describe the representation of the divinity with human characteristics. The word itself is an implicit criticism: it means that God is not like that in reality. It was particularly important to exclude the passion of anger from the understanding of divinity. This led to the development of the idea that God is *apathēs*, without passion. These ideas were influential with early Christian writers, because all Greek education was based on this tradition, as was Roman education later on.

---

[46]Sextus Empiricus, *Pyrrh.* 1.162.
[47]Plotinus, *Enneads* 1.1.2; 5.9.4.

3

Hellenistic Jewish Interpretation
of the Scriptures

*For what greater impiety could there be than to
suppose that the Unchangeable changes?*

PHILO OF ALEXANDRIA, *GOD IS UNCHANGEABLE* 22

BY THE TIME OF JESUS CHRIST, the Jews had become well established in
the Greco-Roman world. There were Greek-speaking Jewish communities
living in cities throughout the Mediterranean area. Two of the most important of these were located in Antioch and Alexandria, the capital cities
first of the Greek kingdoms of Syria and Egypt and then of the Roman
provinces of Syria and Egypt. Already in the third century before Christ
the Jews of Alexandria seem to have translated the law of Moses into Greek.
This meant that it became known to non-Jews as well in the Hellenistic
world. One result of this was the need to defend the Jewish Scriptures and
to explain them to a cultured, philosophically oriented, non-Jewish public
such as that of Alexandria.[1]

---

[1]See H. Hegermann, "The Diaspora in the Hellenistic Age," in *The Cambridge History of Judaism*, ed. W. D.
Davies and L. Finkelstein, *The Hellenistic Age* (Cambridge: Cambridge University Press, 2008), 2:115-66.
See also E. J. Bickerman, *The Jews in the Greek Age* (Cambridge, MA: Harvard University Press, 1988); J.
M. G. Barclay, *Jews in the Mediterranean Diaspora: From Alexander to Trajan* (323 BCE–117 CE) (Berkeley:
University of California Press, 1998); J. R. Bartlett, *Jews in the Hellenistic World: Josephus, Aristeas, the
Sibylline Oracles, Eupolemus* (Cambridge: Cambridge University Press, 1985); and Victor Tcherikover,

Such is the background for the earliest Hellenistic Jewish writings that explain or present the law of Moses. The document known as the *Letter of Aristeas* (or Pseudo-Aristeas, written about 170 B.C.) describes how the law of Moses came to be translated into Greek supposedly at the request of the king of Egypt, Ptolemy, who wished to have it in his famous library at Alexandria. The translation according to this account was made somewhat miraculously by seventy translators sent from Jerusalem for this purpose. In addition the letter contains an apology for the law of Moses and some indications as to how the law is to be interpreted. The author is particularly concerned to explain the dietary laws and the distinction between clean and unclean animals. First of all he lays down a general principle regarding the law: "In general everything is similarly constituted in regard to natural reasoning, being governed by one supreme power, and in each particular everything has a profound reason for it, both the things from which we abstain and those of which we partake."[2] Then he gives various examples. He admonishes: "Do not take the contemptible view that Moses enacted this legislation because of an excessive preoccupation with mice and weasels or suchlike creatures. The fact is that everything has been solemnly set in order for unblemished investigation and amendment of life for the sake of righteousness." The birds that are forbidden and called "impure" are wild and carnivorous and behave unjustly toward the domesticated birds. Their prohibition is in fact a way of teaching a moral lesson.

> By calling them impure, he has thereby indicated that it is the solemn binding duty of those for whom the legislation has been established to practice righteousness and not to lord it over anyone in reliance upon their own strength, nor to deprive him of anything, but to govern their lives righteously, in the manner of the gentle creatures among the aforementioned birds which feed on those plants which grow on the ground and do not exercise a domination leading to the destruction of their fellow creatures.

Hellenistic Civilization and the Jews (Philadelphia: Jewish Publication Society of America, 1959).
[2]Quotations from this work are taken from R. J. H. Shutt, trans., "Letter of Aristeas," in James H. Charlesworth, *The Old Testament Pseudepigrapha*, ed. James H. Charlesworth, *Expansions of the "Old Testament" and Legends, Wisdom and Philosophical Literature, Prayers, Psalms and Odes, Fragments of Lost Judeo-Hellenistic Works* (Peabody, MA: Hendrickson, 2010), 2:22-23.

In other words, it would be unworthy of the one supreme power to be concerned merely about mice and weasels. These merely represent the higher moral principles with which the supreme power is concerned. They are symbols for the true and more profound moral teaching of the law. Similarly the permission to eat cloven-hoofed animals is in fact an exhortation to remember God, for "all cloven-footed creatures and ruminants quite clearly express, to those who perceive it, the phenomenon of memory." The author seems to be anxious that the non-Jewish readers should not think that the laws of the Jewish Scriptures manifest a trivial concept of God. Implicitly (and to a certain extent explicitly) it is the concept of God that governs his explanations. "So he exhorts us to remember how the aforesaid blessings are maintained and preserved by divine power under his providence, for he has ordered every time and place for a continual reminder of the supreme God and upholder of all."

The early Christian writers had a high regard for these Jewish Hellenistic authors, and we know of others like Aristobulus because they were quoted by Christian authors such as Clement of Alexandria and Eusebius of Caesarea. The fragments preserved by Clement and Eusebius come from an apologetic and didactic work addressed to the young king Ptolemy VI Philometor (184–145 B.C.).[3] This second-century Jewish interpreter likewise seems to have felt it necessary to defend Moses from the charge of *alogia*, that is, unreasonable or senseless interpretations, especially taking literally the many anthropomorphisms found in the Scriptures. Eusebius reports that in his work dedicated to Ptolemy the king, Aristobulus "explained why indications are given of hands and arms and face and feet and walking about throughout our Law with respect to the divine power."[4] He states: "And I wish to exhort you to receive the interpretations according to the laws of nature and to grasp the fitting conception of God and not to fall into the mythical and human way of thinking about God." Again it is the conception of God that provides the key to interpreting the

---

[3]Martin Hengel, *Judaism and Hellenism: Studies in Their Encounter in Palestine During the Early Hellenistic Period* (Philadelphia: Fortress, 1974), 1:164. Hegermann, "Diaspora in the Hellenistic Age," p. 144.

[4]Translations of Aristobulus are from Adela Yarbro Collins in Charlesworth, *Expansions of the "Old Testament" and Legends*, pp. 837-42.

Scriptures correctly. For Aristobulus it is clear that one must search for a deeper meaning in these writings. They cannot be taken at face value. As a programmatic statement he notes that Moses uses "words that refer to other matters": "For our lawgiver Moses proclaims arrangements of nature and preparations for great events by expressing that which he wishes to say in many ways, by using words that refer to other matters (I mean matters relating to outward appearances). . . . But to those who have no share of power and understanding, but who are devoted to the letter alone, he does not seem to explain anything elevated." This may be directed against Jews who opposed allegorical interpretation as well as against non-Jews who mocked the unsophisticated and anthropomorphic representations of the supreme being in the Jewish Scriptures.

One obvious anthropomorphism that cannot be taken literally is the reference to the "hands" of God.

> Now "hands" are clearly thought of even in our own time in a more general way. For when you, being king, send out forces, wishing to accomplish something, we say, "The king has a mighty hand," and the hearers are referred to the power which you have. Now Moses indicates this also in our Law when he speaks thus: "God brought you out of Egypt with a mighty hand," and again he says that God said to him, "I will send forth my hand and I will strike the Egyptians." . . . For it is possible for people speaking metaphorically to consider that the entire strength of human beings and their active powers are in their hands. Therefore the lawgiver has employed a metaphor well for the purpose of saying something elevated, when he says that the accomplishments of God are his hands.

Another anthropomorphism that can hardly be taken literally is the suggestion that God engages in physical movement. "It is said too in the book of the Law that there was a descent of God upon the mountain, at the time when he was giving the Law, in order that all might see the action of God. . . . Therefore the descent was not local; for God is everywhere." Unfortunately we have only fragments from Aristobulus's once extensive work, but the fragments suggest a well-developed method for interpreting the passages containing anthropomorphic ways of speaking in which the central element was a lofty conception of the divinity.

From the same Alexandrian Jewish community, but almost two hundred years later, however, we do have the very extensive writings of Philo, a contemporary of Jesus Christ and of St. Paul, another Greek-speaking Jew from the Diaspora. Philo seems to have belonged to a prominent and wealthy Jewish family of Alexandria. We know little about his life other than what can be gleaned from his numerous works, a large part of which are devoted to the explanation of the Scriptures. It is clear that he had received the best kind of education then available in the Hellenistic world, but he remained a convinced and faithful Jew. He appears to have functioned as a rabbi (an institution then developing) in the Alexandrian Jewish community, then one of the largest and most flourishing in the Diaspora. We know that he was sent to Rome in about A.D. 41 as the head of a delegation to plead the cause of the Jews before the emperor Caligula against the Roman governor Flaccus, who had instigated the pogrom of A.D. 38. These matters are described in two of Philo's works, the *Embassy to Gaius* and the *In Flaccum*, and by Flavius Josephus in his *Antiquities of the Jews* (18.8.1). Philo produced numerous treatises on themes in the law of Moses, such as the cherubim, the sacrifices of Abel and Cain, the confusion of languages and the migration of Abraham. He also cites some of the prophets. Other works include *The Life of Moses*, the *Allegories of the Laws* and *Questions and Answers on the Books of Genesis and Exodus*. Philo's works were preserved by early Christian writers, who often cite him with approval as a wise man or a trustworthy witness. These include Clement of Alexandria, Origen, Didymus of Alexandria and Ambrose of Milan.[5] In the late fifth-century collection of short excerpts of interpretation of scriptural passages known as the *catena* (chain), there are many passages from Philo, but they are ascribed to "Philo the bishop" since the compilers assumed that this writer, who seemed so Christian in spirit, must be a Christian bishop.

In the exegetical writings of Philo, the criterion of what is "worthy of"

---

[5]See David T. Runia, *Philo in Early Christian Literature: A Survey*, Compendia Rerum Iudaicarum ad Novum Testamentum (Minneapolis: Fortress, 1993).

or "fitting for" God comes to be widely applied to the interpretation of the Scriptures. For example, with reference to Genesis 2:7, "the LORD God formed man from the dust of the ground, and breathed into his nostrils the breath of life," he writes, "for God forbid that we should be infected with such monstrous folly [*atopia*] as to think that God employs for inbreathing organs such as mouth or nostrils; for God is not only not in the form of man, but belongs to no class or kind." He then explains that the expression "breathe into" must be understood to mean that God sent his spirit into the human intellect so that humanity could have knowledge of God. The expression also has an ethical sense, because, just as the face is the dominant part of the body, so is the intellect the dominant part of the soul and God gives his spirit to this part.[6]

Commenting on the statement in Genesis 3:8 that the man hid himself from God, Philo writes: "Were one not to interpret it allegorically, it would be impossible to accept the statement, for God fills and penetrates all things, and has left no spot void or empty of his presence."[7] Philo applies the terminology of what is "fitting" or "appropriate" extensively in his interpretations, making use especially of the terms *theoprepēs* ("what is fitting to or suited to the deity") and *hieroprepēs* ("what is fitting to the holy"), *anoikeion* ("inappropriate"), and so on. The concept of *anthrōpopathēs* (as if having human passions) seems to originate with Philo, who regards it as even less fitting than anthropomorphism.[8] As already explained in the previous chapter, in Greek philosophy God was already held to be *apathēs*, that is, without passions.

In Exodus 13:11-13 God is said to have sworn an oath: "When the LORD has brought you into the land of the Canaanites, as he swore to you and your ancestors, and has given it to you, you shall set apart to the LORD all that first opens the womb." Philo comments: "But when he tells us that God swore an oath, we must consider whether he lays down that such a thing can with truth be ascribed to God, since to thousands it seems un-

---

[6]Philo, *Leg.* 1.36-39; LCL 226:171.
[7]Ibid., 3.4.3; LCL 226:303.
[8]In the Thesaurus Linguae Graecae all seven instances of the word up to the first century A.D. are from Philo.

worthy [*anoikeion*] of Him."⁹ He explains that our conception of an oath is that it is an appeal to God on some disputed matter. But nothing is disputed with God. He needs no other witness, for there is no other god who is his peer. There is nothing better than the "Cause," just as "there is nothing equal to Him, or even but a little below."¹⁰ The difference between God and humans is one of kind and nature. As Philo sees it, "men have recourse to oaths to win belief, when others deem them untrustworthy; but God is trustworthy in His speech as elsewhere, so that His words in certitude and assurance differ not a whit from oaths. And so it is that while with us the oath gives warrant for our sincerity, it is itself guaranteed by God. For the oath does not make God trustworthy; it is God that assures the oath."¹¹

The impossibility of God's swearing an oath in the same sense that humans do leads Philo to make an extended reflection on human ways of thinking about God. Moses represented God as binding himself by an oath in order to convince "created man" of his weakness and to offer help and comfort. The more general reflection that follows is worth quoting in full.

> We are not able to cherish continually in our souls the thought which sums up so worthily the nature of the Cause, that "God is not as man" (Num 23:19) and thus rise superior to all the human conceptions of him. In us the mortal is the chief ingredient. We cannot get outside ourselves in forming our ideas; we cannot escape our inborn infirmities. We creep within our covering of mortality, like snails into their shells, or like the hedgehog we roll ourselves into a ball, and we think of the blessed and the immortal in terms of our own natures. We shun indeed in words the monstrosity of saying that God is of human form, but in actual fact we accept the impious thought that He is of human passions [*anthrōpopathos*]. And therefore we invent for Him hands and feet, incomings and outgoings, enmities, aversions, estrangements, anger, in fact such parts and passions as can never belong [*anoikeia*] to the Cause. And of such is the oath—a mere crutch for our weakness.¹²

⁹Philo, *Sacr.* 38.91; LCL 227:165.
¹⁰Ibid., 38.92; LCL 227:165.
¹¹Ibid., 38.93; LCL 227:165.
¹²Ibid., 29.94-96; LCL 227:165-167.

This passage is of great interest because of its general and programmatic nature. No human limitations or failings can be attributed to God. All passages in the Scriptures that seem to attribute human form or passions to God must be interpreted in such a way that the meaning is one worthy of God or suited to the divine nature.

Commenting on a different passage where God is said to have sworn an oath, Philo defends the fittingness of the assertion. In Genesis 22:16-17 the text has: "By myself I have sworn, says the Lord: Inasmuch as you have carried out this matter and for my sake have not spared your beloved son, I will indeed bless you with blessings, and I will make your offspring as numerous as the stars of heaven and as the sand that is by the seashore."[13] Philo explains: "Good is it both that He confirmed the promise by an oath, and that He did so by an oath befitting God [*theoprepei*]; you mark that God swears not by some other thing, for nothing is higher than He, but by Himself, who is best of all things."[14] He observes that some have said that it is inappropriate (*anoikeion*—the opposite of *theoprepēs*) for God to swear, because an oath is added to assist faith: "They say indeed that an oath is calling God to witness to a point which is disputed; so if it is God that swears, He bears witness to himself, which is absurd, for he that bears the witness must needs be a different person from him on whose behalf it is borne."[15] Philo's answer to this objection, however, is, "First that there is nothing amiss in God bearing witness to Himself. For who else would be capable of bearing witness to Him? Secondly He Himself is to Himself all that is most precious, kinsman, intimate, friend, virtue, happiness, blessedness, knowledge, understanding, beginning, end, whole, everything, judge, decision, counsel, law, process, sovereignty."[16] Again the answer is based on the concept of God.

Philo returns to the question of attributing passions to God in another work, where he cites Genesis 6:7: "I will blot out man whom I made from

---

[13]The translation from the Greek version is by Albert Pietersma and Benjamin G. Wright, eds., *A New English Translation of the Septuagint: And the Other Greek Translations Traditionally Included Under That Title* (Oxford: Oxford University Press, 2007).

[14]Philo, *Leg.* 3.203; LCL 226:439.

[15]Ibid., 3.205; LCL 226:441.

[16]Ibid., 3.205; LCL 226:441.

the face of the earth, from man to beast, from creeping things to fowls of heaven, because I was angry that I made him." He notes that some people who hear these words think that God feels anger, although he is not susceptible to any passions. "For disquiet is peculiar to human weakness, but neither the unreasoning passions of the soul, nor the parts and members of the body in general, have any relation to God."[17] But the question remains as to why Moses used such expressions. The answer is that he did it for pedagogical reasons. He used them to teach and admonish those who could not understand more abstract ways of thinking. Philo explains that all of the commands and prohibitions in the law of Moses must be understood in the light of two principles. One is that "God is not as man" (Num 23:19), and the other is, "like a man He shall train His son" (Deut 8:5). The words of Genesis 6:7 must be understood in the sense of the latter phrase. They are used for "training and admonition, not because God's nature is such." There are two kinds of people, Philo explains: lovers of the soul and lovers of the body.[18] The first have a lofty conception of "the Existent" and do not compare him to any form of created thing: "They have dissociated Him from every category or quality, for it is one of the facts which go to make His blessedness and supreme felicity that His being is apprehended as simple being, without other definite characteristic; and thus they do not picture it with form, but only admit to their minds the conception of existence only." The others, the lovers of the body, "think of the Cause of all in the same terms as of themselves, and do not reflect that while a being which is formed through the union of several faculties needs several parts to minister to the need of each, God being uncreated and the Author of the creation of the others needs none of the properties which belong to the creatures which He has brought into being."[19] These are denounced in strong terms as "the mythical fictions of the impious, who, professing to represent the deity as of human form, in reality represent Him as having human passions."[20]

---

[17]Philo, *Deus* 11.51; LCL 247:37.
[18]Ibid., 11.55; LCL 247:37.
[19]Ibid., 11.56; LCL 247:39.
[20]Ibid., 11.59; LCL 247:41.

For Philo, the correct perception of God is not merely an intellectual question, but above all a moral one. To think of God in terms of human qualities is not only intellectually mistaken but also morally reprehensible. Those who possess "a generously gifted nature and a training blameless throughout" are guided in their reading of the Scriptures by the principle that "God is not as a man" (Num 23:19). Those, however, who have no power of clear vision and are "ill-disciplined and foolish" receive profit from "a master who frightens them, for they fear his threats and menaces and thus involuntarily are schooled by fear."[21] Moses, says Philo, hoped to eradicate the evil "by representing the supreme Cause as dealing in threats and oftentimes showing indignation and implacable anger, or again as using weapons of war for His onslaughts on the unrighteous."[22] This is the only way that the foolish can be corrected. Then he goes on to link the two principles "God is as a man" and "God is not as a man" to fear and love. As Philo sees it, all the admonitions and exhortations in the law refer either to loving or fearing God. The difference between these is directly connected to having the correct conception of God: "to love Him is the most suitable for those into whose conception of the Existent no thought of human parts or passions enters, who pay Him the honor meet for God [= *theoprepēs*] for His own sake only. To fear is most suitable for the others."[23]

In his work *De plantatione* (Noah's work as a planter), Philo cites Genesis 2:8: "God planted a garden in Eden facing the sun-rising and placed there the man whom He had moulded."[24] Then he explains why it is impossible to imagine such a thing taking place literally and why such a conception is impossible to reconcile with a proper understanding of God. To suppose that such things took place literally would be impious. "They are utterly monstrous inventions of men who would overthrow great virtues like piety and reverence by representing Him as having the form and passions of mankind." The solution, he says, is allegory, "the method dear to men with

[21]Ibid., 11.62-63; LCL 247:41-43.
[22]Ibid., 11.68; LCL 247:45.
[23]Ibid.
[24]Philo, *Plant.* 32; LCL 247:229.

their eyes opened."[25] The text itself, he says, supplies us with hints, for it describes the trees in the garden as "trees of Life, of Immortality, of Knowledge, of Apprehension, of Understanding, of the conception of good and evil."[26] These provide clues that what is really being spoken of in the text is not earthly soil but the "reasonable soul, namely its path according to virtue with life and immortality as its end."[27] He concludes: "We must conceive therefore that the bountiful God plants in the soul as it were a garden of virtues and of the modes of conduct corresponding to each of them, a garden that brings the soul to perfect happiness."[28]

Allegory was indeed the principal tool for making the texts theologically acceptable, that is, for interpreting them in a way suitable to the divine nature. It was presumed that the text must have a deeper meaning. In Genesis 8:21 we read: "And the Lord God smelled an odor of fragrance, and the Lord God, when he had given it thought, said, 'I will not proceed hereafter to curse the earth because of the deeds of humans, for the mind of mankind applies itself attentively to evil things from youth; so I will not proceed hereafter to smite all living flesh, as I have done'" (NETS). A more anthropomorphic and anthropopathic depiction of God can hardly be imagined. Both human senses and human passions are attributed to God as well as the idea that God changes his mind. Philo deals with the passage by noting that the idea of repentance on the part of God is a passion incompatible (*anoikeion*) with the divine power. Human decisions are weak and unstable, since their affairs are full of uncertainty. "But for God nothing is uncertain or unknowable, because He is all powerful and stable in his thought."[29] How is it possible then that God could have first sought to destroy the human race by the deluge and then later have said that he would not do so in the future, given that the same wickedness is still found in the human race? Philo answers that "all these kinds of formulas are contained in the Law for the instruction and for the utility of teaching rather

---

[25]Ibid., 35-36; LCL 247:231.
[26]Ibid., 36; LCL 247:231.
[27]Ibid., 37; LCL 247:231.
[28]Ibid.
[29]Philo, *QG* 2.54; LCL 380:134-36.

than for the expression of essential truth." He then explains again[30] that
there are two principal texts in the entire legislation, the one according to
which God is said "not to be like man" and the other according to which
he is said "to be like a man" who educates his son. The first text, "God is
not like man," brings out the essential truth, because not only is God not
like man but he is also not like the sun or the heavens or the sensible world,
but only like God. This happy Being does not admit of any resemblance or
comparison. He is above all, even of happiness and all that is superior. The
second text, that "God is like a man," expresses the need to educate us.

Not only passages in the law that ascribed to God unfitting characteristics
or behavior needed to be allegorized but also passages that described
human behavior inappropriate for holy persons. In Genesis 16 Sarah, who
has not be able to bear children to Abraham, offers her slave girl named
Hagar to Abraham and tells him to beget children by her. Abraham does
so and Hagar becomes pregnant. Sarah then becomes resentful and feels
dishonored by Hagar's success. She complains to Abraham, who permits
her to mistreat Hagar, who then runs away. For Philo such a story was not
edifying and cried out for an interpretation to give it meaning and justify
its inclusion in Scripture. Philo's interpretation was to see in Sarah the
representation of wisdom and virtue. Abraham is the embodiment of the
seeker after wisdom and virtue, and Hagar symbolizes the preliminary
studies necessary for those who seek wisdom (philosophy). This interpretation forms part of a more extensive allegory in which the three patriarchs
Abraham, Isaac and Jacob are expressions of three different approaches to
the acquisition of wisdom. Abraham seeks it through learning. His migra-
tions are to be understood as steps in receiving a divine teaching. Isaac, the
son of Abraham, allegorically represents the intellect, and Sarah, representing virtue, becomes the symbol of the autodidact. Jacob represents the
figure of the ascetic or the one who engages in the acquisition of virtue
through practice.

---

[30]Cf. Philo, *Deus* 11.51, cited earlier.

Philo can then interpret Sarah's invitation to Abraham to make use of her slave girl as an invitation to engage in study.

> "Go in, then," she says, "to my handmaid, the lower instruction given by the lower branches of school lore, that first you may have children by her," for afterwards you will be able to avail yourself of the mistress's company to beget children of higher birth. For grammar teaches us to study literature in the poets and historians, and will thus produce intelligence and wealth of knowledge. It will teach us also to despise the vain delusions of our empty imagination by shewing us the calamities which heroes and demi-gods who are celebrated in such literature are said to have undergone.[31]

Philo then mentions each of the traditional preliminary studies, such as music, dialectic and rhetoric, to show how they contribute to the search for wisdom. They are symbolized by Hagar, who is the handmaid of virtue. Philo sums it up in this statement: "Sarah, virtue, bears, we shall find, the same relation to Hagar, education, as the mistress to the servant maid, or the lawful wife to the concubine, and so naturally the mind which aspires to study and to gain knowledge, the mind we call Abraham, will have Sarah, virtue, for his wife, and Hagar, the whole range of school culture, for his concubine."[32] But how can the ill treatment of Hagar by Sarah be justified? This could be fitted into the allegory as well. The studies represented by Hagar are preliminary studies and not ends in themselves, as is wisdom. It is important not to lose sight of the goal, and so Philo notes: "For instance when first I was incited by the goads of philosophy, to desire her I consorted in early youth with one of her handmaids, Grammar, and all that I begat by her, writing, reading and study of the writings of the poets, I dedicated to her mistress."[33] In the end, however, Hagar in her allegorical meaning must be sent away, or she becomes a distraction: "For some have been ensnared by the love lures of the handmaids and spurned the mistress, and have grown old, some doting on poetry, some on geometrical figures,

---

[31]Philo, *Congr.* 14–15; LCL 261:465.
[32]Philo, *Congr.* 23; LCL 261:469.
[33]Ibid.; LCL 261:495.

some on the blending of musical 'colours,' and a host of other things, and
have never been able to soar to the winning of the lawful wife."[34] The story
of Abraham, Sarah and Hagar is no longer a story about domestic strife but
is elevated through allegory to become the vehicle of teaching about the
spiritual life. Philo is able to summarize the teaching of the story thus:
"And indeed just as the school subjects contribute to the acquirement of
philosophy, so does philosophy to the getting of wisdom. For philosophy
is the practice or study of wisdom, and wisdom is the knowledge of things
divine and human and their causes. And therefore just as the culture of the
schools is the bond-servant of philosophy, so must philosophy be the
servant of wisdom."[35]

From the point of view of the concept of God, the institutions of the
temple and the sacrificial cult and indeed the notion of Jerusalem as the
city of God posed a problem. Philo, using etymological meanings ascribed to the Hebrew names, had interpreted the two names Jacob and
Israel to represent two aspects of the spiritual life, the struggle against vice
and the contemplative life. The name Jacob was interpreted to mean the
"ascetic" or the "athlete" in the sense of one who is in "training," that is,
training for virtue and struggling against vice. Philo based this interpretation on the story of the birth of Jacob in Genesis 25:26, where he emerges
from the maternal womb holding the heel of his brother Esau.[36] *Askēsis*
in its original meaning in Greek is the training of the athlete. Israel,
however, had been interpreted to mean "the one who sees God," or the
contemplative life. In order to arrive at the vision of God it is necessary
to struggle against the passions and vices represented by Esau. The
"athlete" Jacob struggles in Genesis 32 with a "man" after which he is given
the name Israel, "the one who sees God." This interpretation forms the
background for Philo's interpretation of the city of God as the human soul.
He arrives at his meaning through deduction: "And there is another psalm

---

[34]Ibid.; LCL 261:497.
[35]Ibid.
[36]For a more extensive explanation, see Mark Sheridan, "Jacob and Israel: A Contribution to the History
    of an Interpretation," in *From the Nile to the Rhone and Beyond: Studies in Early Monastic Literature and
    Scriptural Interpretation* (Rome: Pontificio Ateneo Sant'Anselmo, 2012), pp. 315-34.

which runs thus: 'The strong current of the river makes glad the city of God' (Ps. xlvi. (xlv.) 4). What city? For the existing holy city, where the sacred temple also is, does not stand in the neighbourhood of rivers any more than of the sea. Thus it is clear that he writes to show us allegorically something different from the obvious."[37]

Philo concludes that

> God's city is the name in one sense for the world which has received the whole bowl, wherein the divine draught is mixed, and feasted thereon and exultingly taken for its possession the gladness which remains for all time never to be removed or quenched. In another sense he uses this name for the soul of the Sage, in which God is said to walk as in a city. For "I will walk in you," he says, "and will be your God" (Lev. xxvi. 12).[38]

This interpretation is reinforced by the etymology of the name Jerusalem.

> Now the city of God is called in the Hebrew Jerusalem and its name when translated is "vision of peace." Therefore do not seek for the city of the Existent among the regions of the earth, since it is not wrought of wood or stone, but in a soul, in which there is no warring, whose sight is keen, which has set before it as its aim to live in contemplation and peace. For what grander or holier house could we find for God in the whole range of existence than the vision-seeking mind, the mind which is eager to see all things and never even in its dreams has a wish for faction or turmoil?[39]

The true dwelling of God, then, is not in a building or in a city but in the human soul that is in peace. Such an interpretation could easily be taken over by Christians, for whom also "the Most High does not dwell in houses made with human hands" (Acts 7:48). Philo interpreted many other passages of the law of Moses allegorically to give them a sense that was acceptable in terms of a true "theological" idea of God for whom all forms of anthropomorphic and anthropopathic behavior were inconceivable to those who had been imbued with the philosophical culture of the Hellenistic world.

---

[37]Philo, *Somn.* 2.246; LCL 275:553.
[38]Ibid., 2.248; LCL 275:555.
[39]Ibid., 2.250-251; LCL 275:555.

THE ANGER OF GOD AND THE CONCEPT OF *APATHEIA*
IN HELLENISTIC JUDAISM

The idea that God could be angry like human beings was excluded from Jewish Hellenistic interpretation no less than from the Greek philosophical tradition. In the *Letter of Aristeas* we read that during a banquet the king asked a guest, "How can one avoid anger?" The explanation includes the following admonition: "You must know that God governs the whole universe with kindliness and without any anger, and you, O King," he says, "must follow him."[40]

Philo deals with the question many times, especially through his use of the term *anthrōpopathos* (with human passions). In his work *On the Creation* (*De opificio mundi*) he also deals with it from the point of view of God's immovability or unchangeability. He comments on the number seven: "It is the nature of 7 alone, as I have said, neither to beget nor to be begotten."[41]

> There is only one thing that neither causes motion nor experiences it, the original Ruler and Sovereign. Of Him 7 may be fitly said to the a symbol. Evidence of what I say is supplied by Philolaus [a Greek philosopher] in these words: "There is, he says, a supreme Ruler of all things, God, ever One, abiding, without motion, Himself (alone) like unto Himself, different from all others." In the region, then, of things discerned by the intellect only 7 exhibits that which is exempt from movement and from passion.[42]

A key point in Philo's understanding of God is that he is unmoved and unchanging, "For only a truly unchanging soul has access to the unchanging God, and the soul that is of such a disposition does in very deed stand near to the Divine power."[43] And he elaborates: "This oracle [Deut 5:31] proves two things, one that the Existent Being who moves and turns all else is Himself exempt from movement and turning; and secondly that

---

[40]*Letter of Aristeas* 254. Trans. Shutt, in *The Old Testament Pseudepigrapha*, ed. James H. Charlesworth (Peabody, MA: Hendrickson, 2010), 2:24.

[41]Philo, *Opif.* 99; LCL 226:79.

[42]Ibid., 100-101; LCL 226:81.

[43]Philo, *Post.* 27; LCL 227:343.

He makes the worthy man sharer of His own nature, which is repose."[44] Philo also devotes a whole treatise to the subject of the unchangeableness of God, in which he exclaims: "For what greater impiety could there be than to suppose that the Unchangeable changes?"[45] This of course excludes the passion of anger as has been noted earlier in this chapter. It should be emphasized that Philo is addressing himself not to pagans but to Jewish readers, to those "whose natural wit is more dense and dull, or whose early training has been mishandled, since they have no power of clear vision, need physicians in the shape of admonishers,"[46] in other words, those who read the text literally and naively.

To summarize: the Hebrew Scriptures were translated into Greek by the third century B.C. in Alexandria, which was quickly becoming the cultural capital of the ancient Greek-speaking world. There Greek speaking Jews interpreted the biblical texts in ways "fitting to God" (*theoprepēs*) or "worthy of God" (*axios tou theou*) in order to exclude the possibility of taking literally the anthropomorphic or anthropopathic features of the texts. Philo of Alexandria seems to be the first to use the latter term, which excludes anger on the part of God. Philo exercised an enormous influence on early Christian interpretation. He was read by authors as diverse and early as Irenaeus of Lyons, Clement of Alexandria, Origen, Eusebius, Didymus of Alexandria and Ambrose of Milan. At the end of the fifth century many of the passages found in the commentaries known by the Latin name *catenae* (chains of commentary) are attributed to "Philo the bishop."

---

[44]Ibid., 28; LCL 227:345.
[45]Philo, *Deus* 22; LCL 247:21.
[46]Ibid., 63; LCL 247:43.

4

The Interpretation of the Scriptures
in the New Testament

A MODEL FOR LATER WRITERS

The Apostle Paul, "teacher of the Gentiles in faith and truth" (1 Tim 2:7)
taught the church which he gathered from the Gentiles how
it ought to interpret the books of the Law.[1]

ORIGEN, *HOMILY 5.1 ON EXODUS*

THE USE OF THE OLD TESTAMENT in the New Testament is a vast and complicated subject.[2] Of course for the authors of the texts that became the New Testament, the writings that came to be called the "Old Testament" by Christian writers were still simply the "Scriptures." These texts were often cited by New Testament authors to validate or confirm their own texts, but they were also sometimes seen to be in contrast to the new

---

[1] The English translations of the homilies on Genesis and Exodus are taken from Origen, *Homilies on Genesis and Exodus*, FC 71, trans. Ronald E. Heine (Washington, DC: Catholic University of America Press, 1982).
[2] On this subject the following works may be mentioned: G. K. Beale and D. A. Carson, *Commentary on the New Testament Use of the Old Testament* (Grand Rapids: Baker Academic, 2007); R. T. France, *Jesus and the Old Testament: His Application of Old Testament Passages to Himself and His Mission* (Downers Grove, IL: InterVarsity Press, 1971); Richard N. Longenecker, *Biblical Exegesis in the Apostolic Period* (Grand Rapids: Eerdmans, 1974); idem, *New Wine into Fresh Wineskins: Contextualizing the Early Christian Confessions* (Peabody, MA: Hendrickson, 1999); Kenneth Berding and Jonathan Lunde, eds., *Three Views on the New Testament Use of the Old Testament* (Grand Rapids: Zondervan, 2008).

teaching. Many of these scriptural texts cited in the New Testament were actually reinterpreted or given a new meaning in the light of the teaching and life of Jesus. The old scriptural texts were used to interpret the figure of Jesus Christ, but in the process they were also given new meaning by the figure of Jesus. The authors of the New Testament wanted to show continuity, but they also wanted to show the superiority of the teaching of Jesus and of the new covenant generally. Here we can touch only on a few places where they show the latter.

It has been asserted that there is never any suggestion in the Gospels that Jesus opposed the Torah and that the conflicts portrayed always have to do with the correct interpretation of Scripture as opposed to misunderstanding or false application of the law by other teachers. "The Judaism of Jesus' day was a Torah-centric religion. To gain any hearing among his people Jesus' teaching also had to be Torah-centric." It is likewise asserted that Jesus was convinced that the law was the word of God and that he was "the fulfillment of that Law."[3] However, the fact is that we do not have direct access to Jesus' teachings or his conviction, but only through the writings of the New Testament, which are not verbatim reports, but are filled with theological interpretation. To understand these assertions as well as the conflicts over the law reported in the New Testament, it is necessary to keep in mind the distinction between Moses considered as lawgiver and Moses understood as the author of the entire Pentateuch, the first five books of "Moses." In some texts "Moses" refers to the laws and in others to the entire first five books of the Bible, of which he had been understood to be the author for several centuries. When Jesus is quoted in Matthew 5:17 as saying that he did not come to abolish the law and the prophets, what is meant is Scripture as such, not individual precepts. He goes on to say that he has come to "fulfill" them, that is, the Law and the Prophets, or what was considered to be Scripture. This is a strong assertion, indeed, a huge innovation, which his opponents certainly would have seen as a new and unacceptable teaching, indeed, a major source of conflict.

---

[3]E. Earle Ellis, *The Old Testament in Early Christianity: Canon and Interpretation in the Light of Modern Research* (Tübingen: J. C. B. Mohr, 1991), p. 138.

There are a number of New Testament texts that present Jesus as one greater than Moses or as the fulfillment of the Scriptures. It is hardly surprising, then, that many early Christian writers came to regard Jesus as the key with which to interpret the Old Testament Scriptures, especially those that had not already received an interpretation in the New Testament. From Origen's point of view the entire Scriptures are the word of Christ, and Christ is the key to understanding all of them. He means not only those words that formed his teaching after the incarnation but also Moses and the prophets, who were filled with the spirit of Christ.[4]

The subject of this chapter is not so much the general question of how the older texts were used in the New Testament writings, but rather how certain New Testament interpretations of Old Testament texts were later understood as a model for further interpretation. In other words, our interest here is in how these texts were understood and used by the early Christian interpreters to guide their own interpretations. This is true especially of Pauline texts, for Paul's explanations of certain key texts had an enormous influence on the development of Christian interpretation. Another way of putting it would be to speak of the "Christianization" of the older Scriptures by early Christian interpreters, a process already underway in the New Testament writings, but one that became more urgent in the light of the crisis caused by Marcion, which has already been mentioned in the first chapter. The texts assembled in this chapter are meant to illustrate that process. For the most part, the texts are presented with little or no commentary in the belief that they can speak for themselves.[5]

SOME TEXTS FROM THE GOSPELS

Although in Matthew's Gospel Jesus is portrayed as saying that he did not come to change the law (Mt 5:17), shortly thereafter he is portrayed as criticizing a law and even seeming to contradict it: "It was also said,

---

[4]See Mark Sheridan, "Scripture," in *The Westminster Handbook to Origen*, ed. John Anthony McGuckin (Louisville, KY: Westminster John Knox, 2004), pp. 197-201.

[5]In this chapter material has been used from Mark Sheridan, ed., *Genesis 12–50*, ACCS OT 2 (Downers Grove, IL: InterVarsity Press, 2002), and other volumes of the ACCS. For a fuller account of Origen's understanding of Paul's rules of interpretation, see Sheridan, *Genesis 12–50*, pp. xxv-xxxix.

'Whoever divorces his wife, let him give her a certificate of divorce.' But I say to you that every one who divorces his wife, except on the ground of unchastity, causes her to commit adultery; and whoever marries a divorced woman commits adultery" (Mt 5:31-32; cf. 19:3-9; Deut 24:1). In the second occurrence of this teaching, Jesus is presented using the principle of interpreting Scripture by means of Scripture. The principle is based on the presupposition that God is the principal author of all the Scriptures. In this case, he cites Genesis against Deuteronomy. Genesis, also written down by Moses, is quoted as having priority over later laws given by Moses. Jesus is seen by Chromatius of Aquileia as restoring God's original design.

> In all things our Lord and Savior reforms for the better the justice of the ancient law. Indeed, it seems that long ago a license for divorce was granted by Moses on tenuous grounds to the Jewish people who were living licentiously and serving their pleasures. This was due not to the system of law but to the unbridled pleasure of a carnal people unable to uphold the righteousness of the law according to rigorous standards.
>
> This concession was allowed, according to what the Lord himself said in another place in his reply to the inquiring Sadducees. For when they asked why Moses had allowed a bill of divorce to be given, the Lord answered, "Moses, by reason of the hardness of your hearts, permitted you to put away your wives, but it was not so from the beginning" (Mt 19:8). And now, not without good reason does our Lord and Savior, with that license removed, restore the precepts of his former constitution. For he orders that chaste wedlock be preserved by indissoluble law, showing that the law of marriage was first instituted by himself. For he said, "What therefore God has joined together, let no one put asunder" (Mt 19:6; Mk 10:9).[6]

John Chrysostom takes a different approach that presupposes a Christian has absorbed the teaching in general of Jesus (although the allusion is also the Sermon on the Mount):

> How can one who is meek and a peacemaker and poor in spirit and merciful cast out his wife? How can one who reconciles be alienated from her that is his own? . . . Even in this case he makes one exception: "for the cause of

---

[6]*Tractate on Matthew* 1.1-3; CCL 9a:309.

fornication." One who does not look with unchaste eyes upon another woman will certainly not commit fornication. By not committing fornication he will give no occasion that they should become alienated. Thus you see Jesus presses his point without reserve and builds up this fear as a bulwark, urging on the husband great danger, who if he does cast her out, makes himself accountable for her adultery.[7]

Jesus was also critical of the dietary laws. In Matthew 15:11, he states: "It is not what goes into the mouth that defiles a person, but it is what comes out of the mouth that defiles." His critical attitude toward some of the laws seems to have been a principal cause of conflict with his contemporaries: "Then the disciples approached and said to him, 'Do you know that the Pharisees took offense when they heard what you said?'" (Mt 15:12). Origen testifies to the ongoing nature of the dispute in his own time.

We are accused by the Jews and Ebionites[8] of being violators of the laws that we read in Leviticus and Deuteronomy concerning clean and unclean food. But by means of what is said in this passage we are clearly taught by the Savior not to think that the simple meaning of these laws is the aim intended in the Scripture. For Jesus says, "Not that which enters into the mouth defiles a person but that which comes out of the mouth." Especially significant is what is said in the Gospel of Mark: "Thus he declared all foods clean" (Mk 7:19). Since all this is so, it is obvious that we are not defiled when we eat things that are said to be unclean by Jews, who want to serve the letter of the law. Instead, we are defiled when we say whatever happens to be on our mind and we talk about things that we should not talk about, even though our lips should be bound "with perception" and we should make for them "a measuring balance and a standard of measure." The spring of sins comes to us from such talking.[9]

---

[7]*Homilies on the Gospel of Matthew* 17.4; PG 57:260; NPNF 1 10:119**. A single asterisk (*) indicates that a previous English translation has been updated to modern English or amended for easier reading. The double asterisk (**) indicates either that a new translation has been provided or that some extant translation has been significantly amended.

[8]Jewish Christians about whom very little is known with certainty. On the basis of early Christian assertions, they are thought to have accepted Jesus as Messiah, but not as divine, and to have insisted on the observance of Jewish dietary laws.

[9]*ComMt* 11.12; GCS 40:52-53; ANF 9:440.

JESUS IS GREATER THAN MOSES AND THE PROPHETS

In several texts in the New Testament Jesus is said to be greater than various Old Testament figures including Moses, David, Solomon and Jonah.

> The people of Nineveh will rise up at the judgment with this generation and condemn it, because they repented at the proclamation of Jonah, and see, something greater than Jonah is here! The queen of the South will rise up at the judgment with this generation and condemn it, because she came from the ends of the earth to listen to the wisdom of Solomon, and see, something greater than Solomon is here! (Mt 12:41-42)

Origen offers an allegorical interpretation in which the queen of the South is the church making spiritual offerings and the true Solomon is Christ.

> The church of the Gentiles, which in truth is gathered "from the ends of the earth," fulfills the place of the queen of the south, not providing gifts in "perishable things, silver" and spices, but faith, the incense of knowledge, the outpouring of an offering, the sweat of the virtues and the blood of martyrdom. For with such gifts the true Solomon is pleased, who is Christ, "our peace" (Eph 2:14). For "Solomon" is interpreted as "peaceful."[10]

Jonah was a favorite symbol of Christ, but Christ was far superior, especially because of the reference to the resurrection. Both John Chrysostom and Cyril of Alexandria dwell on the negative aspects of Jonah's behavior in order to develop the superiority of Jesus.

> JOHN CHRYSOSTOM: For Jonah was a servant, but I am the Master; and he came forth from the great fish, but I rose from death. He proclaimed destruction, but I am come preaching the good tidings of the kingdom. The Ninevites indeed believed without a sign, but I have exhibited many signs. They heard nothing more than those words, but I have made it impossible to deny the truth. The Ninevites came to be ministered to, but I, the very Master and Lord of all, have come not threatening, not demanding an account, but bringing pardon. They were barbarians, but these—the faithful— have conversed with unnumbered prophets. And of Jonah nothing had been prophesied in advance, but of me everything was foretold, and all the

---

[10]Fragment 277; GCS 41.1:124.

facts have agreed with their words. And Jonah indeed, when he was to go forth, instead ran away that he might not be ridiculed. But I, knowing that I am both to be crucified and mocked, have come nonetheless. While Jonah did not endure so much as to be reproached for those who were saved, I underwent even death, and that the most shameful death, and after this I sent others again. And Jonah was a strange sort of person and an alien to the Ninevites, and unknown; but I a kinsman after the flesh and of the same forefathers.[11]

CYRIL OF ALEXANDRIA: If Jonah then is taken as a type of Christ, he is not so taken in every respect—he was sent to preach to the Ninevites, but he sought to flee from the presence of God (Jon 1:2-3). And he is seen to shrink from going to the east. The Son also was sent from God the Father to preach to the nations, but he was not unwilling to assume this ministry.

The prophet appeals to those sailing with him to throw him into the sea (Jon 1:12), then he was swallowed by a great fish, then after three days he was given back up and afterwards went to Nineveh and fulfilled his ministry. But he was embittered beyond measure when God took pity upon the Ninevites. Christ willingly submitted to death, he remained in the heart of the earth, he came back to life and afterward went up to Galilee and commanded that the preaching to the Gentiles should begin. But he was not grieved to see that those who were called to acknowledge the truth were being saved.

Thus just as bees in the field, when flitting about the flowers, always gather up what is useful for the provision of the hives, so we also, when searching in the divinely inspired Scriptures, need always to be collecting and collating what is perfect for explicating Christ's mysteries and to interpret the Word fully without cause for rebuke.[12]

Acts 3:22-25 (from the speech of Peter):

Moses said, "The Lord your God will raise up for you from your own people a prophet like me. You must listen to whatever he tells you. And it will be that everyone who does not listen to that prophet will be utterly rooted out from the people" [Deut 18:15, 18]. And all the prophets, as many as have

---

[11]*Homilies on the Gospel of Matthew* 43.2; PG 57:459; NPNF 1 10:274.
[12]Fragment 162; MKGK 205.

spoken, from Samuel and those after him, also predicted these days. You are the descendants of the prophets and of the covenant that God gave to your ancestors, saying to Abraham, "And in your descendants all the families of the earth shall be blessed."

Both Origen and Eusebius assert that Jesus is "the prophet" spoken of by Moses. He is a prophet and lawgiver for all the nations (the Gentiles) in contrast to Moses, the lawgiver of the Jews.

> ORIGEN: And inasmuch as there were many prophets in Israel—there was one in particular, who had been prophesied by Moses, who was specially expected in accordance with the saying, "The Lord our God shall raise up a prophet like me for you from your brothers; him you shall hear. And it shall be that every soul that will not hear that prophet shall be destroyed from his people"—they ask a third time, not if he is a prophet, but if he is "the prophet" (Jn 1:21).[13]

> EUSEBIUS OF CAESAREA: . . . this Moses himself for this very reason said that another prophet would be raised up "like unto him"; and publishes the good news that he should be a lawgiver for all the nations. He speaks of Christ in a riddle. He orders his followers to obey him in these prophetic words. "A prophet shall the Lord your God raise up to you from your brethren, like unto me, you shall hear him [whatsoever he says unto you]. And it shall be that every soul who will not hear that prophet shall be cast out of its race" (Dt 18:15, 19). And that this prophet, who is clearly the Christ, should come forth from the Jews and rule all nations, he proclaims again when he says: "How fair are thy dwellings, O Jacob, and thy tents, O Israel, as shady groves, and as a garden by a river, and as tents which God pitched. There shall come a man out of his seed, and he shall rule over many nations, and his kingdom shall be exalted" (Num 24:5).

> . . . These, then, are the reasons why we have accepted and loved as belonging to ourselves the sacred books of the Hebrews, including as they do prophecies relating to us Gentiles. And the more so, since it was not Moses only who foretold the coming of the Lawgiver of the Gentiles after him, but really the whole succession of the prophets, who proclaimed the same truth

---

[13]*ComJn* 6.45; FC 80:181.

with one voice, as David, when he said: "Appoint, O Lord, a Lawgiver over them: let the nations know that they are but men" (Ps 9:20).[14]

Hebrews 3:3-6:

Yet Jesus is worthy of more glory than Moses, just as the builder of a house has more honor than the house itself. (For every house is built by someone, but the builder of all things is God.) Now Moses was faithful in all God's house as a servant, to testify to the things that would be spoken later. Christ, however, was faithful over God's house as a son, and we are his house if we hold firm the confidence and the pride that belong to hope.

The letter to the Hebrews asserts most clearly that Jesus is superior to Moses and all the Old Testament figures, including the patriarchs. He is the priest according to the order of Melchizedek and is the fulfillment of all the Old Testament institutions in himself. It has been called the most "supersessionist" of all the New Testament writings. Both John Chrysostom and Ephrem underline this superiority.

JOHN CHRYSOSTOM: Being about to place him before Moses in comparison, Paul led his discourses to the law of the high priesthood; for they all had a high esteem for Moses. . . . Therefore he begins from the flesh and goes up to the Godhead, where there was no longer any comparison. He began from the flesh, from his human nature, by assuming for a time the equality, and says, "as Moses also was faithful in all God's house." Nor does he at first show his superiority, lest the hearers should start away and straightway stop their ears. For although they were believers, yet nevertheless they still had strong feeling of conscience as to Moses.[15]

EPHREM THE SYRIAN: But since he said, "as Moses," do not think that he is as Moses; "the glory of this" high priest "is greater than that of Moses inasmuch as the maker of a house has greater honor than the house." Similarly the honor of the Lord and the Son is greater than that of the servant Moses. "Every house was built by someone," but "he who created Moses" and "built all things is God. And Moses was certainly faithful," but as an assistant, "as a servant was faithful

---

[14]*Dem. evang.* 1.3-4. Eusebius, *The Proof of the Gospel, Being the Demonstratio Evangelica of Eusebius of Cæsarea*, trans. W. J. Ferrar (London: SPCK; New York: Macmillan, 1920), pp. 20-21*.
[15]*On the Epistle to the Hebrews* 5.4; NPNF 1 14:390.

to testify to the things that were to be spoken later." In truth Christ is not a faithful servant like Moses, but "as a son" he was faithful, and not over the shrine of the temple but over the souls of people. In fact, "we are his house if we stand firm in his confidence" and are not brought into disorder while "in the glory of his hope." But if we transgress, we cause his suffering.[16]

PAUL

By far the most important texts of the New Testament that provided guidance for the later interpretation of the Scriptures were those of Paul. The relationship of Paul to the Scriptures of Israel changed as he came to "know Christ." He was raised as a Pharisee but came to regard legal observance as an obstacle to the preaching of the gospel among the Gentiles. The conflict over the Gentile mission led to his polemic against imposing the law on the Gentiles in Galatians and Romans. His arguments in his letters to the Galatians and the Romans go beyond expediency and assert that the law of Moses as a code of observances is no longer valid. Paul also uses the principle of what is fitting to God: what is considered unfitting to or unworthy of God must be interpreted allegorically. This assumption appears to underlie Paul's citation of Deuteronomy 25:4 ("You shall not muzzle an ox while it is treading out the grain") in 1 Corinthians 9:8-10. He applies this text allegorically to his own situation with the comment: "Is it for oxen that God is concerned? Or does he not speak entirely for our sake?" (1 Cor 9:9-10). This echoes the sentiment of pseudo-Aristeas (see chap. 3) that God could hardly be concerned with legislating for mice and weasels. The implications of this Pauline interpretation of one law would be developed extensively by Origen, who accepted the provisions of the Mosaic law as "Scripture" but insisted that they had to be given a spiritual rather than literal interpretation.[17]

Some of the key Pauline texts. Galatians 4:22-26:

For it is written that Abraham had two sons, one by a slave woman and the other by a free woman. One, the child of the slave, was born according to

---

[16]*Commentary on the Epistle to the Hebrews*; EHA 202.
[17]See Mark Sheridan, "Old Testament," in McGuckin, *Westminster Handbook to Origen*, pp. 159-62.

the flesh; the other, the child of the free woman, was born through the promise. Now this is an allegory: these women are two covenants. One woman, in fact, is Hagar, from Mount Sinai, bearing children for slavery. Now Hagar is Mount Sinai in Arabia and corresponds to the present Jerusalem, for she is in slavery with her children. But the other woman corresponds to the Jerusalem above; she is free, and she is our mother.

This text was particularly important for early Christian interpreters because it contained the word "allegory." Alexandrian and later Antiochene writers interpreted the word differently.[18] When Origen arrives at Genesis 21:9-10 in his homilies on Genesis, he says that he defers explicit commentary because the apostle has already indicated how these things are to be understood, and he quotes Galatians 4:21-24. He then notes that, despite the distinction made by Paul between the flesh and the promise, Isaac was in fact born according to the flesh. Sarah did in fact give birth and Isaac was circumcised in the flesh. Paul's interpretation is remarkable because he says that these things, which undoubtedly occurred according to the flesh, are to be understood allegorically: "This indeed is what is astonishing in the apostle's understanding, that he called things 'allegorical' that are quite obviously done in the flesh. His purpose is that we might learn how to treat other passages, and especially these in which the historical narrative appears to reveal nothing worthy of the divine law."[19] Two points should be noted in this connection: first, that Origen, who is often accused of neglecting or denying the literal level of the text, is here insisting on its reality. As he sees it, the interpretation Paul has offered, and which is to serve as a model for others, does not obliterate the literal meaning of the historical narrative but is superimposed on it and presupposes it. Second, the phrase "anything worthy of the divine law" indicates an important exegetical principle for Origen, one that may be detected also in Paul.

Origen makes reference to this text elsewhere, especially when he wishes to emphasize the possibility or need of an allegorical interpretation

---

[18]For more on the distinction between Alexandrian and Antiochene writers, see chap. 5 below.
[19]Origen, HomGn 7.2.

that does not invalidate the literal meaning of the text.[20] He cites it in the context of a lengthy discussion about the need to distinguish between those texts or prescriptions of the law that are not to be observed in any case according to the letter, those that are not to be completely changed by allegory but are to be observed as formulated in the scriptures and those that can stand according to the letter but for which one must also seek an allegorical interpretation.[21]

The later Antiochene writers, beginning with Diodore of Tarsus and followed by Chrysostom, Theodore of Mopsuestia and Theodoret, attempted to restrict the use of allegory and even tried to redefine the word. They associated the word "allegory" with interpretations drawn from ancient philosophy and tried to insist that only the word "type" (*typos*) should be used for historical allegory. Thus John Chrysostom is forced by this logic to insist that Paul had used the word "improperly": "*Allegory* is used improperly for typology. His meaning is this: 'This story does not say only what is evident but relates other things as well; hence it is called *allegory*.'"[22] Jerome was well acquainted with the works of Cicero, who had defined allegory as follows: the text says one thing, but the meaning is something different: "*Allegory* is properly a term in the art of grammar. How it differs from metaphor and other figures of speech we learn as children. It presents one thing in words and signifies another in sense. . . . Understanding this, Paul (who had a certain knowledge of secular literature also) used the name of the figure of speech and called it *allegory* according to the usage of his own circle."[23]

The polemic of Theodore of Mopsuestia represents another step in which the anachronistic distinction introduced between "allegory" and "type" is projected onto the past writers in order to condemn them.

> Those who are at great pains to pervert the meaning of the divine Scriptures . . . abuse this saying of the apostle's, as though they thought that they could derive from it the power to suppress the entire sense of holy Scripture in

---

[20]See *ComJn* 22.67-74; *HomGn* 13.3; *ComRm* 2.13 (907 BC); *HomJos* 9.8; *HomGn* 6.1.
[21]Origen, *HomNum* 11.1.
[22]John Chrysostom, *Homily on Galatians*, 4.24; IOEP 4:73.
[23]Jerome, *Epistle to the Galatians*, 2.4.24; PL 26:389B-C (471).

their aspirations to speak "allegorically," as if in the manner of the apostle. They fail to see how great a difference there is between their own position and that of the apostle in this passage. For the apostle does not deny the history or pick apart the events of the distant past, but he has stated them as they happened at the time, while using for his own purpose the interpretation of these events. . . . He would not have said "referred to one who was born" if he had not believed that person had really existed. There cannot be a simile if one takes away the historical reality itself.[24]

Nevertheless, despite this attempt to distinguish between typology and allegory (for which there was no previous precedent), the Pauline text continued to influence later interpretation.

JEROME: Hagar, who is interpreted as "sojourning," "wandering" or "tarrying," gives birth to Ishmael. . . . No wonder that the Old Covenant, which is on Mount Sinai, which is in Arabia and nearby to Jerusalem, is stated and alleged in writing to be ephemeral and not perpetual. The sojourning of Hagar stands in contrast with perpetual possession. The name of Mount Sinai means "tribulation," while Arabia means "death."[25]

AMBROSIASTER: Jerusalem, which he calls our mother, represents the Lord's mystery, through which we are reborn into freedom, just as she is free. And she is called heavenly because heaven is her seat. Those to whom she gives birth will be there with her.[26]

JOHN CASSIAN: One and the same Jerusalem can be understood in a fourfold manner. According to history it is the city of the Jews. According to allegory it is the Church of Christ. According to anagogy it is the heavenly city of God, "which is the mother of all." According to tropology it is the soul of the human being, which under this name is frequently either reproached or prasied by the Lord.[27]

This last interpretation by Cassian provided a paradigm of multilevel interpretation for Latin medieval writers. The distinction of these four levels of

---

[24]*Commentary on the Letters of St. Paul*, Galatians 5; TEM 1:73-74.
[25]*Epistle to the Galatians* 2.4.25-26; PL 26:390C-D [472-73].
[26]*Epistle to the Galatians* 4.26; CSEL 81.3:51-52.
[27]*Conferences* 14.8.4; ACW 57:510.

interpretation is first found a little earlier in the writings of Gregory of Nyssa, but without an explanation.[28] For Cassian, the word "tropologically" (from the Greek *tropologia*) refers to an interpretation in terms of the human soul, whereas the term "anagogically" (from the Greek *anagōgia*) refers to an interpretation regarding future things to come in the next world.

First Corinthians 9:8-10:

> Do I say this on human authority? Does not the law also say the same? For it is written in the law of Moses, "You shall not muzzle an ox while it is treading out the grain." Is it for oxen that God is concerned? Or does he not speak entirely for our sake? It was indeed written for our sake, for whoever plows should plow in hope and whoever threshes should thresh in hope of a share in the crop.

For Origen this is one among several texts that indicate how Old Testament provisions of the law are to be interpreted. In answer to Celsus's objections to Christian allegorical interpretation, he observes: "He did not examine their utterances and appearances to see what they mean. For he would have seen that 'God is not concerned about oxen' even where He seems to be laying down laws about oxen or other irrational animals. But laws which in outward appearance are concerned with irrational animals were written for the sake of men and contain certain teaching about nature."[29] In his earlier work *On First Principles* (*De Principiis*), Origen had cited the same passage and stated: "Here he shows clearly that God who gave the law says the words 'You shall not muzzle the mouth of the ox when he treads out the corn' for our sake, that is, for the sake of the apostles, and that his care was not for the oxen but for the apostles, who were preaching the gospel of Christ."[30] Later in this work, citing the same passage, he observes: "And most of the interpretations adapted to the multitude which are in circulation and which edify those who cannot understand the higher

---

[28]Gregory of Nyssa, *Homilies on the Canticle of Canticles*, prologue; PG 44.
[29]Origen, *Contra Celsum* 5.36, trans. Henry Chadwick (London: Cambridge University Press, 1953), pp. 292-93.
[30]Origen, *PArch* 2.4.2.

meanings have the same character."[31] In his homilies on other books of the law, Origen invokes the text as a principle, saying: "In a similar way God does not care about sheep or birds and other animals, but one should interpret whatever is written about them as having been written for human beings."[32] And after citing this among other similar texts, Origen exclaims: "The Law, which Paul names 'spiritual,' is thus understood and Jesus himself is the one who recites these things in the ears of all the people, admonishing us that we not follow 'the letter that kills' but that we hold fast 'the life-giving spirit.'"[33] Other writers followed his example.

> CHRYSOSTOM: Why does Paul mention this, when he could have used the example of the priests? The reason is that he wanted to prove his case beyond any shadow of doubt. If God cares about oxen, how much more will he care about the labor of teachers?[34]

> AMBROSIASTER: The whole of Scripture applies to us by way of analogy.[35]

First Corinthians 10:1-11:

> I do not want you to be unaware, brothers and sisters, that our ancestors were all under the cloud, and all passed through the sea, and all were baptized into Moses in the cloud and in the sea, and all ate the same spiritual food, and all drank the same spiritual drink. For they drank from the spiritual rock that followed them, and the rock was Christ. Nevertheless, God was not pleased with most of them, and they were struck down in the wilderness. Now these things occurred as examples for us, so that we might not desire evil as they did. Do not become idolaters as some of them did; as it is written, "The people sat down to eat and drink, and they rose up to play." We must not indulge in sexual immorality as some of them did, and twenty-three thousand fell in a single day. We must not put Christ to the test, as some of them did, and were destroyed by serpents. And do not complain as some of them did, and were destroyed by the destroyer. These

---

[31]Ibid., 4.2.5.

[32]Origen, *HomNum* 17.2; Origen, *Homilies on Numbers*, trans. Thomas P. Scheck, ed. Christopher A. Hall, ACT (Downers Grove, IL: IVP Academic, 2009), p. 103.

[33]Origen, *HomJos* 9.8.

[34]*Homilies on the Epistles of Paul to the Corinthians* 21.5; NPNF 1 12:121.

[35]*Commentary on Paul's Epistles*; CSEL 81.3:99.

things happened to them to serve as an example, and they were written down to instruct us, on whom the ends of the ages have come.

In the fifth homily on Exodus, Origen relates briefly the events of Exodus 12–17: that the children of Israel departed from Egypt, from Ramesse, then from Socoth (Rameses and Succoth in the NRSV), that they were preceded by the cloud and followed by the rock from which they drank water and finally they crossed the Red Sea and came to the desert of Sinai. The Jews, he says, accept this simply as a historical narrative. Then he cites 1 Corinthians 10:1-4 to show "what sort of rule of interpretation the apostle Paul taught us about these matters." His conclusion is framed as a question: "Do you not see how much Paul's teaching differs from the literal meaning? What the Jews supposed to be a crossing of the sea, Paul calls a baptism; what they supposed to be a cloud, Paul asserts is the Holy Spirit."[36] His further conclusion is also framed in a question: "Does it not seem right that we apply similarly to other passages this kind of rule which was delivered to us in a similar way in other passages?"[37]

Origen then gives his own interpretation of this part of Exodus. He has already established that the exodus from Egypt is to be interpreted spiritually, that is, in terms of the journey of the individual soul. Ramesse means, he says, "the commotion of a moth."[38] He then moves, by association with the word "moth," to the text of Matthew 6:20: "there where the moth destroys" and incorporates this into the Pauline interpretation.

> Depart from Ramesse, therefore, if you wish to come to this place that the Lord may be your leader and precede you "in the column of the cloud" and "the rock" may follow you, which offers you spiritual food and "spiritual drink" no less. Nor should you store treasure "there where the moth destroys and thieves dig through and steal." This is what the

---

[36]FC 71:276.
[37]Ibid.
[38]*Ramesse quae interpretatur commotio tineae.* This etymology is also found in Philo, *Post.* 55. See also Franz Wutz, *Onomastica sacra: Untersuchungen zum Liber interpretationis nominum hebraicorum des Hl. Hieronymus* (Leipzig: J. C. Hinrichs, 1914–1915), p. 140.

Lord says clearly in the Gospels: "If you wish to be perfect, sell all your possessions and give to the poor, and you will have treasure in heaven; and come, follow me." This therefore is to depart from Ramesse and to follow Christ.[39]

Origen has read here the content of New Testament teaching into an Old Testament text. The use of an etymology generates a meaning, which then serves as a bridge to a New Testament text, using the principle of interpreting Scripture by Scripture, in this case by association through the hook word (the word found in both texts), "moth."

Origen often cites 1 Corinthians 10, especially 1 Corinthians 10:6 and 1 Corinthians 10:11, to emphasize that the Scriptures were written "for us," and reach their fulfillment in the present time (the time of the church), which is also understood as the end of the ages. This basic assumption of the "actuality" of the Scriptures Origen shared with other ancient interpreters. Since the text is "for us," it must also have a meaning that is "useful" to us, a criterion of interpretation that had already been developed by Philo and was suggested by the affirmation that "all scripture is . . . useful" (2 Tim 3:16). That for Origen generally means what is helpful for moral or spiritual nourishment.[40]

This text is often cited as an introduction to moral exhortation, which is indeed the original Pauline context of 1 Corinthians 10:1-11. Thus in commenting on the expression "by mud and bricks" (Ex 1:14), Origen states: "These words were not written to instruct us in history, nor must we think that the divine books narrate the acts of the Egyptians. What has been written 'has been written for our instruction' and admonition."[41] There follows a moral exhortation in which the king of Egypt "who knew not Joseph" is interpreted as the devil. Most Christian interpreters followed Origen's lead in interpreting the passage from Exodus. Some examples are cited here verse by verse to illustrate how early Christian writers after Origen interpreted this passage.

---

[39]FC 71:277.
[40]See Sheridan, "Scripture," p. 198.
[41]Origen, *HomEx* 1.5.

10:1 *The cloud and the sea*

CYRIL OF JERUSALEM: There Moses was sent by God into Egypt; here Christ was sent from the Father into the world. Moses' mission was to lead out of Egypt a persecuted people; Christ's was to rescue all the people of the world who were under the tyranny of sin. There the blood of a lamb was the charm against the destroyer; here, the blood of the unspotted Lamb, Jesus Christ, is appointed your inviolable sanctuary against demons.[42]

THEODORET OF CYRRHUS: These events, he is saying, are a type of ours: the sea resembled the font, the cloud the grace of the Spirit, Moses the priest, the rod the cross, Israel suggesting the baptized, while the Egyptians in pursuit acted as a type of the demons and Pharaoh in person was an image of the devil; after the crossing, you see, the Israelites were freed from the power of the Egyptians, as in a type they also received the manna from heaven.[43]

MAXIMUS OF TURIN: What took place, as the apostle says, was the mystery of baptism. Clearly this was a kind of baptism, where the cloud covered the people and water carried them. But the same Christ the Lord who did all these things now goes through baptism before the Christian people in the pillar of his body—he who at that time went through the sea before the children of Israel in the pillar of fire. . . . Through this faith—as was the case with the children of Israel—the one who walks calmly will not fear Egypt in pursuit.[44]

10:2 *Baptized into Moses*

CYPRIAN: The Jews had already obtained that most ancient baptism of the law and of Moses.[45]

AMBROSIASTER: Paul says the Jews were under the cloud in order to point out that everything that happened to them is meant to be understood as a picture of the truth which has been revealed to us. Under the cloud they

---

[42]*Mystagogical Lecture* 1.1.3; FC 64:154.
[43]Theodoret, *Commentary on the Letters of St. Paul*, trans. Robert C. Hill (Brookline, MA: Holy Cross Orthodox Press, 2001), 1:199.
[44]*Sermon 100.3*; ACW 50:227.
[45]*Letter 73, The Baptismal Controversy* 17; LCC 5:166.

were protected from their enemies until they were delivered from death, analogous to baptism. For when they passed through the Red Sea they were delivered from the Egyptians who died in it, and their death prefigured our baptism, which puts our adversaries to death as well.[46]

AUGUSTINE: The history of the exodus was an allegory of the Christian people that was yet to be.[47]

THEODORE OF MOPSUESTIA: The sea is a figure of baptism with water; the cloud of the grace of baptism in the Spirit.[48]

GENNADIUS OF CONSTANTINOPLE: The cloud was a figure standing for the grace of the Spirit. For just as the cloud covered the Israelites and protected them from the Egyptians, so the Spirit's grace shields us from the wiles of the devil. Likewise, just as the crossing of the sea protected them from their enemies and gave them real freedom, so baptism protects us from our enemies. That was how the Israelites came to live under the law of Moses. This is how we, in baptism, are clothed with the Spirit of adoption and inherit the covenants and confessions made in accordance with the commands of Christ.[49]

10:3 *Supernatural food*

GREGORY OF NYSSA: The divine apostle also, in calling the Lord "spiritual food and drink," suggests that he knows that human nature is not simple, but that there is an intelligible part mixed with a sensual part and that a particular type of nurture is needed for each of the elements in us—sensible food to strengthen our bodies and spiritual food for the well-being of our souls.[50]

AMBROSE: All those who ate that bread [manna] died in the desert, but this food which you receive, this "living bread which came down from heaven," furnishes the energy for eternal life. Whoever eats this bread "will not die forever," for it is the body of Christ (Jn 6:49-58).... That manna was subject to corruption if kept for a second day. This is foreign to every corruption.

---

[46]*Commentary on Paul's Epistles*; CSEL 81.3:107.
[47]*The Usefulness of Belief* 8; LCC 6:297. Cf. 1 Cor 10:1-11.
[48]*Pauline Commentary from the Greek Church*; NTA 15:185.
[49]*Pauline Commentary from the Greek Church*; NTA 15:418.
[50]*On Perfection*; FC 58:107*.

Whoever tastes it in a holy manner shall not be able to feel corruption. For them water flowed from the rock. For you blood flows from Christ. Water satisfied them for the hour. Blood satisfies you for eternity.[51]

AMBROSE: What we eat, what we drink, the Holy Spirit expresses to you elsewhere, saying; "Taste and see that the Lord is sweet. Blessed is the one who trusts in him" (Ps 33:9). Christ is in that sacrament, because the body is Christ's. So the food is not corporeal but spiritual.[52]

THEODORE OF MOPSUESTIA: Paul calls the food supernatural because it gave those who ate it the power of the Holy Spirit. However, it did not of itself make them spiritual people.[53]

10:4 *Supernatural drink*

EPHREM THE SYRIAN: I considered the Word of the Creator and likened it to the rock that marched with the people in Israel in the wilderness; it was not from the reservoir of water contained within it that it poured forth for them glorious streams. There was no water in the rock, yet oceans sprang forth from it. Just so did the Word fashion created things out of nothing.[54]

AMBROSIASTER: The manna and the water which flowed from the rock are called spiritual because they were formed not according to the law of nature but by the power of God working independently of the natural elements. They were created for a time as figures of what we now eat and drink in remembrance of Christ the Lord.[55]

GREGORY OF NYSSA: We also will be a rock, imitating, as far as possible in our changing nature, the unchanging and permanent nature of the Master.[56]

AUGUSTINE: All symbols seem in some way to personify the realities of which they are symbols. So, St. Paul says, "The rock was Christ," because the rock in question symbolized Christ.[57]

---

[51] *The Mysteries* 8.48; FC 44:22-23*.
[52] *The Mysteries* 8:56; FC 44:27.
[53] *Pauline Commentary from the Greek Church*; NTA 15:185.
[54] *Hymns on Paradise* 5.1; HOP 102.
[55] *Commentary on Paul's Epistles*; CSEL 81.3:108.
[56] *On Perfection*; FC 58:108.
[57] *City of God* 18.46; FC 24:168.

CHRYSOSTOM: Why does Paul say these things? He was pointing out that just as the Israelites got no benefit from the great gift which they enjoyed, so the Corinthian Christians would get nothing out of baptism or holy communion unless they went on and manifested a life worthy of that grace.[58]

CAESARIUS OF ARLES: Surely this refers more to his physical body than to his divinity, for the hearts of the thirsty people were satisfied by the endless stream of his blood.[59]

10:5 *God's displeasure*

ORIGEN: Paul wants to remind us that we are not saved merely because we happen to have been the recipients of God's free grace. We have to demonstrate that we are willing recipients of that free gift. The children of Israel received it, but they proved to be unworthy of it, and so they were not saved.[60]

CHRYSOSTOM: The Israelites were not in the land of promise when God did these things to them. Thus it was that he visited them with a double vengeance, because he did not allow them to see the land which had been promised to them, and he punished them severely as well.[61]

10:6 *Not desiring evil*

ORIGEN: These things were written as examples for us, so that when we read about their sins we shall know to avoid them.[62]

CHRYSOSTOM: Just as the gifts are symbolic, so are the punishments symbolic. Baptism and holy Communion were prefigured in prophecy. In the same way the certainty of punishment for those who are unworthy of this gift was proclaimed beforehand for our sake, so that we might learn from these examples how we must watch our step.[63]

---

[58]*Homilies on the Epistles of Paul to the Corinthians* 23.3; NPNF 1 12:133.
[59]*Sermon* 117.2; FC 47:178.
[60]*Commentary on 1 Corinthians* 4.45.2-5; JTS 9:29.
[61]*Homilies on the Epistles of Paul to the Corinthians* 23.4; NPNF 1 12:134.
[62]*Commentary on 1 Corinthians* 4.46; JTS 9:29.
[63]*Homilies on the Epistles of Paul to the Corinthians* 23.4; NPNF 1 12:134.

Second Corinthians 3:15-18:

> Indeed, to this very day whenever Moses is read, a veil lies over their minds;
> but when one turns to the Lord, the veil is removed. Now the Lord is the
> Spirit, and where the Spirit of the Lord is, there is freedom. And all of us,
> with unveiled faces, seeing the glory of the Lord as though reflected in a
> mirror, are being transformed into the same image from one degree of glory
> to another; for this comes from the Lord, the Spirit.

One of the Pauline texts most frequently cited by Origen not only as an
example of Pauline exegesis but also as a virtual program of interpretation
is that of 2 Corinthians 3:7-18.[64] In commenting on Exodus 34:33-34,
where the veil over the glorified face of Moses is mentioned, Origen describes Paul's interpretation as "magnificent."[65] Then he proceeds to dwell
especially on the significance of the "veil" and the question of how it can
be removed. Only if one leads a life superior to the common mean can one
contemplate the glory on the face of Moses. Moses still speaks with glorified face, but we cannot see it because we lack sufficient zeal. The veil
remains over the letter of the Old Testament (2 Cor 3:14). Only if one is
converted to the Lord will the veil be removed (2 Cor 3:16). Origen then
explains that this veil can be interpreted to mean preoccupation with the
affairs of this world, with money, the attraction of riches. To be converted
to the Lord means to turn our back on all these things and dedicate ourselves to the word of God, meditating on his law day and night (Ps 1). He
notes that parents who want their children to receive a liberal education
do everything to find teachers, books and so on and spare no expense to
achieve this goal. The same must be done in pursuit of the understanding
of the Scriptures. As for those who do not even bother to listen to the
proclamation of the Scriptures but engage in idle conversation in the
corners of the church while they are being read, not only a veil but also a
wall is placed over their hearts.[66]

---

[64]This section, on Origen's interpretation of the veil in 2 Corinthians 3, is borrowed from the author's article, "Old Testament" in *The Westminster Handbook to Origen*, ed. John Anthony McGuckin (Louisville:
Westminster John Knox, 2004), pp. 160-61.

[65]Origen, *HomEx* 12.1.

[66]Ibid.

When the veil is taken away, however, Christ is revealed as already present in the entire Old Testament. In commenting on the verse of the Canticle in which the bridegroom is pictured "leaping upon the mountains, / bounding over the hills" (Song 2:8) Origen applies it to the interpretation of the Scriptures.

> This foretelling, of which we read in the Old Testament, has a veil on it, however; but when the veil is removed for the Bride, that is, for the Church that has turned to God, she suddenly sees Him leaping upon those mountains—that is, the books of the Law; and on the hills of the prophetical writings. He is so plainly and so clearly manifested that He springs forth, rather than merely appears. Turning the pages of the prophets one by one, for instance, she finds Christ springing forth from them and, now that the veil that covered them before is taken away, she perceives Him breaking out and emerging from individual passages in her reading, and bursting out of them in a manifestation that is now quite plain.[67]

The "veil" as interpreted by Origen is often simply the literal historical account or the "letter."[68] In order to remove this veil, however, the coming of Christ was indispensable. In fact Origen goes so far as to say that the "divine character" of the prophetic writings and the spiritual meaning of the law of Moses were revealed only with the coming of Christ. Previously it was not possible to bring forth convincing arguments for the inspiration of the Old Testament. The light contained in the law of Moses, covered by a veil, shown forth at the coming of Christ, when the veil was removed and it became possible to have "knowledge of the goods of which the literal expression contained the shadow."[69]

Both Origen and later interpreters interpreted the veil in a moral sense as well in an intellectual one. Lack of belief was seen as an obstacle to the correct interpretation of the Old Testament texts, to seeing the christological sense beneath the letter.

---

[67]Origen, *ComCt* 3.
[68]For other examples of the use of this text, see Origen, *HomGn* 2.3; 7.1; 12.1; *HomLev* 1.1; *HomNum* 26.3.
[69]Origen, *PArch* 4.1.6; translation from Origen, *On First Principles,* trans. and ed. G. W. Butterworth (New York: Harper & Row, 1966).

JEROME: The curtain of the temple is torn, for that which had been veiled in Judea is unveiled to all the nations; the curtain is torn and the mysteries of the law are revealed to the faithful, but to unbelievers they are hidden to this very day. When Moses, the Old Testament, is read aloud by the Jews on every Sabbath, according to the testimony of the apostle: "the veil covers their hearts." They read the law, true enough, but they do not understand because their eyes have grown so dim that they cannot see. They are, indeed, like those of whom Scripture says: "They have eyes but see not; they have ears but hear not."[70]

CHRYSOSTOM: The purpose of the veil was not to hide Moses but to prevent the Jews from seeing him, for they were unable to do so. But when we turn to the Lord, the veil is naturally taken away. When Moses talked with the Jews, he had his face covered, but when he talked with God, the veil was removed. Likewise when we turn to the Lord, we shall see the glory of the law and the face of the Lawgiver uncovered. And not only this, we shall then be in the same frame of reference as Moses.[71]

CYRIL OF ALEXANDRIA: Yet the shadows bring forth the truth, even if they are not at all the truth themselves. Because of this, the divinely inspired Moses placed a veil upon his face and spoke thus to the children of Israel, all but shouting by this act that a person might behold the beauty of the utterances made through him, not in outwardly appearing figures but in meditations hidden within us. Come, therefore, by taking off the veil of the law and by setting the face of Moses free of its coverings, let us behold the naked truth.[72]

THEODORET OF CYRRHUS: The same is true for you as well. When you believe in Christ, the veil of your unbelief will be taken away.[73]

Hebrews 8:4-5 and Hebrews 10:1, "copy and shadow":

Now if he were on earth, he would not be a priest at all, since there are priests who offer gifts according to the law. They offer worship in a sanctuary that is a sketch and shadow of the heavenly one; for Moses, when he was about to erect the tent, was warned, "See that you make everything according to the pattern that was shown you on the mountain."

---

[70]*Homily 66 on Psalm 88* (89); FC 57:68.
[71]*Homilies on the Epistles of Paul to the Corinthians* 7.4; NPNF 1 12:313.
[72]Letter 41; FC 76:172-73.
[73]*Commentary on the Second Epistle to the Corinthians* 305; PG 82:398.

> Since the law has only a shadow of the good things to come and not the true form of these realities, it can never, by the same sacrifices that are continually offered year after year, make perfect those who approach.

The use of the word "shadow" in these two texts from the letter to the Hebrews to designate the institutions of the Old Testament guaranteed that they would be important for an understanding of the relationship between the two testaments and as a principle of interpretation. Origen, making use of the principle of interpreting Scripture by means of Scripture mentioned earlier, manages to assimilate the notion of "shadow" in the letter to the Hebrews to the notion of our whole life as a shadow found in Job and then with the idea that our life on earth, when we see things reflected darkly as if in a mirror (1 Cor 13:12), is a shadow of things yet to come.

> And the apostle says with reference to the law, that they who have circumcision in the flesh, "serve as a copy and shadow of heavenly things." And elsewhere, "Is not our life upon the earth a shadow?" (cf. Job 8:9). If, then, not only the law which is upon the earth is a shadow, but also all our life which is upon the earth is the same, and we live among the nations under the shadow of Christ, we must see whether the truth of all these shadows may not come to be known in that revelation, when no longer through a glass, and darkly, but face to face, all the saints shall deserve to behold the glory of God, and the causes and truth of things. And the pledge of this truth being already received through the Holy Spirit, the apostle said, "Yes, though we have known Christ after the flesh, yet now henceforth we know Him no more" (2 Cor 5:16).[74]

Origen also connects the idea that Moses was shown a "form and pattern" (Ex 25:40) of the cultic objects he was to produce with the understanding that what he produced were only shadows of the heavenly patterns. This notion he then connects also with the understanding of the law as a kind of schoolmaster, as Paul argues in Galatians.

> In which land I believe there exist the true and living forms of that worship which Moses handed down under the shadow of the law; of which it is said,

---

[74]Origen, *PArch* 2.6.7; ANF 4:284.

that "they serve unto the example and shadow of heavenly things"—those, viz., who were in subjection in the law. To Moses himself also was the injunction given, "Look that thou make them after the form and pattern which were shown you on the mount" (Ex 25:40). From which it appears to me, that as on this earth the law was a sort of schoolmaster to those who by it were to be conducted to Christ, in order that, being instructed and trained by it, they might more easily, after the training of the law, receive the more perfect principles of Christ; so also another earth, which receives into it all the saints, may first imbue and mould them by the institutions of the true and everlasting law, that they may more easily gain possession of those perfect institutions of heaven, to which nothing can be added; in which there will be, of a truth, that Gospel which is called everlasting, and that Testament, ever new, which shall never grow old.[75]

John Chrysostom, on the other hand, explains the idea of the law as shadow by making a comparison between a line drawing and a colored image.

For as in painting, so long as one only draws the outlines, it is a sort of "shadow," but when one has added the bright paints and laid in the colors, then it becomes "an image." Something of this kind also was the law.[76]

My subject in this chapter has not been the interpretation of the Old Testament as a whole in the New Testament, but rather some of those areas where Jesus or New Testament authors are seen to correct, complement or complete Scripture. The New Testament authors did not attempt to interpret the Scriptures as a whole. Their use was quite selective: texts that were useful for interpreting the figure of Jesus or where he had criticized or been in conflict with the traditional teaching and later, as in the case of Paul, texts useful for resolving disputes in the early church. It should also be kept in mind that the New Testament authors were not aware that they were New Testament authors, although they may have been trying to offer authoritative interpretations. It is only in the early third century that we find commentaries on whole books of the Old Testament. This made it

---

[75]Ibid., 3.6.8; ANF 4:347-48.
[76]John Chrysostom, *On the Epistle to the Hebrews* 17.5; NPNF 1 14:448.

necessary to confront texts by now considered as Scripture that were problematic, that is, difficult to reconcile with the teaching of Jesus. As I have already noted, Marcion played a key role in determining what would be considered Scripture and how it would be interpreted.

In antiquity Christian interpreters read the Old Testament Scriptures through the eyes, so to speak, of New Testament texts. The Old Testament was never read as if it had a separate existence apart from the interpretation given to it by Jesus and the authors of the writings that form the New Testament. As Origen and many other writers saw it, Paul had given rules and examples of how to interpret the old writings. It was the task of Christian authors to continue this work. A passage from Origen's homilies on Joshua may serve to illustrate this outlook: "Therefore, Jesus reads the Law to us when he reveals the secret things of the Law. For we who are of the catholic Church do not reject the Law of Moses, but we accept it if Jesus reads it to us. For thus we shall be able to understand the Law correctly, if Jesus reads it to us, so that when he reads we may grasp his mind and understanding."[77]

The context of this comment is Joshua 8:35: "There was no word, out of all that Moses commanded, which Jesus did not read in the ears of the whole church of Israel." For Origen, Joshua was a figure, a type of Jesus, and the fact that the names were identical in Greek made this identification easier. Joshua reading the whole of the law to the people was a figure of Jesus interpreting the whole of the Scriptures to the church.

Although Origen was the first to try to work out such a Christian reading of the Scriptures in detail through his many commentaries and homilies, he was not the first to express the basic principle. It can be seen already perhaps in the response of Ignatius of Antioch to the Philadelphians: "to my mind it is Jesus Christ who is the original documents. The inviolable archives are his cross and death and his resurrection and the faith that came by him."[78] In the writings of Irenaeus of Lyons it becomes clearer that Jesus Christ is the *hypothesis* (the subject of the Scriptures) and

---

[77]Origen, *HomJos* 9.8; FC 105:104.
[78]Ignatius, *Letter to the Philadelphians* 8.2; trans. from John J. O'Keefe and R.R. Reno, *Sanctified Vision: An Introduction to Early Christian Interpretation of the Bible* (Baltimore: Johns Hopkins University Press, 2005), pp. 27-28.

through him the whole economy of salvation can be understood. He also employs the concept of "recapitulation": "He has therefore, in his work of recapitulation, summed up all things, both waging war against our enemy, and crushing him who had at the beginning led us away captives in Adam."[79] For Justin Martyr the "mysteries" of Christ are the key to reading the Scriptures: "Nobody will be able to receive Abraham's heritage, except those whose way of thinking is in utter conformity with the faith of Abraham through the acknowledgement of all the mysteries."[80] As has been observed, "This conviction that Christ fulfilled and clarifies the scriptures animated the entire patristic exegetical project."[81]

Summary: The ancient church read the Old Testament through the interpretations found already in the New Testament, never as a separate body of texts. For Origen and many others who followed his lead, Paul had provided both examples and norms to be followed in the interpretation of these older texts. Paul had supplied the notions of type (symbol), allegory and shadow that made it possible for early Christian interpreters to make sense, a Christian sense, of the Old Testament texts. The conviction that the texts had a Christian sense was also the presupposition for much of the "theological" interpretation of which we are speaking in this book.

---

[79]Irenaeus, *Adv. haer.* 5.11.1; O'Keefe and Reno, *Sanctified Vision*, p. 39.

[80]Justin, *Dialogue with Trypho* 44; O'Keefe and Reno, *Sanctified Vision*, pp. 41-42.

[81]From O'Keefe and Reno, *Sanctified Vision* p. 42. For an excellent exposition of this point, see chap. 2, "Christ Is the End of the Law and the Prophets." One may also usefully consult Ronald E. Heine, *Reading the Old Testament with the Ancient Church: Exploring the Formation of Early Christian Thought* (Grand Rapids: Baker Academic, 2007). He observes: "In the understanding of the church fathers, the Old Testament is dependent on Christ for its meaning in the way that a compass is dependent on the magnetic field of the North Pole. The latter is not a part of the compass but all its readings depend on it. The church fathers understood the law, the prophets, and the psalms to point toward Christ. They approached the Old Testament with the assumption that its overarching purpose was to communicate a message about Christ" (p. 194).

5

The Early Christian Writers

And so, since these things cannot without horrible sacrilege be literally
understood of him who is declared by the authority of Holy Scripture to be
invisible, ineffable, incomprehensible, inestimable, simple, and uncomposite,
the disturbance of anger (not to mention wrath) cannot be attributed
to that immutable nature without monstrous blasphemy.

JOHN CASSIAN, *INSTITUTES* 8.4[1]

IN THE PREVIOUS CHAPTERS A FEW of the more important early Christian
writers such as Origen and John Chrysostom have already been mentioned
in order to illustrate our theme. The purpose of this chapter is to fill out
the picture of early Christian interpretation by offering a wider selection
of authors and more examples of how they used the technical terminology
already described in the earlier chapters to deflect what they regarded as
harmful interpretations, that is, those considered unworthy of God.

It may be useful to mention that the Bible of the early church was Greek.
That is true of the Old Testament as well as the New Testament, which was
written in Greek. The Greek translation of the Old Testament used by the
church is known as the Septuagint ("seventy"), because of the legend
found first in the *Letter of Aristeas* (second century B.C.) that it had been

---

miraculously translated by seventy elders sent to Alexandria from Jerusalem for that purpose. Greek was the lingua franca (i.e., the common language) of the Roman Empire, and most of the Jewish communities in the
Diaspora (at least in the Roman Empire), such as that of Paul in Tarsus,
were Greek speaking. So also were many cities in the West, or they had
large Greek-speaking populations such as Rome. The church at Rome
spoke Greek into the third century, and the liturgy was not translated into
Latin until the third century. Although there existed a partial Latin translation earlier known as the *Vetus Latina*, the standard Latin translation by
Jerome, known as the Vulgate, was not made until the late fourth century
and did not come into common use until the fifth century. There exists far
more early Christian writing and biblical commentary in Greek than in
Latin. The translations of the Greek works of Origin made by Jerome and
Rufinus of Aquileia influenced later Latin commentators such as Augustine,
who did not have access to the Greek originals. Therefore mention is made
here first of Greek writers.

CLEMENT OF ALEXANDRIA

Although Clement did not write commentaries on the Scriptures, he did
make extensive use of them and developed the concept of what is "fitting
to God" or "worthy of God" as a key to interpretation. To him we are in-
debted for transmitting several of the passages from Xenophanes quoted
in chapter two, to which he has added the characterizations of "anthropomorphic" and "anthropopathic."

> Now, as the Greeks represent the gods as possessing human forms
> [*anthrōpomorphous*], so also do they as possessing human passions
> [*anthrōpopatheis*]. And as each of them depict their forms similar to them-
> selves, as Xenophanes says, "Ethiopians as black and apes, the Thracians
> ruddy and tawny"; so also they assimilate their souls to those who form
> them: the Barbarians, for instance, who make them savage and wild; and
> the Greeks, who make them more civilized, yet subject to passion.
>   Wherefore it stands to reason, that the ideas entertained of God by
> wicked men must be bad, and those by good men most excellent. And

therefore he who is in soul truly kingly and gnostic, being likewise pious and free from superstition, is persuaded that He who alone is God is honourable, venerable, august, beneficent, the doer of good, the author of all good things, but not the cause of evil.[2]

Clement himself offers an extended critique of the Homeric gods and passes in review the previous philosophical criticism of Greek mythology. Clement's key to interpreting the Scriptures is to be found in his concept of the "pedagogue," that is, the divine Logos (Word). He is described as follows:

our Instructor is like His Father God, whose son He is, sinless, blameless, and with a soul devoid of passion; God in the form of man, stainless, the minister of His Father's will, the Word who is God, who is in the Father, who is at the Father's right hand, and with the form of God is God. He is to us a spotless image; to Him we are to try with all our might to assimilate our souls. He is wholly free from human passions; wherefore also He alone is judge, because He alone is sinless.[3]

One should note the emphasis on freedom from human passions. The Logos, who becomes incarnate in Jesus Christ, was also active in the Law and the Prophets. Here of course he is clearly taking his cue from Paul, who had characterized the law as a pedagogue (Gal 3). "Accordingly, of old He instructed by Moses, and then by the prophets. Moses, too, was a prophet."[4] The law was given "and terror ensued for the prevention of transgressions and for the promotion of right actions, securing attention, and so winning to obedience to the true Instructor, being one and the same Word."[5] But God was acting as a Father: "So that from this it is clear, that one alone, true, good, just, in the image and likeness of the Father, His Son Jesus, the Word of God, is our Instructor; to whom God has entrusted us, as an affectionate father commits his children to a worthy tutor, expressly charging us, 'This is my beloved Son: hear Him.'"[6] It is in this context, then, that one must interpret actual passages of the law. God is acting as a Father toward his

---

[2]Clement, *Strom.* 7.4.22; ANF 2:528-29.
[3]Clement, *Paed.* 1.2.4; ANF 2:209-10.
[4]Ibid., 1.11; ANF 2:234.
[5]Ibid.
[6]Ibid.

children through his Word. Biblical descriptions of God's anger and threats can then be treated as expressions of his love for humanity. To the question of how God can be angry and punish, if he loves humankind, Clement answers:

> For this mode of treatment is advantageous to the right training of the children, occupying the place of a necessary help. For many of the passions are cured by punishment, and by the inculcation of the sterner precepts, as also by instruction in certain principles. For reproof is, as it were, the surgery of the passions of the soul; and the passions are, as it were, an abscess of the truth, which must be cut open by an incision of the lancet of reproof. Reproach is like the application of medicines, dissolving the callosities of the passions, and purging the impurities of the lewdness of the life; and in addition, reducing the excrescences of pride, restoring the patient to the healthy and true state of humanity. Admonition is, as it were, the regimen of the diseased soul, prescribing what it must take, and forbidding what it must not. And all these tend to salvation and eternal health.[7]

The approach is thus quite similar to that of Philo and Origen. God acts like a father toward children, and he is motivated by his love for humankind. He is not really angry.

ORIGEN OF ALEXANDRIA

Although there were many earlier writers in the church such as Ignatius of Antioch, Justin Martyr and Irenaeus of Lyons, Origen of Alexandria (ca. 184–254) was by far the most important and the most influential in the development of early Christian interpretation of the Scriptures. He was the first to develop and codify a set of rules and procedures for the interpretation of Scripture and the first to provide running commentaries on most of the books both of the Old Testament and the New Testament. We know a great deal about his life and work because the first church historian, Eusebius of Caesarea, dedicated the sixth book of his *Ecclesiastical History* to Origen. Origen had spent the last period of his life teaching and writing in Caesarea; Eusebius knew his disciples and probably had access to the library

---

[7]Ibid., 1.8; ANF 2:225.

he had collected. Because of controversies over his ideas later at the end of the fourth century and again in the early sixth century, many of Origen's works were lost, at least in the original Greek. However, many of them survived in Latin translation through the work of Jerome and Rufinus of Aquileia at the end of the fourth and the beginning of the fifth century.

Origen thought of himself as following the example of Paul in interpreting the Scriptures, and he frequently invoked Pauline texts to justify his procedures.[8] At the beginning of his fifth homily on Exodus, Origen states that Paul "taught the church which he gathered from the Gentiles how it ought to interpret the books of the Law."[9] According to Origen, Paul was aware of the possibility that the books of the law might be incorrectly interpreted by the Gentile converts because of their lack of familiarity with this literature. The danger from Paul's perspective (and Origen's) was that the Gentile converts would interpret the books of the law literally, as had the Jews. "For that reason," says Origen,

> [Paul] gives some examples of interpretation that we also might note similar things in other passages, lest we believe that by imitation of the text and document of the Jews we be made disciples. He wishes, therefore, to distinguish disciples of Christ from disciples of the Synagogue by the way they understand the Law. The Jews, by misunderstanding it, rejected Christ. We, by understanding the Law spiritually, show that it was justly given for the instruction of the church.[10]

In this quotation two phrases in particular should be noted: "examples of interpretation" and "understanding the Law spiritually." From Origen's point of view, Paul has first given examples of how to interpret the Scriptures. Origen is suggesting that we should analyze these examples and imitate the principles and procedures that Paul used in order to continue the work of interpreting the Scriptures. Second, this program of interpretation can be described as "understanding the Law spiritually." The two

---

[8]For a more extensive discussion of these texts, see the introduction to Mark Sheridan, *Genesis 12–50*, ACCS OT 2 (Downers Grove, IL: InterVarsity Press, 2002), pp. xxvi-xxxiv.
[9]Origen, *HomEx* 5.1; FC 71:275.
[10]Ibid.

ideas are united in a similar phrase later in the same homily, when Origen
speaks of the "seeds of spiritual understanding received from the blessed
apostle Paul."[11] When this program is carried out, then the Scriptures
appear in their true light as "given for the instruction of the Church." They
are not in fact a Jewish but a Christian book, since the Scriptures have been
given "for us." This latter idea is an important principle, which governs the
whole process of spiritual interpretation.

However, as might be expected from one strongly influenced by the
Greek philosophical tradition and by Philo, the concept of what is worthy
of God plays a significant role in his exegetical work. Already in his earlier
work *Peri Archon* (*De Principiis*), where the more general principles are set
forth, Origen uses this concept both as a theological principle and as an
exegetical tool. In the first book, he asserts that the idea of the Father begetting the Son must be understood as "some exceptional process, worthy
of God [*deo dignum*], to which we can find no comparison whatever."[12]
Speaking of participation in the Holy Spirit, he suggests that through grace
a person may make such progress "that the life which he received from
God shall be such as is worthy of God [*deo dignum*], who gave it to be pure
and perfect."[13]

In the second book, treating the question of the unity of the testaments,
he discusses the statements of the Old Testament where God is said to be
angry and points out that similar things can be found also in the New Testament. This leads to the general conclusion: "whenever we read of the
anger of God, whether in the Old or the New Testament, we do not take
such statements literally, but look for the spiritual meaning in them, endeavoring to understand them in a way that is worthy of God" (*deo
dignum*).[14] Origen states a similar principle in an even more general way
in the fourth book of this work, which is of course dedicated to the principles of interpretation of the Scriptures.

---

[11]FC 71:277.
[12]Origen, *PArch* 1.2.4; translation from Origen, *On First Principles*, trans. and ed. G. W. Butterworth (New York: Harper & Row, 1966), pp. 17-18.
[13]Ibid., 1.3.8; Butterworth, p. 38.
[14]Ibid., 2.4.4; Butterworth, p. 100.

> For we recognise that the letter is often impossible and inconsistent with itself, that is, that things, not only irrational but even impossible are occasionally described by it; but that we are to realise that with this external story are interwoven certain other matters which, when considered and comprehended in their inward meaning, provide us with a law which is useful to men and worthy of God [*deo dignam*].[15]

This is of course the well-known and controversial principle of *defectus litterae* ("the missing literal sense"), in which the *inrationabilia* ("senseless," *alogon* in Greek) and the *inpossibilia* ("impossible," *adynaton* in Greek) serve as triggers for a spiritual interpretation.[16] It is worth underlining the double criterion for meaning, at least as we have it in the Latin text. It must be "useful to men" and "worthy of God."

In practice Origen uses this principle frequently. In the homilies on Genesis, for example, he notes that the circumcision of the church is honorable, holy and worthy of God (*deo dignam*), whereas that taken literally is unseemly, detestable, disgusting and vulgar.[17] Likewise preaching on the marriage of Isaac in Genesis 24, Origen comments that if one interprets these things figuratively "he will find a marriage worthy of God [*nuptias Deo dignas*]; for his soul is united with God."[18] In fact, for Origen the criterion of "worthy of God" becomes not only a tool for dealing with difficult passages but also a motivation for finding a meaning for the entire text that is worthy of God. All of the Scriptures are the work of the Holy Spirit, and all of them have a spiritual meaning, if not a literal one.[19] Hence a meaning worthy of God or of the word of God or of the Holy Spirit can be found for all of them. After citing at length the prescriptions of Leviticus for sin offerings, Origen remarks that, if one holds only to the literal sense of the passage, it becomes an obstacle and cause of ruin for the Christian religion, but if one discovers a sense worthy of God (*digne Deo*), to whom

---

[15]Ibid., 4.3.4; Butterworth, p. 294.
[16]For further explanation of this principle, see Sheridan, *Genesis 12–50*, pp. xxxvi-xxxviii.
[17]Origen, *HomGn* 3.6. See also 3.5, where he speaks of a circumcision "worthy of the word of God" (*dignam circumcisionem uerbi Dei*).
[18]Ibid., 10.5; FC 71:166.
[19]Ibid., 4.2.4-5.

the Scriptures are attributed, then one can become a spiritual Jew.[20] Similarly at the end of an explanation of the prophecy of Balaam in Numbers, Origen exhorts the congregation to pray that that he will be able to explain the others as well in a manner worthy of God and of the Holy Spirit, who has inspired them.[21]

EUSEBIUS OF CAESAREA

Eusebius is perhaps better known as the father of church history, but he also wrote commentaries on the Psalms and other biblical books. He was interested in the correct interpretation of the Scriptures also because of his apologetic works, the *Preparation of the Gospel* (*Praeparatio evangelica*) and the *Proof of the Gospel* (*Demonstratio evangelica*), works preliminary to the *Ecclesiastical History*, which is in fact a continuation of the apologetic works designed to show the triumph of Christianity. In the *Preparation* he speaks of the portrayal of the gods with human passions in the works of Homer: "Then as to wanderings, and drunken fits, and amours, and seduction of women, and plots against men, and countless things, which are in truth shameful and unseemly practices of mortal men, how could any one refer these to the universal elements, acts which bear upon their very face mortality and human passion [*anthrōpopathēs*]?"[22] He shows also that he is well acquainted with the defense of Homer through allegorical explanations: "If therefore the gods are to speak true in certifying the human passions [*anthrōpopatheias*] attributed to them, they who set these aside must be false; but if the physical explanations of the philosophers are true, the testimonies of the gods must be false."[23] These explanations of the philosophers are not convincing, and the portrayals of the gods are not fitting to deity: "Well then! it is manifest even to themselves that their lifeless images are no gods; and that their mythical theology offers no explanation that is respectable and becoming to deity [*theoprepē*], has been shown in

---

[20]Origen, *HomLev* 5.1.
[21]Origen, *HomNum* 16.9.
[22]Eusebius, *Praep. evang.* 3.3.21. The following translations of Eusebius are taken from Eusebius of Caesarea, *Praeparatio Evangelica*, trans. E. H. Gifford (Grand Rapids: Baker Book House, 1981).
[23]Ibid., 3.15.2.

the first book, as likewise in the second and third it has been shown that neither does their more physical and philosophical interpretation of the legends contain an unforced explanation."[24]

Finally he must acknowledge the presence of similar things in the Bible: "Now you may find in the Hebrew Scriptures also thousands of such passages concerning God as though He were jealous, or sleeping, or angry, or subject to any other human passions [*anthrōpopatheias*], which passages are adopted for the benefit of those who need this mode of instruction."[25] Here too we see the notion of the divine "condescension" (*synkatabasis*) in the writing of Scripture.

DIDYMUS OF ALEXANDRIA

In the later fourth century Didymus, blind from the age of four, was one of the most erudite and popular teachers of the church. Both Jerome and Rufinus went to hear his lectures in Alexandria. He had a prodigious memory and could cite not only the biblical books from memory but also the works of Philo, Origen and many others. He wrote (or dictated) many commentaries, and we also have lecture notes from his course on the Psalms. Didymus was well acquainted with the traditional terminology used in the interpretation of the Scriptures and employed it often. In a passage on Genesis 6:7 he comments:

> That said, it is appropriate to see the sense of these words: "God repented of having made man on the earth and he thought it over" and "I have become angry that I have made them" (Gen 6:6, 7), which is parallel to: "I repent of having anointed Saul king" (1 Sam 15:35). It is necessary to say that this is to attribute to God human passions [*anthrōpopathōs*] and that the sense is not that which the words suppose. When the Scripture speaks metaphorically of hands, of feet, of eyes or of ears, one must not think that God has a human form, but we interpret obviously his hands as his powers of acting, his eyes as the fact that nothing escapes him and each member is like a power of God.[26]

---

[24]Ibid., 4.1.6.
[25]Ibid., 12.31.2.
[26] Didymus, *In Genesim*, on Gen 6:7; SCh 244:42-44.

God is not changeable, and thus any expression that suggests otherwise must be interpreted in terms of what we know to be the true nature of God.

> The same thing goes for the expressions: "He thought it over" and "he re-pented." We interpret them as is fitting for an immutable being. When men want to show to those whom they are instructing the importance of sin, to make them understand that they have committed great errors and that they are not worthy of receiving instruction, they say to them, "I am sorry to have taught you that" in order to make them aware of the sin; thus it is said of God that "he repents," not because he is subject to a passion, but to show the greatness of the sin. He was not in fact ignorant of the fact that men would be sinners, but in his goodness he wanted to see whether [or not they would convert] in virtue of the laws inscribed in their thought. Let us take an image to show that there is no passion in God himself, but in those who change their feelings in his regard.[27]

In his lectures on the Psalms, commenting on Psalm 36:13 (LXX), "but the Lord will laugh at him, / because he foresees that his day will come" (NETS), Didymus explains: "Such words said in regard to God cannot be taken in such a way as to attribute to God these sentiments. We have to understand their meaning in a way fitting to God [*theoprepōs*]. It was said 'He who resides in the heavens will laugh at them and the Lord will mock them' (Ps 2:4). It is not said with regard to a man, let us not understand it of God in a human manner [*anthrōpopathōs*]."[28]

The terminology relating to what is considered "fitting to" or "worthy of" God can be found in many other Greek writers including Basil the Great, Gregory of Nyssa and especially Cyril of Alexandria. Limits of space pro-hibit a more extensive treatment here.

THE ANTIOCHENE SCHOOL

The phrase "Antiochene school" designates a school of thought rather than an institution, which was characterized by the rejection of allegory or at

---

[27]Ibid.; on Gen 6:7; SCh 244:44.
[28]M. Gronewald, *Didymos de Blinde. Psalmenkommentar*, pt. 5 [*Papyrologische Texte und Abhandlungen* 12. Bonn: Habelt, 1970]: p. 232 (Codex 247, 11).

least of the word. The first author in this category is Diodore of Tarsus in the time of the emperor Julian (A.D. 360–363). John Chrysostom and Theodore of Mopsuestia were disciples of Diodore. Theodoret of Cyrrhus (A.D. 393–457) is usually listed as belonging to this "school," although he is later and the least typical representative of it. Diodore insisted on making the distinction between "types" (from the Greek word *typoi*), which he regarded as legitimate and founded in the writings of Paul, and "allegory," which he identified with philosophical interpretation and rejected. The modern notion of "typology" (a word never found in ancient Greek literature) draws inspiration from this distinction. In this view, Paul would himself have used the word "allegory" improperly. More recent research into the subject suggests that the difference between the two schools of thought should not be exaggerated.[29] They shared many common presuppositions and much common terminology, including that of "fitting to God" (*theoprepōs*), and the notion that Scripture "hints" (*ainittesthai*) in order to indicate hidden or nonliteral meanings.[30] No consensus has emerged regarding the reasons for the emergence of this Antiochene "school" of thought, which has generally been interpreted as criticism of the Alexandrian tradition. One interesting theory, however, is that it was a reaction to the attempt of the emperor Julian (the Apostate) to reintroduce allegorical interpretation of the Homeric epics.[31]

John Chrysostom, the famous preacher from Antioch who became bishop of Constantinople in 398, produced by far the most extensive collection of homilies on biblical texts. Those on Genesis and the Psalms are especially notable. He was untiring in his efforts to get his listeners to understand the text in a way fitting to God. He explained hundreds of times that the biblical

---

[29]See, e.g., P. W. Martens, "Revisiting the Allegory/Typology Distinction: The Case of Origen," *JECS* 16, no. 3 (2008): 283-317; and Martens, "Origen Against History? Reconsidering the Critique of Allegory," *Modern Theology* 28, no. 4 (2012): 635-56.

[30]See chap. 2.

[31]See G. Rinaldi, *Diodoro di Tarso, Antiochia e le ragioni della polemica antiallegorista*, in *Ricerche patristiche in onore di Dom Basil Studer OSB*, Augustinianum 33 (1993): 407-30. For additional information, see Robert C. Hill, *Reading the Old Testament in Antioch* (Leiden: Brill, 2005); Manlio Simonetti, *Lettera e/o allegoria: un contributo alla storia dell'esegesi patristica* (Rome: Institutum Patristicum "Augustinianum," 1985); John J. O'Keefe, "'A Letter That Killeth': Toward a Reassessment of Antiochene Exegesis, or Diodore, Theodore, and Theodoret on the Psalms," *JECS* 8 (2000): 83-104.

texts that represent God in a human way are to be understood as God's adapting himself to the human situation for the sake of instructing and are not to be taken literally. They are all to be interpreted in terms of God's "considerateness" (*synkatabasis*). Chrysostom does not use the term *anthrōpopathēs* to describe the attribution of human passions to God, but assumes it under the critical term *anthrōpomorphos*, a term found many times in his writings. Since Chrysostom has already been mentioned in the first chapter and will be cited often in the next chapter, I mention only two texts here.

> From these words ["in our image"] they want to speak of the divine in human terms [*anthrōpomorphon*], which is the ultimate example of error, namely, to cast in human form him who is without shape, without appearance, without change, and to attribute limbs and forms to the one who has no body. What could match this madness, people not simply refusing to derive any profit from the teachings of the inspired Scriptures, but even incurring severe harm from them?[32]
>
> So recognizing our limitations, and the fact that what is said refers to God, let us accept the words as equivalent to the shape of bodies and the structure of limbs, but understand the whole narrative in a manner appropriate to God [*theoprepōs*]. For the deity is simple, free of parts and shape; should we form an impression from ourselves and want to ascribe an arrangement of limbs to God, we would be in danger of falling into the irreverence pagans are guilty of.[33]

John was concerned above all that the ordinary Christian might misunderstand the nature of God when listening to the biblical texts.

THE ANCIENT CHRISTIAN LATIN WRITERS

Tertullian. Among Latin Christian writers Tertullian is the first to use the criterion of what is fitting to God extensively, particularly in his work *Contra Marcionem.* It may reasonably be inferred that Marcion had also appealed to this norm in his own works.[34] Arguing against Marcion's doctrine of a dual divinity—the Old Testament creator God and the New Testament Savior God, Tertullian states: "But the Christian truth has

---

[32]*Homilies on Genesis* 8.8; FC 74:109.
[33]Ibid., 13.9; FC 74:173.
[34]See Tertullian, *Contre Marcion I*, ed. René Braun, SCh 365 (Paris: Cerf, 1990), p. 46. Braun notes that this criterion is invoked more than thirty times in this work.

distinctly declared this principle, 'God, if he is not one, is not,' because we more properly [*dignius*] believe that that has no existence which is not as it ought to be."[35] He uses the same argument against Marcion's separation of the function of creator from his God. "State some reason worthy of God [*Deo dignam*]," he says, "why he, supposing him to exist, created nothing."[36] The reason, he insists, must be limited to one of two: either he was unwilling to create or unable. "Now, that he was unable, is a reason unworthy of God."[37] Nothing in fact is so "proper and worthy of God" (*propria et Deo digna*) as the testimony of the creation.[38] "The world," says Tertullian, "is not unworthy of God, for God has made nothing unworthy of Himself."[39] Against the Marcionite depreciation of the world, he adds, "And yet, if to have been the author of our creation, such as it is, be unworthy of God, how much more unworthy of Him is it to have created absolutely nothing at all!"[40] He goes on to note and enumerate, against the argument of the unworthiness of the world, all the elements of the world that philosophers have regarded as divine, concluding: "It is, indeed, enough for me that natural elements, foremost in site and state, should have been more readily regarded as divine than as unworthy of God."[41]

Turning to the question of God's goodness and other qualities that can be attributed to him, Tertullian uses similar arguments.

As touching this question of goodness, we have in these outlines of our argument shown it to be in no way compatible with Deity [*minime deo adaequare*],—as being neither natural, nor rational, nor perfect, but wrong, and unjust, and unworthy of the very name of goodness [*bonitatis nomine indignam*],—because, as far as the congruity of the divine character is concerned [*in quantum deo congruat*], it cannot indeed be fitting that that Being should be regarded as God who is alleged to have such a goodness, and that

---

[35]Tertullian, *Marc.* 1.3. All translations of Tertullian are from ANF 3.
[36]Ibid., 1.11.6.
[37]Ibid., 1.11.7.
[38]Ibid., 1.13.1.
[39]Ibid., 1.13.2.
[40]Ibid., 1.13.3.
[41]Ibid., 1.13.5.

not in a modified way, but simply and solely. For it is, furthermore, at this
point quite open to discussion, whether God ought to be regarded as a
Being of simple goodness, to the exclusion of all those other attributes, sen-
sations, and affections, which the Marcionites indeed transfer from their
god to the Creator, and which we acknowledge to be worthy characteristics
of the Creator too [*in Creatore ut deo dignos*], but only because we consider
Him to be God. Well, then, on this ground we shall deny him to be God in
whom all things are not to be found which befit the Divine Being [*quae deo
digna sint*].[42]

Tertullian insists that Marcion's God is hopelessly weak because Marcion
refuses to ascribe to him the function of judge and the emotions that must
accompany such a function, which include anger. He concludes: "If it is
unbecoming for God to discharge a judicial function, or at least only so far
becoming that He may merely declare His unwillingness, and pronounce
His prohibition, then He may not even punish for an offence when it is
committed. Now, nothing is so unworthy of the Divine Being as not to
execute retribution on what He has disliked and forbidden."[43]

In the second book of this work Tertullian returns to the question of
divine punishments and, using the Stoic notion that the only real evil is the
moral one, is able to insist that the divine punishments "are, no doubt, evil
to those by whom they are endured, but still on their own account good,
as being just and defensive of good and hostile to sin. In this respect they
are, moreover, worthy of God."[44] He lists the punishments inflicted on the
Egyptians in Exodus as examples.

Defending the law and the prophets from the Marcionite charge that
they were unworthy of God, Tertullian insists that, quite apart from their
figurative sense, even on the literal level they exercised a positive function
and "the prophets were also ordained by the self-same goodness of God,
teaching precepts worthy of God."[45] Another of the Marcionite objections
to the God of the Old Testament was evidently that he swears oaths (Gen

---

[42]Ibid., 1.25.1-2.
[43]Ibid., 1.26.3.
[44]Ibid., 2.14.3.
[45]Ibid., 2.19.1-2.

22:16; Deut 32:40; Is 45:23). To this Tertullian replies that "He swears by Himself, in order that you may believe God, even when He swears that there is besides Himself no other God at all." And he concludes with the extraordinary statement, "Hence, if He swears both in His promises and His threatenings, and thus extorts faith which at first was difficult, nothing is unworthy of God which causes men to believe in God."[46] This, if taken at face value, considerably broadens the scope of the concept "worthy of God." He invokes a similar principle in considering the question of the incarnation and asserts

> that God would have been unable to hold any intercourse with men, if He had not taken on Himself the emotions and affections of man, by means of which He could temper the strength of His majesty, which would no doubt have been incapable of endurance to the moderate capacity of man, by such a humiliation as was indeed unworthy [*sibi quidem indigna*] of Himself, but necessary for man, and such as on this very account became worthy of God, because nothing is so worthy of God as the salvation of man.[47]

In the end, however, Tertullian gives in to the weight of the philosophical tradition regarding the impassibility (*apatheia*) of God by dividing the burden between Father and Son.[48] All that is regarded as unworthy of God throughout the economy of salvation can be attributed to the Son acting for the unseen Father. He concludes in this often-quoted statement:

> Whatever attributes therefore you require as worthy of God, must be found in the Father, who is invisible and unapproachable, and placid, and (so to speak) the God of the philosophers; whereas those qualities which you censure as unworthy must be supposed to be in the Son, who has been seen, and heard, and encountered, the Witness and Servant of the Father, uniting in Himself man and God, God in mighty deeds, in weak ones man, in order that He may give to man as much as He takes from God.[49]

---

[46]Ibid., 2.26.2.

[47]Ibid., 2.27.1.

[48]For this tradition, see H. Frohnhofen, *Apatheia tou theou. Über die Affektlosigkeit Gottes in der griechischen Antike und bei den griechischsprachigen Kirchenvätern bis zu Gregorios Thaumaturgos*, Europäische Hochschulschriften 23/318 (Frankfurt am Main: Peter Lang, 1987).

[49]Tertullian, *Marc.* 2.27.6.

As has been observed, this is a capitulation more to the philosophical tradition than to the arguments of Marcion.[50] These examples must suffice to illustrate the extensive use made of this principle in the thought of Tertullian. With Tertullian, however, the question of what is worthy or unworthy of God has become a principle of interpreting the Scriptures and not merely an instrument of apologetic for the Christian God against the pagan gods.[51]

Augustine. The same terminology can be found occasionally in the writings of Hilary, Ambrose and Jerome, but it occurs frequently in Augustine, who was of course well acquainted with philosophical criticism of the classical or poetic portrait of the gods found in Cicero and other Latin writers. Augustine uses the criterion of "worthiness" not only for apologetic purposes but also as an instrument of interpretation. Commenting on Psalm 6:1, "Reprove me not, O Lord, in your anger," he writes, "Yet this emotion must not be attributed to God, as if to a soul, of whom it is said, 'but You, O Lord of power, judgest with tranquillity.' Now that which is tranquil, is not disturbed. Disturbance then does not attach to God as judge [*non ergo cadit in deum iudicem perturbation*]: but what is done by His ministers, in that it is done by His laws, is called His anger."[52] Similarly commenting on Psalm 9:13, "For requiring their blood he has remembered," he observes: "But let no one suppose 'He has remembered' to be so used, as though forgetfulness can attach to God [*quasi obliuio cadat in Deum*]; but since the judgment will be after a long interval, it is used in accordance with the feeling of weak men, who think God has forgotten, because He does not act as speedily as they wish."[53] Likewise in commenting on Psalm 41, he notes that mutability does not attach to God (*ista mutabilitas non cadit in deum*).[54] The phrase "worthy of God"

---

[50]Jean-Claude Fredouille, *Tertullien et la conversion de la culture antique*, Études Augustiniennes 47 (Paris: Études Augustiniennes, 1972), pp. 62-161.

[51]On Tertullian's exegesis in general, one may consult T. P. O'Malley, *Tertullian and the Bible: Language, Imagery, Exegesis* (Nijmegen–Utrecht: Dekker & van de Vegt, 1967). However, the author does not deal with our subject.

[52]Augustine, *Enarrat. Ps.* 6.3; NPNF 1 8:16.

[53]Ibid., 9.13; NPNF 1 8:36.

[54]Ibid., 41.7.

also finds ample use in Augustine's works. In the introduction to book four of his unfinished work *Against Julian*, he promises to show that the laws of God are worthy of the governance of God and that the works of God are most worthy of God as Creator (*haec postremo digna esse deo rectore, illa deo dignissima conditore*).[55]

One final passage from Augustine should be quoted because of its similarity to the rules enunciated by Cassian. In the third book of *On Christian Doctrine*, Augustine makes the observation: "Those things, again, whether only sayings or whether actual deeds, which appear to the inexperienced to be shameful, and which are ascribed to God, or to men whose holiness is put before us as an example, are wholly figurative, and the hidden kernel of meaning they contain is to be picked out as food for the nourishment of charity."[56] The principle of interpretation, in other words, must be our concept of God or our knowledge of the character of the person in question.

John Cassian. Although John Cassian (d. ca. 435) did not write commentaries on the Scriptures, he did, as the principal Western monastic author, have considerable influence on later Latin writers. Cassian was concerned with correct interpretation above all because of the influence this could have on the spiritual life of the monks for whom he was writing. The reading and interpretation of the Scriptures belonged to the core activity of the monastic life. Wrong interpretations could seriously mislead and damage the spiritual well-being of the readers. They could influence behavior or be used to defend mistaken behavior. In his fourteenth Conference Cassian sketches out a theory of biblical interpretation that was to have great influence in the Middle Ages.

The quotation from Cassian at the head of this chapter contains strong language—"horrible sacrilege" and "monstrous blasphemy"—to describe literal readings of many biblical passages. However, they accurately express Cassian's concern for correct interpretation, which for him must always be "worthy of God." In dealing with the vice of anger, Cassian observes that there are people who try to defend or excuse their anger by citing the Scrip-

---

[55]Augustine, *Contra Iulianum opus imperfectum* IV; PL 45:1338.
[56]Augustine, *Doctr. chr.* 3.12.18; NPNF 1 2:561-62.

tures and claiming that since God gets angry with wrongdoers, we are justified in doing the same. "They do not understand that, in their eagerness
to concede human beings the opportunity for pernicious vice, they are
mixing the injustice of fleshly passion into the divine limitlessness and the
source of all purity."[57] To answer this mistaken opinion Cassian first cites
the absurdity of taking literally the anthropomorphisms of Scripture.

> For if these things that are said of God are to be accepted according to the
> letter and with a carnal and crass understanding, then he of whom it is said:
> "Behold, he who watches over Israel will neither slumber nor sleep" (Ps
> 121:4) also sleeps, since it is said: "Arise, Lord, why do you sleep?" (Ps 44:23)
> And he stands and sits, since it is said: "Heaven is my seat, and the earth is
> a footstool for my feet" (Is 66:1 LXX)—he who "measures the heavens with
> his palm and encloses the earth in his fist." (Is 40:12) And he gets drunk
> with wine, since it is said: "And the Lord rose up as if from slumber, like a
> strong man drunken with wine" (Ps 78:65)—he "who alone has immor-
> tality and dwells in inaccessible light" (1 Tim 6:16).[58]

All of these anthropomorphic descriptions of God are to be interpreted
metaphorically in a way that is worthy of God. He explains that "by the
term 'mouth' we should understand that conversation of his which he is
wont to carry on softly in the inmost recesses of our souls, or what he spoke
to our fathers and to the prophets."[59] By the attribution of "eyes" to God
"we should be able to recognize that sharp and unobstructed gaze with
which he surveys and views all things, and the fact that nothing that is done
or will be done or that is thought by us is hidden from him."[60]

After listing various other such interpretations, Cassian concludes:
"Thus, when we read of God's anger and wrath, we must not think of it
ἀνθρωποπαθῶς [written in Greek letters in Cassian's text]—that is, in
terms of lowly human disturbances, but in a manner worthy of God, who
is free of all disturbance."[61] Here we see combined once again the two

---

[57]Cassian, *Inst.* 8.2 (translations of Cassian's *Institutes* are all from ACW 58).
[58]Ibid., 8.3.
[59]Ibid., 8.4.2.
[60]Ibid.
[61]Ibid., 8.4.3.

criteria of attributing passions to God and the notion of what is fitting or worthy of God. Cassian does not deny that the perception of God as a just judge may be helpful to sinners: "For human nature is accustomed to fear those who it knows get angry, and it hesitates to offend them."[62] However, the burden of the perception is in the souls of "those who are afraid." It cannot be attributed to God. Rather: "With whatever mildness and gentleness of spirit it may be carried out, this is nonetheless considered high wrath and the cruelest anger by those who are to be deservedly punished."[63] The perception of God as angry, in other words, arises in the soul of the sinner. But this perception becomes an obstacle to growth in the spiritual life if it is used to justify anger on the part of the individual, because the passions are obstacles to union with God, who is free of all passion. The goal is to become like God, free from anger.

Summary: The wide range of texts cited in this chapter from both Greek and Latin early Christian writers illustrates a common approach to the problematic texts of the Bible. These writers use the categories of God's "considerateness," that is, his adapting himself to human ways of speaking, as well as the technical terminology of anthropomorphism, anthropopathism and what is fitting to or worthy of divinity in order to find an acceptable meaning for difficult and dangerous texts. Especially noteworthy is the exclusion of anger as an attribute of God.

---

[62]Ibid., 8.4.4.
[63]Ibid., 8.4.3.

6

Three Classic Cases

He [Moses] did not, like any historian, make it his business to leave
behind for posterity records of ancient deeds for the pleasant
but un-improving entertainment which they give.

PHILO OF ALEXANDRIA, *DE VITA MOYSIS* 2.48[1]

Nor is Scripture devoted so much to historical narratives
as to things and ideas which are mystical.

ORIGEN, *HOMILIES ON GENESIS* 15.1[2]

AS THE TWO QUOTATIONS ABOVE IMPLY, God did not give us the Scriptures just for entertainment. As noted already several times, one of the
basic assumptions of early Christian interpretation was that the real
meaning of the sacred texts must be something useful. The role of the interpreter was to discover the meaning intended "for us" (1 Cor 9:10), a
meaning that should be edifying and convey useful teaching—useful on
the level of faith and morals, that is, and not just as facts about the past.

The three sets of texts to be examined here posed a challenge in different
ways to the concept of a transcendent God. In the previous chapter Eu-

---

[1]LCL 289:471.
[2]FC 71:203.

sebius was quoted as saying that there are thousands of such passages in the Hebrew Scriptures. Here we can only present three of the more notable passages that challenged the ancient interpreter.

GENESIS 1–4: THE STORY OF THE CREATION AND FALL

The early chapters of Genesis contain an extraordinary number of anthropomorphisms. God is depicted creating like a potter, planting a garden like a gardener, punishing repeatedly, having regrets for what He did and so on. Philo of Alexandria had already devoted a number of treatises (twelve in all) to dealing with various subjects found in these accounts. Much early Christian commentary was devoted to dealing with the anthropomorphic presentation of God found in these chapters, in order to develop a properly "theological" understanding of God. Preserving the transcendence of God (that he is not like humans) was a primary aim of the commentary. Early commentators examined every detail of the text. Here we shall look at only a few examples, which illustrate the concern of the commentators to avoid misunderstandings and to preserve the transcendence of God, that is, that he is "not like mankind." The ancient commentators were also sensitive to the charge that this account had a "mythical" character to it and so were eager to show that it had a deeper meaning rather than to insist on its literal reading.

Genesis 1:4.

And God saw that the light was good.

Although the first chapter of Genesis is much less anthropomorphic in its presentation than the account in the second chapter, nevertheless it attributes to God human characteristics including speech, sentiments and reflection. Philo was also aware of the problem of speaking of light and darkness, not to mention day and night, before introducing the creation of the sun and moon and other heavenly bodies. Consequently he introduces the Platonic distinction between the invisible, intelligible universe and the material one in order to explain the text. His Greek text seems to have included a variant reading: "preeminently." The light spoken of before the creation of the sun was therefore an invisible intellectual light.

Of light he says that it is beautiful pre-eminently: for the intelligible as far surpasses the visible in the brilliancy of its radiance, as sunlight assuredly surpasses darkness and day night, and mind, the ruler of the entire soul, the bodily eyes. Now that invisible light perceptible only by the mind has come into being as an image of the Divine Word Who brought it in within our ken: it is a supercelestial constellation, fount of the constellations obvious to sense.[3]

John Chrysostom instead makes use of his usual explanation for the use of anthropomorphic language. It is a sign of the divine condescension that God employs such terminology, but we must not attribute human limitations to God. We must understand the words "in a sense proper to God."

The text says, "God saw that it was good." When you hear that God "saw" and "God praised," take the word in a sense proper to God [*theoprepōs*]. That is to say, the Creator knew the beauty of the created thing before he created it, whereas we are human beings and encompassed with such limitations that we cannot understand it in any other way; accordingly, he directed the tongue of the blessed author to make use of the clumsiness of these words for the instruction of the human race.[4]

For Augustine the anthropomorphisms can all be interpreted in terms of abstract qualities of God. Human language and characteristics are being used of God so that everyone can understand.

We should understand that this sentence does not signify joy as if over an unexpected good but an approval of the work. For what is said more fittingly of God—insofar as it can be humanly said—than when Scripture puts it this way: "he spoke," and "it was made," "it pleased him." Thus we understand in "he spoke" his sovereignty, in "it was made" his power and in "it pleased him" his goodness. These ineffable things had to be said in this way by a man to men so that they might profit all.[5]

AUGUSTINE: "God saw that the light was good," and these words do not

---

[3]*On the Creation* 8.30; LCL 226:25.
[4]*Homilies on Genesis* 4.11; FC 74:58.
[5]*On the Literal Interpretation of Genesis* 5.22; FC 84:158-59.

mean that God found before him a good that he had not known but that he was pleased by one that was finished.[6]

Genesis 1:26-27.

Then God said, "Let us make humankind in our image, according to our likeness; and let them have dominion over the fish of the sea, and over the birds of the air, and over the cattle, and over all the wild animals of the earth, and over every creeping thing that creeps upon the earth."

So God created humankind in his image,
in the image of God he created them;
male and female he created them.

Of all the phrases in the creation narrative the statement that humanity was made in God's image and likeness probably caused the most controversy. It could be interpreted to mean that God had a human form and evidently was so interpreted, if the repeated insistence on the contrary is any indication. For Philo the "image" in question could hardly be the human body, but must be the mind, the "sovereign element of the soul."

> After all the rest, as I have said, Moses tells us that man was created after the image of God and after His likeness. Right well does he say this, for nothing earth-born is more like God than man. Let no one represent the likeness as one to a bodily form; for neither is God in human form, nor is the human body God-like. No, it is in respect of the Mind, the sovereign element of the soul, that the word "image" is used; for the pattern of a single Mind, even of the Mind of the Universe as an archetype, the mind in each of those who successively came into being was moulded. It is in a fashion a god to him who carries and enshrines it as an object of reverence; for the human mind evidently occupies a position in men precisely answering to that which the great Ruler occupies in all the world.[7]

Clement of Alexandria combines Philo's interpretation (with which he was certainly acquainted) with the terminology from the first chapter of John's Gospel, where Jesus is described as the "Word" of God and the "true

---

[6]*Two Books on Genesis Against the Manichaeans* 1.8.13; FC 84:61.
[7]*On the Creation* 23.69; LCL 226:55.

light." This of course implies that the Word of God had a role in the creation, which in fact became standard Christian doctrine.

> For "the image of God" is his Word (and the divine Word, the light who is the archetype of light, is a genuine son of Mind [the Father]); and an image of the Word is the true man, that is, the mind in man, who on this account is said to have been created "in the image" of God and "in his likeness," because through his understanding heart he is made like the divine Word or Reason [*Logos*], and so reasonable [*logikos*].[8]

Origen's interpretation was more complex. He interpreted the two accounts of the creation of humanity in Genesis 1 and Genesis 2 to indicate two different moments in the creation of humans, a first, spiritual creation of souls and a second moment when bodies were created (Gen 2). He also noted that the word "likeness" found in Genesis 1:26 was not repeated in Genesis 1:27. He took this to be significant, an indication that the "likeness" was not present at the beginning, but something to be attained through a person's imitation of God. In a homily on Genesis he also makes use of the idea of the "inner man" (Rom 7:22; Eph 3:14-21) to insist that the image could hardly refer to the human body, but only to the incorporeal, incorruptible and immortal aspects of the human soul.

> For Moses, before all others, points to it when in recording the first creation of man he says, "And God said, Let us make man in our own image and likeness." Then he adds afterwards, "And God made man; in the image of God made he him; male and female made he them, and he blessed them." Now the fact that he said "he made him in the image of God" and was silent about the likeness points to nothing else but this, that man received the honor of God's image in his first creation, whereas the perfection of God's likeness was reserved for him at the consummation. The purpose of this was that man should acquire it for himself by his own earnest efforts to imitate God, so that while the possibility of attaining perfection was given to him in the beginning through the honor of the "image," he should in the end through the accomplishment of these works obtain for himself the perfect "likeness."[9]

---

[8]*Exhortation to the Greeks* 10; LCL 92:215.
[9]Origen, *PArch* 3.6.1; Butterworth, p. 245.

We do not understand, however, this man indeed whom Scripture says was made "according to the image of God" to be corporeal. For the form of the body does not contain the image of God, nor is the corporeal said to be "made" but "formed," as is written in the words that follow. For the text says, "And God formed man," that is fashioned, "from the slime of the earth" (Gen 2:7). But it is our inner man, invisible, incorporeal, incorruptible and immortal, that is made "according to the image of God." For it is in such qualities as these that the image of God is more correctly understood. But if anyone supposes that this man who is made "according to the image and likeness of God" is made of flesh, he will appear to represent God himself as made of flesh and in human form. It is most clearly impious to think this about God.[10]

John Chrysostom is concerned, on the one hand, to refute heretics who want to interpret the "image" in human, material terms and, on the other hand, to maintain the transcendence of God. Reading the text so as to attribute external human form to God is harmful. But Chrysostom sees the meaning of "image" not so much in terms of the human soul as in the sovereignty that God granted to humankind over the inferior creatures. It is in their ability to command that humans resemble God.

> CHRYSOSTOM: Here again, however, other heretics arise assailing the dogmas of the Church; they say, Look: he said, "In our image"—and from these words they want to speak of the divine in human terms, which is the ultimate example of error, namely to cast in human form him who is without shape, without appearance, without change, and to attribute limbs and forms to the one who has no body. What could match this madness, people not simply refusing to derive any profit from the teaching of the inspired Scriptures, but even incurring severe harm from them?[11]

> CHRYSOSTOM: You learnt what is the meaning of "in our image," that it is not in the order of being but a similarity of command, that he spoke not in terms of a formal image but in terms of command—hence the postscript,

---

[10]Origen, *HomGn* 1.13; FC 71:63.
[11]*Homilies on Genesis* 8.8; FC 74:109.

"Let them have control of the fish of the sea and the birds of heaven, the wild beasts and the reptiles of the earth."[12]

CHRYSOSTOM: As the word "image" indicated a similitude of command, so too "likeness," with the result that we become like God to the extent of our human power—that is to say, we resemble him in our gentleness and mildness and in regard to virtue, as Christ also says, "Be like your Father in heaven" (Mt 5:45).[13]

Augustine notes that the "image" is restricted to humans because only God is more exalted than humans. He is also concerned with the interpretation of the word "our" in Genesis 1:26. Originally the word may have referred to the idea of a heavenly court in which God was speaking. Such a possibility was excluded in later Jewish and Christian interpretation. For Christians the plural "our" must refer to the three persons of the Trinity. Humans are made in the image of the triune God, not in the image of one person of the Trinity alone.

Not everything that among creatures bears some likeness to God is rightly called his image, but only that than which God alone is more exalted. That is directly drawn from him, if between himself and it there is no interposed nature.[14]

For God said, "Let us make man in our image and likeness": a little later, however, it is said "And God made man in the image of God." It would certainly not be correct to say "our," because the number is plural, if man were made in the image of one person, whether Father, Son or Holy Spirit. But because he is made in the image of the Trinity, consequently it was said "in our image." Again, lest we choose to believe in three gods in the Trinity, since the same Trinity is one God, he said, "And God made man in his image," as if he were to say "in his [own triune] image."[15]

Ambrose denies that the flesh can be made in the image of God. What is made in the image of God is what can be perceived by the mind. It is the

[12]*Homilies on Genesis* 9.6; FC 74:119.
[13]Ibid., 9.7; FC 74:120.
[14]*On the Trinity* 11.5.8; FC 45:327-28*.
[15]Ibid., 12.6.6; FC 45:348*.

power of reflection. Using the rule of explaining Scripture by means of Scripture, Ambrose introduces quotations from Paul to explain the idea: "our citizenship is in heaven (Phil 3:20)" and the notion that we are being transformed into the image of God from 2 Corinthians 3:18.

> But let us define more accurately the meaning of the phrase "to the image of God." Is it true that the flesh is made "to the image of God"? In that case, is there earth in God, since flesh is of earth? Is God corporeal, that is to say, weak and subject like the flesh to the passions? . . .
>
> The flesh, therefore, cannot be made to the image of God. This is true, however, of our souls, which are free to wander far and wide in acts of reflection and of counsel. Our souls are able to envisage and reflect on all things. We who are now in Italy have in mind what seems to pertain to affairs in the East or in the West. We seem to have dealings with men who dwell in Persia. We envision those who have their homes in Africa, if there happen to be acquaintances of ours who enjoy the hospitality of that land. We accompany these people on their departure and draw near to them in their voyage abroad. We are one with them in their absence. Those who are separated far from us engage us in conversation. We arouse the dead even to mutual interchange of thoughts and embrace them as if they were still living. We even go to the point of conferring on these people the usages and customs of our daily life. That, therefore, is made to the image of God that is perceived not by the power of the body but by that of the mind. It is that power that beholds the absent and embraces in its vision countries beyond the horizon. Its vision crosses boundaries and gazes intently on what is hidden. In one moment the utmost bounds of the world and its remote secret places are under its ken. God is attained, and Christ is approached. There is a descent into hell, and aloft in the sky there is an ascent into heaven. Hear, then, what Scripture says: "But our citizenship is in heaven (Phil 3:20)." Is not that, therefore, in which God is ever-present made to the likeness of God? Listen to what the apostle says in that regard: "We all, therefore, with faces unveiled, reflecting as in a mirror the glory of God, are being transformed into his very image from glory to glory, as through the Spirit of the Lord (2 Cor 3:18)."[16]

---

[16]*Hexaemeron* 6.8.44-45; FC 42:256-58.

Gregory of Nyssa took a different approach. For him the image signifies above all the goodness of God, which he communicated to humankind through his creation. "Image" includes all the gifts that God gave to humans.

> God creates man for no other reason than that God is good; and being such, and having this as his reason for entering upon the creation of our nature, he would not exhibit the power of this goodness in an imperfect form, giving our nature some one of the things at his disposal and grudging it a share in another: but the perfect form of goodness is here to be seen by his both bringing man into being from nothing and fully supplying him with all good gifts. But since the list of individual good gifts is a long one, it is out of the question to apprehend it numerically. The language of Scripture therefore expresses it concisely by a comprehensive phrase, in saying that man was made "in the image of God," for this is the same as to say that he made human nature participant in all good; for if the Deity is the fullness of good, and this is his image, then the image finds its resemblance to the archetype in being filled with all good.[17]

John Cassian relates the story of a monk named Serapion in the context of the so-called anthropomorphist controversy that took place in Egypt in the year 400 because of a letter written by the patriarch Theophilus condemning the practice of thinking about God in human form when praying. This monk was unable to pray without thinking of God in human form and so an effort was made to explain to him that this was contrary to the traditional understanding of the church concerning the interpretation of the phrase "image and likeness." The phrase must be interpreted "not according to the lowly sound of the letter but in a spiritual way."

> Placing him [Serapion] in the midst of all the brothers, he inquired as to how the Catholic churches throughout the East interpreted what is said in Genesis: "Let us make man according to our image and likeness." Then he explained that the image and likeness of God was treated by all the heads of the churches not according to the lowly sound of the letter but in a spiritual way, and he proved this with a long discourse and many examples from Scripture, showing that nothing of this sort could be the case with that

---

[17]*On the Making of Man* 16.10; NPNF 2 5:405.

immeasurable and incomprehensible and invisible majesty—that it could
be circumscribed in a human form and likeness, that indeed a nature that
was incorporeal and uncomposed and simple could be apprehended by the
eye or seized by the mind.[18]

Genesis 2:7.

Then the LORD God formed man from the dust of the ground, and breathed
into his nostrils the breath of life; and the man became a living being.

The second creation account, in Genesis 2, contains even more striking
anthropomorphisms than the first one. The image of God "breathing" into
the man the breath of life is described by Philo as "monstrous folly" if taken
literally and receives an allegorical interpretation as the human soul being
"inspired" by God. For Basil the Great the phrase suggests a share in the
divine grace that allows humans to recognize their likeness to God. John
Chrysostom takes the phrase to refer to the creation of the human soul, but
warns against thinking that the soul came from the substance of God. Augustine also takes the language to be a reference to the human soul and is
similarly concerned that it should not be misunderstood to mean that the
soul is of the same nature as God, since the soul is mutable and God is not.

PHILO OF ALEXANDRIA: "Breathed into," we note, is equivalent to "inspired"
or "be-souled" the soul-less; for God forbid that we should be infected with
such monstrous folly as to think that God employs for inbreathing organs
such as mouth or nostrils; for God is not only not in the form of man, but
belongs to no class or kind. Yet the expression clearly brings out something
that accords with nature. For it implies of necessity three things, that which
inbreathes, that which receives, that which is inbreathed: that which inbreathes is God, that which receives is the mind, that which is inbreathed
is the spirit of breath. What, then, do we infer from these premises? A union
of the three comes about, as God projects the power that proceeds from
Himself through the mediant breath till it reaches the subject. And for what
purpose save that we may obtain a conception of Him? For how could the
soul have conceived of God, had He not breathed into it and mightily laid

---

[18]*Conference* 10.3.2-3; ACW 57:372.

hold of it? For the mind of man would never have ventured to soar so high as to grasp the nature of God, had not God Himself drawn it up to Himself, so far as it was possible that the mind of man should be drawn up, and stamped it with the impress of the powers that are within the scope of its understanding.[19]

BASIL THE GREAT: "And he breathed into his nostrils," that is to say, he placed in man some share of his own grace, in order that he might recognize likeness through likeness. Nevertheless, being in such great honor because he was created in the image of the Creator, he is honored above the heavens, above the sun, above the choirs of stars. For which of the heavenly bodies was said to be an image of the most high God? (Cf. Ps 8:5/Heb 1:5).[20]

CHRYSOSTOM: It was pleasing to God's love of humanity to make this thing created out of earth a participant of the rational nature of the soul, through which this living creature was manifest as excellent and perfect. "And he breathed into his nostrils the breath of life," that is, the inbreathing communicated to the one created out of earth the power of life, and thus the nature of the soul was formed. Therefore Moses added "And man became a living soul"; that which was created out of dust, having received the inbreathing, the breath of life, "became a living soul." What does "a living soul" mean? An active soul, which has the members of the body as the implements of its activities, submissive to its will.[21]

CHRYSOSTOM: In this regard some senseless people, moved by their own reasoning, and having no regard for what is proper to God [*theoprepēs*] nor any appreciation of the considerateness [*synkatabasis*] revealed in these words, try to say that the soul comes from the substance of God.[22]

AUGUSTINE: We ought to understand this passage so that we do not take the words "he breathed into him the breath of life, and man became a living soul" to mean that a part, as it were, of the nature of God was turned into the soul of man. . . . The nature of God is not mutable, does not err and is not corrupted by the stains of vices and sins. . . . Scripture clearly says that

---

[19]*Leg.* 1.36-38; LCL 226:171.
[20]*Homily on Psalm 48*; FC 46:324-25.
[21]*Homilies on Genesis* 12.15; FC 74:166.
[22]Ibid., 13.7; FC 74:172.

the soul was made by the almighty God and that it is therefore not a part of God or the nature of God.[23]

Genesis 2:8.

And the LORD God planted a garden in Eden, in the east.

The idea of God's engaging in so human an activity as planting a garden also caused Philo to insist on the nature of God as far transcending all such human limitations. To attribute them to God would be "great impiety." For John Chrysostom the words must be interpreted in a way fitting to God, that is, that God commanded such a thing to happen.

> PHILO OF ALEXANDRIA: Far be it from man's reasoning to be the victim of so great impiety as to suppose that God tills the soil and plants pleasure gardens. We should at once be at a loss to tell from what motive He could do so. Not to provide Himself with pleasant refreshment and comfort. Let not such fables even enter our mind. For not even the whole world would be a place fit for God to make His abode, since God is His own place, and He is filed by Himself, and sufficient for Himself, filling and containing all other things in their destitution and barrenness and emptiness, but Himself contained by nothing else, seeing that He is Himself One and the Whole.[24]

> CHRYSOSTOM: "God," it says, "planted a garden in Eden in the east." Notice here, dearly beloved, that unless we take the words in a manner appropriate to God [*theoprepōs*], we will inevitably be trapped in a deep pitfall. I mean, what would be likely to be said about this sentence, too, by those rash enough to interpret in human fashion everything said about God?[25]

> CHRYSOSTOM: And when, dearly beloved, you hear that "God planted a garden in Eden in the east," take the word "planted" in a sense appropriate to God [*theoprepōs*], namely, that he commanded this happen.[26]

---

[23]*Two Books on Genesis Against the Manichaeans* 2.8.11; FC 84:106*.
[24]*Allegorical Interpretation* 1.43-44; LCL 226:175.
[25]*Homilies on Genesis* 13.12; FC 74:174
[26]Ibid.; FC 74:175.

Genesis 2:21.

Then he took one of his ribs and closed up its place with flesh.

The creation of woman from a rib of the man was also to be taken in a manner suitable to God, hardly as a literal description of what took place.

CHRYSOSTOM: "God took one of his ribs," the text says. Don't take the words in human fashion; rather, interpret the concreteness of the expression from the viewpoint of human limitations. You see, if he had not used these words, how would we have been able to gain knowledge of these mysteries which defy description? Let us therefore not remain at the level of the words alone, but let us understand everything in a manner proper to God [*theoprepōs*] because applied to God. That phrase, "He took," after all, and other such are spoken with our limitations in mind.[27]

Genesis 3:8.

They heard the sound of the LORD God walking in the garden at the time of the evening breeze.

The idea of God's "walking" could only be considered an absurdity if taken literally. John Chrysostom interprets it to mean that God induced in the man and the woman an experience of anguish. For Augustine it meant the presence of God and the desire to "hide" themselves meant that they were trying to remove themselves from the presence of God.

CHRYSOSTOM: "They heard the sound of the Lord God," the text says, "as he strolled in the garden in the evening; both Adam and his wife hid from the Lord's presence amongst the trees of the garden." Let us not, dearly beloved, pass heedlessly by the words from Sacred Scripture, nor remain at the level of their expression, but consider that the ordinariness of their expression occurs with our limitations in mind and that everything is done in a manner befitting God [*theoprepōs*] for the sake of our salvation. I mean, tell me this: were we prepared to follow the drift of the words without taking what is said in a sense befitting God, [*theoprepōs*] how could many absurdities [*atopa*] be avoided? See now, let us consider this from the very

---

[27]Ibid., 15.8; FC 74:199.

beginning of the reading: "They heard the sound of the Lord God," the text says, "as he strolled in the garden in the evening, and they hid." What are you saying—God strolls? Are we assigning feet to him? Have we no exalted conception of him?[28]

AUGUSTINE: Toward evening God was walking in paradise, that is, he was coming to judge them. He was still walking in paradise before their punishment, that is, the presence of God still moved among them, when they no longer stood firm in his command. It is fitting that he comes toward evening, that is, when the sun was already setting for them, that is, when the interior light of the truth was being taken from them. They heard his voice and hid from his sight. Who hides from the sight of God but he who has abandoned him and is now beginning to love what is his own? For they now were clothed with a lie, and he who speaks a lie speaks from what is his own. This is why they are said to hide near to the tree that was in the middle of paradise, that is, near themselves who were set in the middle rank of things beneath God and above bodies. Hence they became hidden to themselves so that they might be troubled by their wretched errors after they had left the light of truth that they were not. For the human soul can be a partaker in the truth, but the truth is the immutable God above it. Hence whoever turns away from that truth and toward himself, rejoicing not in God who rules and enlightens him but rather in his own seemingly free movements, becomes dark by reason of the lie.[29]

Genesis 3:21.

And the LORD God made garments of skins for the man and for his wife, and clothed them.

Of all the anthropomorphisms in the account, this is perhaps the boldest, to portray God sewing up animal skins to provide garments for the man and the woman. For Origen this is a symbol of human mortality, since the skins were from dead animals. John Chrysostom is careful to insist on an interpretation "befitting God" and suggests that "made" means that God gave orders for such to happen. The garments of skin are a sym-

---

[28]Ibid., 17.3-4; FC 74:223.
[29]*Two Books on Genesis Against the Manichaeans* 2.16.24; FC 84:119-20.

bolic reminder of their disobedience. Gregory of Nyssa interprets the "skins" to mean the form of irrational (animal) nature that we have put on from our "association with disordered passions." Augustine sees the garments of skin as a sign of the loss of innocence and of mortality. It means that humanity has become like the beasts.

ORIGEN: It is said that God made those miserable garments with which the first man was clothed after he had sinned. "For God made skin tunics and clothed Adam and his wife." Therefore, those were tunics of skin taken from animals. For with such as these, it was necessary for the sinner to be dressed. It says, "with skin tunics," which are a symbol of the mortality that he received because of his skin and of his frailty that came from the corruption of the flesh. But if you have been already washed from these and purified through the law of God, then Moses will dress you with a garment of incorruptibility so that "your shame may never appear" (Ex 20:26) and "that what is mortal may be swallowed up by life (2 Cor 5:4)."[30]

CHRYSOSTOM: "The Lord made garments of skin for Adam and his wife, and clad them in them." See the extent of the considerateness [*synkatabasis*] of Sacred [*theia*] Scripture. Still, what I've often said I say again now: let us understand everything in a sense befitting God [*theoprepōs*]. Let us understand "made" in the sense of "gave directions for": he ordered that they be clad in garments of skin as a constant reminder of their disobedience.[31]

GREGORY OF NYSSA: In the same way, when our nature becomes subject to the disequilibrium and paroxysm of disordered passions, it encounters those conditions that necessarily follow the life of the passions. But when it returns again to the blessedness of an ordered emotive life, it will no longer encounter the consequences of evil. Since whatever was added to human nature from the irrational life was not in us before humanity fell into passion, we shall also leave behind all the conditions that appear along with passion. If a man wearing a ragged tunic should be denuded of his garment, he would no longer see on himself the ugliness of what was discarded. Likewise, when we have put off that dead and ugly garment that was made for us from irrational skins (when I hear "skins" I interpret it as the form of

---

[30]*HomLev* 6.2.7; FC 83:120.
[31]*Homilies on Genesis* 18.4; FC 82:5.

the irrational nature that we have put on from our association with disordered passions), we throw off every part of our irrational skin along with the removal of the garment. These are the disruptions of harmony that we have received from "the irrational skin": sexual intercourse, conception, childbearing, dirt, lactation, nourishment, evacuation, gradual growth to maturity, the prime of life, old age, disease and death.[32]

AUGUSTINE: [Adam and Eve], who were stripped of their first garment [of innocence], deserved by their mortality garments of skin. For the true honor of man is to be the image and the likeness of God that is preserved only in relation to him by whom it is impressed. Hence, he clings to God so much the more, the less he loves what is his own. But through the desire of proving his own power, man by his own will falls down into himself as into a sort of [substitute] center. Since he, therefore, wishes to be like God, hence under no one, then as a punishment he is also driven from the center, which he himself is, down into the depths, that is, into those things wherein the beasts delight. Thus, since the likeness to God is his honor, the likeness to the beasts is his disgrace.[33]

GENESIS 16: SARAH AND HAGAR

Although the stories of Abraham, Sarah and Hagar did not involve God directly in the same way that the anthropomorphic depictions of the primeval history did, nevertheless, because they formed part of Sacred Scripture, they needed to be explained in such a way that God did not seem to be condoning behavior that could be considered immoral. Whatever may have been the customs lying behind these stories when they received their written form several centuries earlier, by the time of Jesus, Paul and Philo they appeared to be scandalous. The story of Sarah's offering her slave girl to her husband, Abraham, posed a challenge to biblical interpreters both Jewish and Christian. The text of Genesis 16:1-4 states:

Now Sarai, Abram's wife, bore him no children. She had an Egyptian slave-girl whose name was Hagar, and Sarai said to Abram, "You see that

---

[32]*On the Soul and Resurrection*; NPNF 2 5:464-65.
[33]*On the Trinity* 12.11.16; FC 45:358.

the LORD has prevented me from bearing children; go in to my slave-girl; it may be that I shall obtain children by her." And Abram listened to the voice of Sarai. So, after Abram had lived ten years in the land of Canaan, Sarai, Abram's wife, took Hagar the Egyptian, her slave-girl, and gave her to her husband Abram as a wife. He went in to Hagar, and she conceived; and when she saw that she had conceived, she looked with contempt on her mistress.

It appeared that Sarah and Abraham had agreed to adultery for the sake of obtaining an heir. The principal solution was to interpret the text allegorically, and in this Philo was the leader. For Philo Sarah represented wisdom and Hagar the preliminary studies that one must pursue before philosophy (the pursuit of wisdom). Whereas Philo had offered a moral allegory of the story (see chap. 3), Paul offered an allegorical reading of the text in terms of two covenants and two peoples, that is, in terms of the plan of salvation.

The Pauline interpretation is found in Galatians 4:22–5:1.

For it is written that Abraham had two sons, one by a slave woman and the other by a free woman. One, the child of the slave, was born according to the flesh; the other, the child of the free woman, was born through the promise. Now this is an allegory: these women are two covenants. One woman, in fact, is Hagar, from Mount Sinai, bearing children for slavery. Now Hagar is Mount Sinai in Arabia and corresponds to the present Jerusalem, for she is in slavery with her children. But the other woman corresponds to the Jerusalem above; she is free, and she is our mother. For it is written,

"Rejoice, you childless one, you who bear no children,
    burst into song and shout, you who endure no birth pangs;
for the children of the desolate woman are more numerous
    than the children of the one who is married."

Now you, my friends, are children of the promise, like Isaac. But just as at that time the child who was born according to the flesh persecuted the child who was born according to the Spirit, so it is now also. But what does the scripture say? "Drive out the slave and her child; for the child of the slave will not share the inheritance with the child of the free woman." So then, friends, we are children, not of the slave but of the free woman. For freedom Christ has set us free. Stand firm, therefore, and do not submit again to a yoke of slavery.

It will be recalled from chapter four earlier that this is one of the key texts invoked by Origen precisely because it contains the word "allegory" and also because it presumes the literal sense of the passage in Genesis. Paul's allegorical reading of the text presumes that the reader has in mind the whole story of Genesis 16–21, from the begetting of Ishmael to his being sent away with his mother, Hagar. It also presumes the reader has in mind the whole story of the giving of the law on Mount Sinai as well as the polemic against observance of the law on the part of the Gentiles in the preceding part of the letter to the Galatians. In this rather dense passage Paul then associates Hagar with the giving of the law on Mount Sinai. He has already explained earlier in the letter that the law was like a pedagogue, a temporary measure until the heir came of age. He also states that "heirs, as long as they are minors, are no better than slaves" (Gal 4:1). The heir means the offspring of Abraham, those who inherited the promise made to Abraham. The faith of Abraham and of those who believe in Jesus had been contrasted with observance of the law: "the law was our disciplinarian until Christ came, so that we might be justified by faith" (Gal 3:24). Hagar is then not only associated with the bondage of the law but also with the earthly Jerusalem in contrast with the Jerusalem "above," which is implicitly represented by Sarah. We, like Isaac, are children of the free woman, Sarah, and not of the slave, and therefore we are not in bondage to the law.

Christian interpretation of the story of Abraham, Sarah and Hagar in Genesis shows the influence of the allegorical interpretations of both Philo and Paul, but also adds a moralizing interpretation of the literal text. Didymus the Blind finds the text useful in this sense and actually manages to discover praiseworthy virtues being exercised in the story by Abraham and Sarah.

The apostle saw in these women the type of the two covenants, in accordance with the rule of allegory, but since what the text narrates actually took place, the literal sense also deserves consideration. The saints entered the married life not to pursue pleasure but for the sake of children. There is in fact a tradition that says they would go with their wives only when the time was suitable for conception. They would not go with them during the lactation period, when they were nursing their young, or when they were with child, because they regarded neither of these times as suitable for coming together. . . .

When Sarah, therefore, who was wise and holy, had observed for a long time that in spite of coming together with her husband she was not conceiving, she abstained from conjugal relations, and since she knew that it was in the order of things that he should have children, she gave him her slave girl as a concubine. This shows the moderation and the absence of jealousy of Sarah and the passionlessness of Abraham, who chose this solution at his wife's instigation and not on his own initiative and who yielded to her request only in order to give birth to children. The literal sense too, then, is useful according to the considerations offered above.[34]

But Didymus also makes ample use of the allegorical interpretations from Paul and Philo, especially the latter, who had interpreted Sarah to represent virtue and philosophy and Abraham as the symbol for the man who seeks wisdom through learning. In this perspective it is altogether proper for Abraham to mate with Hagar because she represents the studies preliminary to philosophy. Didymus even enriches this allegorical interpretation by introducing the idea that the law contains the shadow of better things to come. The shadow, according to Didymus, is the letter of the law and the institutions described by the law. Thus he manages to weave together the philosophical-ethical perspective of Philo with the perspective of the plan of salvation.

As for the anagogical (mystical) teaching, one could explain the text by recalling that Paul allegorically transposed the two women into the two covenants (Gal 4:22-31). Philo also used allegory here but gave the text another application: he understood Sarah to represent perfect virtue and philosophy, because she was a free woman and wife, of noble birth and living with her husband in lawful union. Now virtue lives with the wise

---

[34]*On Genesis* 235; SCh 244:200-202.

man in lawful union so that he can give birth from her to a divine progeny: "Wisdom," in fact, "begets a man of discernment" (Prov 10:23 LXX). In Scripture the devout and holy man is addressed with the words "your wife is like a fruitful vine.... Your children are like olive shoots around the table. So shall the man be blessed who fears the Lord" (Ps 128:3-4 [127:3-4 LXX]).

Sarah then is allegorically transposed into perfect and spiritual virtue. Hagar, the Egyptian slave, symbolizes, according to Philo, the preliminary exercises,[35] and, in Paul, "the shadow" [of good things to come] (Heb 10:1).

> It is not possible, in fact, to understand anything of the spiritual or elevated ideas without the shadow that is the letter or without a preliminary study of the introductory sciences, for one must first bear children from inferior unions. In the era of the shadow, they offered actual animal sacrifices, they celebrated Passover in an external and tangible way, they received physical circumcision, and all of this was preparing them gradually so that eventually they could "offer to God a sacrifice of praise" (Ps 50:14 [49:14 LXX]), which pertains to the free woman. As the zeal of the wise impels them to go on to the higher realities in due order, virtue impels them, by divine intention, to make use first of the introductory sciences and to have children from them. Since it is impossible, in fact, for one who has just recently approached virtue so successfully to attain perfection as to have children through her too, virtue counsels such a one to subject himself first to the preparatory disciplines so that by this path he might perfectly grasp her, if he is able.[36]

Didymus also manages to combine ingeniously Paul's reproof to the Galatians that they had turned back to the things of flesh (circumcision and other legal observances) after they had received the Spirit with Philo's condemnation of those who become so enthralled with the preliminary studies, such as music and mathematics, that they forget about the search for wisdom. The Galatians forgot that the true circumcision was that of the heart and were content to live with the shadow, that is, the letter of the law.

---

[35]Philo develops this allegorical interpretation especially in *De Congressu Eruditionis Gratia* 1–9, although he employs it elsewhere as well. Hagar represents the studies preliminary to philosophy in the Greek system of education: grammar, music, mathematics, rhetoric, etc. The word used here by Didymus, "preliminary exercises" (*progymnasmata*), actually refers to the exercises used to learn the components of rhetoric.

[36]*On Genesis* 235-36; SCh 244:202-204.

Likewise Philo's students forgot about the true goal of their studies and were content to remain with those that were only preliminary.

> Virtue's purpose was, as we have said, that the wise man do training exercises first in preliminary education and shadow so that later, with this training behind him, he might arrive at greater things—which is the proper procedural order. It is likewise illogical that after the knowledge of perfect things one should turn back to petty things. This is in fact what the apostle Paul writes to the Galatians, who, after the gospel had been preached to them, wanted to live with the shadow, which is the law. . . . They had been taken in by a certain Ebion,[37] who wanted to practice Judaism after having become a Christian and who was so successful in persuading others that the apostles gave him this surname to show his poverty. Ebion, in fact, means "poor," and he was so called because of the perversion and poverty of his ideas. As for the fact that the Galatians were of pagan origin, Paul writes, "Formerly, when you did not know God, you were in bondage to beings that by nature are not gods, but now you have come to know God, or rather to be known by God" (Gal 4:8-9). He reproached them, as I said, in these terms (to produce now the text I announced): "Having begun with the Spirit, are you now ending with the flesh?" (Gal 3:3). Indeed, when once they had given a wholly divine beginning to their edifice, they were looking for figures in an inappropriate manner, for they were searching for them when it was no longer their time. For we must understand why the visible circumcision was given and until what time it was appropriate to practice it. If one has understood this, he has had children from the concubine and is able, after this, to comprehend the circumcision of the heart that is effected by the Spirit. This holy man, upon the advice of virtue, went in to the slave girl whom she had placed at his disposal, as we have explained, and the slave girl conceived. But after this, it is inappropriate to remain with her beyond the time of her favor. Many indeed, having made use of the preparatory exercises in view of the perfect teaching, never go beyond this point, thus giving birth to a progeny of slavery, and in a certain sense dishonor virtue. . . . One dishonors virtue, then, who gives other things precedence over it. For if one chooses virtue, not for its own sake but for the sake of

---

[37]Paul does not say this. The information about Ebion is found in Origen, *PArch* 4.3.8.

something else—praise, for example, or glory—then in a certain sense one is dishonoring the good, which in itself is not susceptible to dishonor.[38]

Ambrose, taking a rather different approach from Didymus, excuses Abraham's conduct on the grounds that the law against adultery had not yet been promulgated in the time of Abraham. Therefore Abraham could not be said to have violated the law. Ambrose was of course aware of the account of the institution of marriage in the first part of Genesis and allowed that although "in paradise God had praised marriage, he had not yet condemned adultery." His major concern, however, is to warn converts that what they did as pagans is not permitted to them as Christians. As pagans they were in a situation similar to Abraham before the giving of the law.

> Some might still be struck by the fact that Abraham had a relationship with his slave girl when he was already conversing with God, as it is written: "Sarah said to Abraham, 'See now, the Lord has prevented me from bearing children; go in to my maid to make children from her.'" And this is exactly what happened. But we should consider first of all that Abraham lived prior to the law of Moses and before the gospel; adultery, it seems, was not yet prohibited at this time. The penalty for the crime goes back only to the time of the law, which made adultery a crime. So there is no condemnation for the offense that precedes the law but only one based on the law. Abraham then cannot be said to have violated the law since he came before the law. Though in paradise God had praised marriage, he had not condemned adultery. In fact, he does not wish the death of sinners (cf. Ezek 33:11), and for this reason he promises the reward without exacting the penalty. Indeed, God prefers to stimulate with mild proddings than to terrify with severe threats. If you too sinned, when you were a pagan, you have an excuse. But now you have come to the church and have heard the law, "You shall not commit adultery" (Ex 20:14 [20:13 LXX]), you no longer have an excuse for the offense. However, since this discourse is directed also to those who are inscribed to receive the grace of baptism, if anyone has committed such a grave sin, let him be sure that he will be pardoned, but as one who has committed an offense. Let him know, however, that for the future he is obliged

---

[38]*On Genesis* 237-38; SCh 244:206-208.

to abstain. Indeed, in the case of the adulterous woman spoken of in the Gospel, whom the scribes and Pharisees presented to the Lord, the Lord forgave her former sins but said, "Go, and from now on be careful not to sin any more" (Jn 8:11). In saying this to her, he says it to you. You have committed adultery as a pagan; you have sinned as a catechumen. The sin is forgiven you, remitted through baptism; go, and in the future, see that you do not sin. Such is the first defense of Abraham.[39]

Whether the passage was interpreted allegorically or given a moralizing interpretation, it was clear that it had to be somehow neutralized, so that it could not be misinterpreted and be used to justify behavior that was considered immoral.

WIPING OUT THE NATIONS: DEUTERONOMY AND JOSHUA

A major problem for early Christian writers was posed by the repeated commands attributed to God in Deuteronomy, Joshua and Judges to wipe out, destroy utterly, put to the sword the inhabitants of the Promised Land. The ethnocentric in-group morality expressed in these books was in sharp contrast to the universalist outlook of the gospel. The portrait of a violent and vengeful God could not easily be reconciled with the preaching of Jesus Christ. The language itself of "utterly destroy them," "put all its males to the sword," "not leave any that breathed" was as shocking to ancient sensibilities as it is to modern ones, which have witnessed the genocidal horrors of the twentieth century. To appreciate the extent of the problem it is necessary to pass in review the texts in question.

Already in the book of Deuteronomy the people are prepared and taught what they must do in the future:

> When the LORD your God brings you into the land that you are about to enter and occupy, and he clears away many nations before you—the Hittites, the Girgashites, the Amorites, the Canaanites, the Perizzites, the Hivites, and the Jebusites, seven nations mightier and more numerous than you—and when the LORD your God gives them over to you and you defeat them, then you must utterly destroy them. Make no covenant with them

---

[39]*On Abraham* 1.4.23; CSEL 32.1:517-18.

and show them no mercy. Do not intermarry with them, giving your daughters to their sons or taking their daughters for your sons, for that would turn away your children from following me, to serve other gods. Then the anger of the LORD would be kindled against you, and he would destroy you quickly. But this is how you must deal with them: break down their altars, smash their pillars, hew down their sacred poles, and burn their idols with fire. (Deut 7:1-5)

And later in the same book they are reminded of this command, "When the LORD your God has cut off the nations whose land the LORD your God is giving you, and you have dispossessed them and settled in their towns and in their houses" (Deut 19:1):

When you draw near to a town to fight against it, offer it terms of peace. If it accepts your terms of peace and surrenders to you, then all the people in it shall serve you at forced labor. If it does not submit to you peacefully, but makes war against you, then you shall besiege it; and when the LORD your God gives it into your hand, you shall put all its males to the sword. You may, however, take as your booty the women, the children, livestock, and everything else in the town, all its spoil. You may enjoy the spoil of your enemies, which the LORD your God has given you. Thus you shall treat all the towns that are very far from you, which are not towns of the nations here. But as for the towns of these peoples that the LORD your God is giving you as an inheritance, you must not let anything that breathes remain alive. You shall annihilate them—the Hittites and the Amorites, the Canaanites and the Perizzites, the Hivites and the Jebusites—just as the LORD your God has commanded, so that they may not teach you to do all the abhorrent things that they do for their gods, and you thus sin against the LORD your God. (Deut 20:10-18)

To be sure, the theological concern is with the preservation of the pure monotheistic faith, and the fear expressed is that of syncretistic religion. But this can hardly justify such a violent, inhuman solution. Even the differentiation between those who surrender peacefully and those who resist does not remove the horror, for the first are to be reduced to forced labor in any case.

In the book of Joshua these commands are recorded as having been carried out, first of all with the "fall of Jericho" in Joshua 6:20-21.

> So the people shouted, and the trumpets were blown. As soon as the people heard the sound of the trumpets, they raised a great shout, and the wall fell down flat; so the people charged straight ahead into the city and captured it. Then they devoted to destruction by the edge of the sword all in the city, both men and women, young and old, oxen, sheep, and donkeys.

The same record of human butchery is repeated after each stage of the "conquest" in Joshua 10:34-43.

> From Lachish Joshua passed on with all Israel to Eglon; and they laid siege to it, and assaulted it; and they took it that day, and struck it with the edge of the sword; and every person in it he utterly destroyed that day, as he had done to Lachish.
>
> Then Joshua went up with all Israel from Eglon to Hebron; they assaulted it, and took it, and struck it with the edge of the sword, and its king and its towns, and every person in it; he left no one remaining, just as he had done to Eglon, and utterly destroyed it with every person in it.
>
> Then Joshua, with all Israel, turned back to Debir and assaulted it, and he took it with its king and all its towns; they struck them with the edge of the sword, and utterly destroyed every person in it; he left no one remaining; just as he had done to Hebron, and, as he had done to Libnah and its king, so he did to Debir and its king.
>
> So Joshua defeated the whole land, the hill country and the Negeb and the lowland and the slopes, and all their kings; he left no one remaining, but utterly destroyed all that breathed, as the LORD God of Israel commanded. And Joshua defeated them from Kadesh-barnea to Gaza, and all the country of Goshen, as far as Gibeon. Joshua took all these kings and their land at one time, because the LORD God of Israel fought for Israel. Then Joshua returned, and all Israel with him, to the camp at Gilgal.

And then finally in Joshua 11 the Lord's command is said to have been fully accomplished.

> All the spoil of these towns, and the livestock, the Israelites took for their booty; but all the people they struck down with the edge of the sword, until

they had destroyed them, and they did not leave any who breathed. As the
LORD had commanded his servant Moses, so Moses commanded Joshua,
and so Joshua did; he left nothing undone of all that the LORD had commanded Moses.

So Joshua took all that land: the hill country and all the Negeb and all
the land of Goshen and the lowland and the Arabah and the hill country of
Israel and its lowland, from Mount Halak, which rises toward Seir, as far as
Baal-gad in the valley of Lebanon below Mount Hermon. He took all their
kings, struck them down, and put them to death. Joshua made war a long
time with all those kings. There was not a town that made peace with the
Israelites, except the Hivites, the inhabitants of Gibeon; all were taken in
battle. For it was the LORD's doing to harden their hearts so that they would
come against Israel in battle, in order that they might be utterly destroyed,
and might receive no mercy, but be exterminated, just as the LORD had
commanded Moses. (Josh 11:14-20)

The principal Christian response to these texts was to transfer everything on to the plane of the spiritual life through moral or spiritual allegory.
In its most fully developed form this allegorical interpretation is found in
the writings of John Cassian, the early fifth-century Latin monastic writer
who synthesized and transmitted the interpretive tradition to the West.
Cassian explains that the seven nations represent seven "carnal vices." The
interpretation begins with the command of the Lord through Moses: "do
not say to yourself, 'It is because of my righteousness that the LORD has
brought me in to occupy this land'; it is rather because of the wickedness
of these nations that the LORD is dispossessing them before you. It is not
because of your righteousness or the uprightness of your heart that you are
going in to occupy their land; but because of the wickedness of these nations" (Deut 9:4-5). This is in effect a warning against "that pernicious
opinion and presumption of ours, by which we want to attribute everything that we do to our free will and to our own effort." It is really about an
essential point in the development of the spiritual life of the Christian.

When you have enjoyed a notable success in warring against the carnal
vices and you see that you have been freed from their filthiness and from

the world's way of life, you should not be puffed up with the success of the struggle and the victory and ascribe this to your own strength and wisdom, believing that you were able to obtain victory over evil spirits and carnal vices through your own efforts and application and free will. There is no doubt that you would never have been able to prevail over these if the Lord's help had not fortified and protected you.[40]

Cassian then states clearly that these vices are "the seven nations whose lands the Lord promised to give to the children of Israel when they left Egypt."[41] We must interpret them figuratively as the apostle taught when he said that everything that happened to them "in a figure" was written for our instruction (1 Cor 10:6). After repeating the command to utterly destroy the seven nations by name in Deuteronomy 7:1-2, Cassian explains that the reason they are said to be "more numerous than you are, and stronger than you" is that "there are more vices than virtues."[42] They are counted in the list as seven, but when it is a question of destroying them, they are said to be innumerable. From this sevenfold stock and root of vices "sprout murder, wranglings, heresies, thefts, false witness, blasphemies, overeating, drunkenness, slander, silliness, immodest speech, lies, perjuries, foolish talk, buffoonery, restlessness, greediness, bitterness, uproar, indignation, contempt, murmuring, temptation, despair and many others."[43] Cassian's speaker goes on to explain that when the eight principal vices are utterly destroyed, then so are all the others that spring from them and he lists the vices that come from each of the eight. The interlocutor in the dialogue, Germanus, notices of course that there has been a switch from the seven nations to the eight vices, and he asks, "Why, then, are there eight vices that attack us, when Moses enumerates seven nations that are opposed to the people of Israel?" The giver of the conference, Serapion, replies that it is the firm opinion of everyone that there are eight principal vices. This allows Cassian to extend the allegory to Egypt, which represents the first vice to be combated, gluttony. But Egypt is different from

---

[40]*Conferences* 5.15.4; ACW 57:196.
[41]*Conferences* 5.16.1; ACW 57:196.
[42]*Conferences* 5.16.2; ACW 57:197.
[43]Ibid.

the other seven, because the order was not given to destroy it. Why not? The answer lies on the allegorical level rather than on the literal one. Egypt was not ordered to be destroyed like the other seven nations, because

> with whatever spiritual ardor we may be inflamed and have entered the desert of the virtues, we can never rid ourselves of the proximity and the service of gluttony and of a certain daily contact with it. For the desire for food and for things to eat will always live in us an inborn and natural quality, although we should make a sincere effort to cut off its superfluous appetites and desires. Since these cannot be destroyed altogether, they should be avoided by a certain turning away.[44]

This, Serapion explains, is why "fasts should be moderate so that it is not necessary, because of an excessive abstinence which has been taken on through fleshly weakness or infirmity, to return to the land of Egypt—that is, to the former fleshly desire of gourmandizing, which we rejected when we renounced this world."[45] Egypt then is not to be destroyed because the link with the body, the necessity of taking in food, cannot be eliminated. However, the seven nations, representing the other principal temptations or vices, are to be destroyed. No compromise can be made with them. Food can be taken in moderation, but not anger or greed or vainglory or pride. For these there is no such thing as moderation. If one does not seek to eliminate them completely, one will become their victim. The difference is important and is explained by reference to other verses of Scripture: "You shall not abhor the Egyptian, because you were a sojourner in his land" (Deut 23:7 LXX). Serapion explains: "For food that is necessary for the body is not refused without hurting it and involving the soul in sin. But the movements of those seven perturbations, which are harmful in every respect, must be completely uprooted from the recesses of our soul."[46] Additional verses from the New Testament can be cited to support this view: "Let all bitterness and wrath and anger and clamor and slander be put away from you, with all malice" (Eph 4:31). Likewise, "Fornication and all im-

---

[44]Ibid., 5.19.1; ACW 57:199.
[45]Ibid.
[46]Ibid., 5.19.3; ACW 57:199.

purity or covetousness must not even be named among you, as is fitting among saints. Let there be no filthiness, nor silly talk, nor levity, which are not fitting" (Eph 5:3-4). Here Cassian is invoking the well-known principle of "interpreting the Scriptures by means of the Scriptures," which allows Old Testament texts to be illuminated by New Testament ones.

Cassian's interpretation of the command to destroy the seven nations, which served both to remove from the literal level a command that could not be reconciled with the goodness and justice of God as well as to make it useful for Christian teaching, comes at the end of a long process of development.

Origen of Alexandria had already offered extensive indications for interpreting these biblical passages in his homilies on the book of Joshua. In his first homily, Origen plays on the similarity (identity in Greek) between the name of Joshua and the name Jesus, noting that "the book does not so much indicate to us the deeds of the son of Nun, as it represents for us the mysteries of Jesus my Lord. For he himself is the one who assumes power after the death of Moses; he is the one who leads the army and fights against Amalek. What was foreshadowed there on the mountain by lifted hands was the time when 'he attaches [them] to his cross, triumphing over the principalities and powers on it' (Col 2:14-15)."[47] In other words, the text is to be interpreted in the light of the New Testament and as foreshadowing it. Joshua is a type of and prefigures Jesus. The stories in the book of Joshua must be read in reference to ourselves. Thus it is said in Joshua 1:3: "Every place you have set the soles of your feet will be yours."[48] Origen says: "let us consider what is promised to us in these words."[49] He explains that "there are certain diabolical races of powerful adversaries against whom we wage a battle and against whom we struggle in this life. However many of these races we set under our feet, however many we conquer in battle, we shall seize their territory, their provinces, and their realms, as Jesus our Lord apportions them to us."[50] These races are the fallen angels, some of whom "incite pride, jealousy, greed, and lust and instigate these evil things.

---

[47]Origen, *HomJos* 1.3; FC 105:29.
[48]*HomJos* 1.6; FC 105:33.
[49]Ibid.
[50]Ibid.

Unless you gain mastery over their vices in yourself and exterminate them from your land—which now through the grace of baptism has been sanctified—you will not receive the fullness of the promised inheritance."[51] The meaning of the text for us is not about distant historical events in a faraway land, but the land is to be understood as within us. It is in our souls that the battles take place. Commenting on the phrase "the land rested from wars" (Josh 11:23), Origen explains, "It is certain that also this land of ours, in which we have struggles and endure contests, will be able to rest from battles by the strength of the Lord Jesus alone. Within us, indeed, are all those breeds of vices that continually and incessantly attack the soul. Within us are the Canaanites; within us are the Perizzites; here are the Jebusites."[52]

For Origen, the notion of the land to be conquered had to be reinterpreted. It was not the land that Moses gave, but "that which I am giving you"[53] (Josh 1:2). The real speaker of these words is not Joshua, son of Nun, but Jesus the Christ, who is prefigured by Joshua. In the Greek text on which Origen was commenting, the names are identical. Origen asks with a rhetorical flourish: "What land?" and answers: "Doubtless, the land about which the Lord says, 'Blessed are the meek, who will possess the land as their inheritance'"[54] (Mt 5:5). Here Origen is implicitly invoking the principle of interpreting the Scriptures by means of the Scriptures, which meant that New Testament texts could be used to discover the deeper meaning of the Old Testament texts. The statement of Joshua 1:3, "Every place, wherever you will ascend with the soles of your feet, I shall give to you," must then be interpreted in the light of the beatitude. Then Origen can ask:

> What are the places we ascend with the soles of our feet? The letter of the Law is placed on the ground and lies down below. On no occasion, then, does the one who follows the letter of the Law ascend. But if you are able to rise from the letter to the spirit and also to ascend from history to a higher understanding, then truly you have ascended the lofty and high place that

you will receive from God as your inheritance. For if in these things that are written you perceive types and observe figures of heavenly things, and with reflection and intuitive feeling "you seek those things that are above, where Christ is sitting at the right hand of God" (Col 3:1), then you will receive this place as your inheritance.[55]

Having established that the book of Joshua is basically about the spiritual life and that the "land" in question is a spiritual territory, Origen is able to use many details of the text to teach about various aspects of the spiritual journey. For example, Rahab (Josh 2:1) can be interpreted as a figure of the church, and the crossing of the Jordan as a figure of baptism (Josh 3:15-17). Here we shall mention only those that have to do with the question of wiping out the nations.

The fall of Jericho set the pattern for the conquest of the land. And it provides the pattern for spiritual progress. "Let us go forth to the war," says Origen, "so that we may subdue the chief city of this world, malice, and destroy the proud walls of sin."[56] He elaborates: "Perhaps what I am about to say will seem strange to you, but nevertheless it is true: You require nothing from without, beyond your own self; within you is the battle that you are about to wage; on the inside is that evil edifice that must be overthrown; your enemy proceeds from your heart." What then does it mean to capture Jericho? First the meaning of Jericho on the spiritual level must be established. "We frequently find Jericho to be placed in Scripture as a figure of this world."[57] To establish this meaning Origen appeals to other texts in the Scriptures where Jericho is mentioned. Origen sees the man who "had descended from Jerusalem to Jericho" (Lk 10:30) as "a type of that Adam who was driven from Paradise into the exile of this world,"[58] and the blind men in Jericho (Mt 20:29-30) "bore the sign of those who continue to be overwhelmed in this world by the blindness of ignorance, to whom the Son of God comes."[59]

---

[55]Ibid.
[56]Ibid., 5.2; FC 105:61.
[57]Ibid., 6.4; FC 105:72.
[58]Ibid.
[59]Ibid.

Thus the stage is set for the fall of Jericho, "the sign of the present age."[60] Origen begins his interpretation with the trumpets: "For when the noise of the trumpets resounded, immediately the circle of walls was thrown down."[61] What were the trumpets? Origen finds a clue where other trumpets are mentioned in Numbers 10:2 and Psalm 98:6: "But when our Lord Jesus Christ comes, whose arrival that prior son of Nun designated, he sends priests, his apostles, bearing 'trumpets hammered thin,' the magnificent and heavenly instruction of proclamation. Matthew first sounded the priestly trumpet in his Gospel."[62] After mentioning the other Evangelists and authors, he concludes: "And now that last one comes, the one who said, 'I think God displays us apostles last,' and in fourteen of his epistles, thundering with trumpets, he casts down the walls of Jericho and all the devices of idolatry and dogmas of philosophers, all the way to the foundations."[63] The command to destroy everything that is devoted (anathema; Josh 6:18) is interpreted in the same context.

One of the more seemingly cruel and bloody episodes of the conquest of the land is related in Joshua 8:21-26 concerning the destruction of Ai.

> When Joshua and all Israel saw that the ambush had taken the city and that the smoke of the city was rising, then they turned back and struck down the men of Ai. And the others came out from the city against them; so they were surrounded by Israelites, some on one side, and some on the other; and Israel struck them down until no one was left who survived or escaped. But the king of Ai was taken alive and brought to Joshua.
>
> When Israel had finished slaughtering all the inhabitants of Ai in the open wilderness where they pursued them, and when all of them to the very last had fallen by the edge of the sword, all Israel returned to Ai, and attacked it with the edge of the sword. The total of those who fell that day, both men and women, was twelve thousand—all the people of Ai. For Joshua did not draw back his hand, with which he stretched out the sword, until he had utterly destroyed all the inhabitants of Ai.

---

[60]Ibid., 7.1; FC 105:74.
[61]Ibid.
[62]Ibid.
[63]Ibid.; FC 105:75.

Origen appears to reject the literal level ("these things that follow truly pertain more to the truth of a mystery than that of history"[64]) and transposes all on to the spiritual plane, where it becomes acceptable.

> When the Jews read these things,[65] they become cruel and thirst after human blood, thinking that even holy persons so struck those who were living in Ai that not one of them was left "who might be saved or who might escape." They do not understand that mysteries are dimly shadowed in these words and that they more truly indicate to us that we ought not to leave any of those demons deeply within, whose dwelling place is chaos and who rule in the abyss, but destroy them all. We slay demons, but we do not annihilate their essence. For their work and endeavor is to cause persons to sin. If we sin, they have life; but if we do not sin, they are destroyed. Therefore, all holy persons kill the inhabitants of Ai; they both annihilate and do not release any of them. These are doubtless those who guard their heart with all diligence so that evil thoughts do not proceed from it, and those who heed their mouth, so that "no evil word" proceeds from it.[66]

When the whole story has been transferred to the level of the interior spiritual conflict, Origen has no hesitation in recommending the utter destruction of the inhabitants of Ai: "Let us thrust Ai through with the edge of the sword, and let us extinguish all the inhabitants of chaos, all opposing powers."[67]

Origen did not doubt for an instant that "the wars that are waged through Jesus, and the slaughter of kings and enemies must also be said to be 'a shadow and type of heavenly things,' namely, of those wars that our Lord Jesus with his army and officers—that is, the throng of believers and their leaders—fights against the Devil and his angels."[68] His interpretation of the rest of the wars of conquest related in the book of Joshua is consistently on the spiritual level. Regarding the wars and battles described

---

[64]Ibid., 8.5; FC 105:90.

[65]From Origen's point of view, the fundamental error of the Jews was to read the Scriptures too literally rather than to interpret them figuratively. This had prevented them from recognizing Jesus as the Messiah. See *PArch* 4.2.1.

[66]*HomJos* 8.7; FC 105:92.

[67]Ibid., 8.7; FC 105:92-93.

[68]Ibid., 12.1; FC 105:120. See also Theodoret, *Questiones in Octateuchum,* In Iosuam, praef., 1.

in Joshua 10:28-43, Origen comments, citing 1 Corinthians 10:11:

> "All these things, which happened figuratively to them, were written for us,
> for whom the end of the ages has arrived." When he who is "outwardly a
> Jew" reads these things, that is, someone who has the exterior circumcision
> in the flesh, he thinks it is nothing else but wars being described, the de-
> struction of enemies, and the Israelites conquering and seizing the
> kingdoms of nations under the leadership of Jesus [= Joshua]. For he does
> not know what it is "to be a Jew secretly" by the circumcision of the heart
> (Rom 2:28-29). But the one who is "a Jew secretly," that is, a Christian, who
> follows Jesus, not as the son of Nun but as the Son of God, understands that
> all these things are mysteries of the kingdom of heaven. He affirms that even
> now my Lord Jesus Christ wars against opposing powers and casts out of
> their cities, that is, out of our souls, those who used to occupy them.[69]

He then offers a variety of interpretations of the various cities on the spiritual level and concludes that it is better to understand the Israelite wars in
this way, "for in this manner, what is said will also appear more devout and
more merciful, when he is said to have so subverted and devastated individual cities that 'nothing that breathed was left in them, neither any who
might be saved nor any who might escape [Josh 8:22; 10:40].'"[70] This last
sentence must be understood of my own soul, "so that nothing of a mali-
cious inclination may continue to breathe in me, nothing of wrath."[71]

Again in Joshua 11:8-20, with regard to the kings in the north and in the
south, the Canaanites in the east and the west, the Amorites, the Hittites,
the Perizzites and the Jebusites in the hill country, and the Hivites under
Hermon in the land of Mizpah, it is said that the Lord gave them into the
hand of Israel, who "struck them down, until they had left no one remaining" (Josh 11:8). In addition Joshua "hamstrung their horses, and
burned their chariots with fire" (Josh 11:9). Then they destroyed Hazor:
"And they put to the sword all who were in it, utterly destroying them; there
was none left who breathed, and he burned Hazor with fire" (Josh 11:11).

---

[69]Ibid., 13.1; FC 105:125.
[70]Ibid., 13.3; FC 105:127.
[71]Ibid.

The dilemma for the Christian interpreter is summed up by Origen: "Unless those physical wars bore the figure of spiritual wars, I do not think the books of Jewish history would ever have been handed down by the apostles to the disciples of Christ, who came to teach peace, so that they could be read in the churches."[72] Once again he insists that "we do not have to wage physical wars," but rather "the struggles of the soul have to be exerted against spiritual adversaries."[73] The command to hamstring their horses receives particular attention. We must understand the horses, together with their chariots, "as the passions of the body—that is, lust, petulance or pride, and fickleness, by whom the unhappy, just as a rider, is borne and carried to great dangers."[74] It is these that must be wiped out. "If we wage war properly under the leadership of Jesus, we ought to cut off their vices in ourselves and, taking the 'spiritual sword' (Eph 6:17) hamstring the whole stable of pernicious vices."[75] And "setting fire to their chariots" means to "cut ourselves off from every spirit of arrogance and exaltation."[76] The phrase "nothing that draws breath maybe left behind" must be interpreted to mean that "not even the impulse of wrath retains a place within you."[77]

Commenting on Joshua 11:12 ("And Jesus put all their kings to death by the sword"), Origen explains on the basis of Romans 6:12 ("Sin has reigned" in everyone) that everyone had some particular "king" in him that ruled over him. In one it was avarice, in another pride, in another lust and so on. And he concludes: "Thus a kingdom of sin was in every one of us before we believed. But afterwards, Jesus came and struck down all the kings who possessed kingdoms of sin in us, and he ordered us to destroy all those kings and to leave none of them. For if someone should keep any of them alive within, that person will not be able to be in the army of Jesus."[78] When the kings are identified with vices, it is obvious why they must be destroyed.

---

[72]Ibid., 15.1; FC 105:138.
[73]Ibid., 15.3; FC 105:142.
[74]Ibid.
[75]Ibid.; FC 105:143.
[76]Ibid.
[77]Ibid.
[78]Ibid., 15.4; FC 105:145.

"Wiping out the nations" and destroying their kings forms part of a broader spiritual program that Origen developed as an allegory of the entire story of the exodus from Egypt until the arrival in the Promised Land in his homilies on Exodus, Leviticus and Numbers. The whole program is summarized in homily 27 on Numbers, where Origen explains that the Lord had descended into this world through forty-two generations (Mt 1:17), and forty-two places are mentioned at which the Israelites stopped on their way to the Promised Land: "Therefore, those who ascend from Egypt make forty-two stages, the same number as these forty-two stages of generations that Christ made when he descended to the Egypt of this world."[79] The whole story becomes an allegory of the spiritual life, the ascent with Christ to the place from which he came.

Summary: Three quite different sets of texts, each of which presented different challenges to interpretation, have been presented here with early Christian interpretations. The Genesis creation narrative, because of the repeated anthropomorphisms, had to be interpreted in a way "fitting to God." The story of Abraham and Sarah had to be interpreted in a way fitting to holy persons, models for imitation. Finally the story of the conquest had to be interpreted in such a way that God could not be thought to have commanded such unspeakable cruelty.

---

[79]Origen, *HomNum*, 27, 3.1; Origen, *Homilies on Numbers*, trans. Thomas P. Scheck (Downers Grove, IL: IVP Academic, 2009), p. 170.

7

The Special Problem of the Psalms

The teaching of the New Testament is not like that, however:
we are bidden to give food and drink to our enemies,
to pray for those who abuse us.

JOHN CHRYSOSTOM, COMMENTARY ON PSALM 137

BY THE FOURTH CENTURY, IF NOT BEFORE, that most heterogeneous of all the books of the Old Testament, the book of Psalms, had become the Christian prayer book.[1] It was used extensively in the liturgy and recited frequently in its entirety by monks and nuns. However, the Psalms, produced over a period of hundreds of years and inspired by different theologies, often contained sentiments difficult to reconcile with the teaching of Jesus Christ. It was necessary to give them a Christian meaning. That is what the authors of the extended commentaries produced from the time of Origen on were attempting to do. Many of the Psalms already received an interpretation in the New Testament writings, where they had been cited as prophetic writings, for David, the reputed author of the psalms, had also been a prophet. Such was the interpretation of Psalm 109 (110) in Acts and in Hebrews (see Acts 2:34; Heb 1:3, 13; 8:1; 10:12).

---

[1]From the fourth century we have many examples of monastic communities reciting the book of Psalms as their communal prayer, as well as notices of individuals who recited the whole Psalter in a day or night. But the earliest example of extended commentary is that of Origen in the third century. We have numerous commentaries from the fourth century.

It has been estimated, however, that at least seventy passages in the Psalms posed a challenge for Christian interpreters and continue to do so today. I will attempt to explain how early Christian interpreters dealt with only some of the more obvious questions. Many commentaries on the Psalms have survived from Christian antiquity, but many others have been lost. Only a small portion of what Origen produced in this area has been transmitted. But we have commentaries or homilies or lectures by Eusebius, Didymus, Chrysostom, Theodoret, Ambrose, Augustine and Cassiodorus. These writers employed a variety of strategies in explaining the Psalms, including trying to determine who was speaking in the psalm, whether it was a prophecy about some future event or one already fulfilled, as Psalm 109 (110) had already been read in the New Testament. They also frequently resorted to various kinds of allegory. What follows here is a selection of some of the more problematic passages in the book of Psalms from a Christian point of view and the comments from early Christian writers to show how they dealt with the texts. For those accustomed to translations based on the Hebrew text of the Psalms, it may be useful to keep in mind that the ancient interpreters were using the Greek text known as the Septuagint, as explained at the beginning of chapter five, and that the Septuagint's numbering of verses and chapters differs in many places from those of the Hebrew text and most English Bibles. Where they differ I have used the Septuagint's numbering first and provided the Hebrew/English numbering in parentheses. The Greek differed in many details from the preserved Hebrew text. Therefore the psalms have been cited in a modern English translation of the Greek Septuagint version.[2]

Psalm 7:7-8 (6-7)

> Rise up, O Lord, in your wrath;
>> be exalted at the deaths of my enemies,
>> and awake, O my God, with the ordinance you commanded.

---

[2]Albert Pietersma and Benjamin G. Wright, eds., *A New English Translation of the Septuagint: And the Other Greek Translations Traditionally Included Under That Title* (New York: Oxford University Press, 2007).

And a congregation of people will surround you,
    and above this return on high!

Because of the superscription to the psalm: "A psalm of David, which he sang to the Lord about the words of Hushai the Benjaminite," it was assumed that the psalm was written by David as a song of thanksgiving upon learning of the failure of the rebellion of Absalom. The problem with the verse is that it could be understood to attribute physical movement, as well as anger, to God. For John Chrysostom it was necessary to insist that the notion of God's anger must be understood in a way fitting to God: "Now, what is the force of that phrase *in your anger*? This once again must be taken in a sense appropriate to God [*theoprepēs*]. I mean, in God anger is not a passion, but retribution and punishment."[3] Chrysostom was also concerned that people should not imagine God's presence to be localized, and he employed the same criterion of what is "appropriate" to God.

> Do not get the idea of anything human here, either; I mean, even if the expression is like that, the sense is appropriate to God. So what is the meaning of *will encircle you*? It means it will sing your praises, praise you, do you great honor. Since, you see, when they did this in choir, they stood in a circle in the temple around the altar, and offered thanksgiving this way, he implied their praise by reference to the manner of their standing.[4]

Augustine, however, used a different approach, suggesting that the psalmist was not praying against human enemies but against the devil and his angels, who hold the "ungodly" in their power. God's "anger" in this case then means only that God removes the "ungodly" from the power of the devil by making them just. This is perceived as a punishment by the devil, who wishes to maintain his power.

> Or does the Psalmist pray thus not against men, but against the devil and his angels, whose possession sinners and the ungodly are? He then does not pray against him in wrath, but in mercy, whosoever prays that that possession may be taken from him by that Lord "who justifies the ungodly." For

---

[3] John Chrysostom, *Commentary on the Psalms*, trans. Robert C. Hill (Brookline, MA: Holy Cross Orthodox Press, 1998), 1:124.
[4] Ibid., 1:125.

when the ungodly is justified, from ungodly he is made just, and from being the possession of the devil he passes into the temple of God. And since it is a punishment that a possession, in which one longs to have rule, should be taken away from him: this punishment, that he should cease to possess those whom he now possesses, the Psalmist calls the anger of God against the devil.[5]

Cassiodorus follows Augustine's explanation, but adds that the psalmist knew that God is "most gentle," an allusion to Matthew 11:28, and notes the use of "human and metaphorical language" to guard against a literal reading.

The first bids Him rise up in anger, in other words to take vengeance. But he does not actually provoke God to anger, for he knew that God is most gentle, especially as he had earlier said of himself: *If I have rendered to them that repaid me evils.* These things are recounted in human and metaphorical language; in fact this vengeance which is called anger ought rather to be attributed to the devil, who is punished whenever a sinner in thrall is rescued from him.[6]

PSALM 57(58):11

A righteous one will be glad when he sees vengeance done;
  he will wash his hands in the blood of the sinner.

This verse seemed to ancient Christian interpreters to be suggesting rejoicing at the sight of the suffering of enemies and offered a particularly repugnant image of what seemed cruelty toward sinners. In fact the previous verses of the psalm also offered rather cruel images. Eusebius felt it necessary to insist that the rejoicing was not in seeing the wicked suffer, but in the justice of God. The image of washing with blood must be interpreted in the sense of being purified by seeing the punishment of the wicked.

When he sees the end of the wicked and the vengeance against them, at that point he will rejoice, not in the sense that he enjoys the ruin of the wicked, but because he rejoices in the just judgment of God. "He will wash his feet

---

[5]Augustine, *Expositions on the Book of Psalms*; NPNF 1 8:52-53.
[6]Cassiodorus, *Explanation of the Psalms*; ACW 51:103.

in the blood of the wicked." Not as if he is bloodthirsty or one who loves war, but in the sense that he is purified by their punishment and changes for the better seeing their punishment.[7]

Theodoret of Cyrrhus also understands the "rejoicing" to be not at the expense of the sinners but in the recognition of divine providence, but he takes a different approach to the image of washing in blood, insisting that it should be understood not as washing "in blood" but "of blood" to show the innocence of the virtuous.

> "The righteous will rejoice on seeing vindication; he will wash his hands in the blood of the sinner"; the student of virtue, on the other hand, will rejoice to see the evildoer punished, not to mock him but in recognition of divine providence, which is reluctant to ignore those wronged by them. Now, he washes his hands, not for having soiled and besmirched them with blood, but to show he is innocent and has no association with the other's wickedness; he is not, in fact, washing them in blood, as some suggested, but washing them of blood, for the reason of having nothing in common with him.[8]

Augustine had particular difficulty with the notion of washing hands in the blood of the sinner. It was to be interpreted spiritually in the sense that seeing the punishment of the wicked leads the just to live more cleanly in the future.

> But what is, "in the blood of the sinner he shall wash his hands"? When a just man sees the punishment of a sinner, he grows himself; and the death of one is the life of another. For if spiritually blood runs from those that are dead within, do you, seeing such vengeance, wash therein your hands; for the future live more cleanly. And how shall he wash his hands, if he is a just man? For what does he have on his hands to be washed, if he is just? "But the just man of faith shall live" (Rom 1:17). Just men therefore he has called believers: and from the time that you believed, at once you began to be called just. For there has been made a remission of sins. Even if out of that remaining part of your life some sins are yours, which cannot but flow in,

---

[7]Eusebius, *Commentary on the Psalms*; PG 23:529.
[8]Theodoret, *Commentary on the Psalms*; FC 101:335.

like water from the sea into the hold; nevertheless, because you have believed, when you shall have seen him that altogether is turned away from God to be slain in that blindness, there falling upon him that fire so that he see not the sun—then do you that now through faith see Christ, in order that you may see in substance (because the just man lives of faith), observe the ungodly man dying, and purge yourself from sins. So you shall wash in a manner your hands in the blood of the sinner.[9]

Cassiodorus also saw clearly the contradiction between the sentiments expressed in the verse and the teaching of Jesus. Recognizing that the image is one of savagery, he interprets the "hands" to refer to the deeds of the just, which are corrected by the punishment of the sinner, and so the innocent are warned to behave.

"He shall wash his hands in the blood of sinners." How can this be, that He who has bidden us pray for our enemies maintains that the hands of the holy will be washed in the blood of sinners? If we look at this more carefully, it will afford an example of correction rather than savagery; for when the blood of a sinner is shed, the hands—in other words, the deeds—of the most just man undergo correction. When the guilty man perishes, the innocent man is warned to behave more carefully and more studiously. So it happens that the blood of the sinner cleanses the just man's hands in a holy rather than a cruel way.[10]

PSALM 62:10-12 (63:9-11)

The psalm begins with a pious expression of longing for God.

O God, my God, early I approach you;
   my soul thirsted for you
How many times did my flesh thirst for you
   in a land, desolate and trackless and waterless? (Ps 62:2 [63:1])

But it concludes with an expression of desire for bloody vengeance against unnamed enemies.

---

[9]Augustine, *Expositions on the Book of Psalms*; NPNF 1 8:235*.
[10]Cassiodorus, *Explanation of the Psalms*; ACW 52:50.

But they sought my soul for no good reason;
>they shall enter into the deepest parts of the earth;
they shall be given over to a sword's power;
>prey for foxes they shall be.
But the king shall be glad in God;
>everyone who swears by him shall be commended,
>because the mouth of people speaking unjust things was stopped up.
>>(Ps 62:10-12 [63:9-11])

Eusebius of Caesarea offers a historical reading and suggests a spiritual one. According to him, it is a psalm of David when he was in the desert of Judea. Alluding to Hebrews 11:38, he says that David was wandering about like the other prophets among deserts and mountains, caves and caverns, and he sang this psalm, having the opportunity in the desert to dedicate himself to the divine philosophy. Psalm 62:9 (63:8), "My soul clung to you; / your right hand upheld me," is interpreted with the help of Paul (1 Cor 6:17, 16): "he who is united to the Lord becomes one spirit with him, as also he who joins himself to a prostitute becomes one body with her" (translations from Eusebius). This allows him to conclude that the expression of Psalm 62:9 (63:8), "My soul clung to you," means that he had dedicated himself to chastity and purity. By contrast, the phrase of Psalm 62:10 (63:9), "they shall enter into the deepest parts of the earth," can be interpreted of those who think of earthly things.

Given that they thought of the things of earth and belonged to that which is below, they will receive the just reward for what they have done. Whoever is united to God, whose soul has adhered to him, will have the hope of the kingdom of heaven, while those who live in contrary way and think of the things below, will be thrown into the ditch of which we have spoken elsewhere.[11]

Finally the reference to the king in Psalm 62:12 (63:11) means that

once the just man has become perfect because of the progress made in virtue, the king rejoices and exults, that is the only-begotten Son of God, giving thanks to his own Father, who gave such great gifts to human nature.[12]

---

[11]Eusebius, *Commentary on the Psalms*; PG 23:613.
[12]Ibid.

Augustine focuses on the expressions "deepest parts of the earth" ("lower places of the earth" in Augustine) and "foxes." Using the principle of interpreting the Scriptures by means of the Scriptures, that is, finding other passages of Scripture with the same or similar words, he introduces a christological interpretation of the psalm. It is to be interpreted as prophecy of things now fulfilled rather than of the future.

"But themselves in vain have sought my soul. They shall go unto the lower places of the earth" (v. 9). Earth they were unwilling to lose, when they crucified Christ: into the lower places of the earth they have gone. What are the lower places of the earth? Earthly lusts. Better it is to walk upon earth, than by lust to go under earth. For every one that in prejudice of his salvation desires earthly things, is under the earth: because earth he has put before him, earth upon himself he has put, and himself beneath he has laid. They therefore fearing to lose earth, said what of the Lord Jesus Christ, when they saw great multitudes go after Him, forasmuch as He was doing wonderful things? "If we shall have let Him go alive, there will come the Romans, and will take away from us both place and nation." They feared to lose earth, and they went under the earth: there befell them even what they feared. For they willed to kill Christ, that they might not lose earth; and earth they therefore lost, because Christ they slew. For when Christ had been slain, because the Lord Himself had said to them, "The kingdom shall be taken from you, and shall be given up to a nation doing righteousness:" there followed them great calamities of persecutions: there conquered them Roman emperors, and kings of the nations: they were shut out from that very place where they crucified Christ, and now that place is full of Christian praisers: it has no Jew, it has been cleared of the enemies of Christ, it has been fulfilled with the praisers of Christ. Behold, they have lost at the hands of the Romans the place, because Christ they slew, who to this end slew, that they might not lose the place at the hands of the Romans. Therefore, "They shall enter into the lower places of the earth."

"They shall be delivered unto the hands of the sword" (v. 10). In truth, thus it has visibly befallen them, they have been taken by storm by enemies breaking in. "Portions of foxes they shall be." Foxes he calls the kings of the world, that then were when Judea was conquered. Hear in order that you may know and perceive, that those he calls foxes. Herod the king the Lord

Himself has called a fox. "Go," He says, "and tell that fox." See and observe, my brethren: Christ as King they would not have, and portions of foxes they have been made. For when Pilate the deputy governor in Judea slew Christ at the voices of the Jews, he said to the same Jews, "Your King shall I crucify?" Because He was called King of the Jews, and He was the true King. And they rejecting Christ said, "We have no king but Caesar." They rejected a Lamb, chose a fox: deservedly portions of foxes they were made.[13]

The interpretation of Cassiodorus is both historical and allegorical. The psalm refers to past events and to the present situation of the church. The "church" (she) is understood to be speaking in the psalm.

Psalm and *David* often point to the Lord Christ, and often denote the Church, for Christ is in His members, and the members are contained in their Head. If the Head suffers anything, so do the members; again if the members are disturbed, the Head undoubtedly suffers with them.... When she [the Church] says they, she points to those who tried to snuff out Christ with their evil opposition. In Him, as is shown beyond all doubt, all men are healed and live. They sought her soul in vain when by false charges they decided to shed His blood, but He was to rise again after three days into eternal glory.[14]

PSALM 82:14-19 (83:13-18)

O my God, make them like a wheel
    like a straw in the wind.
Like a fire that will blaze through a forest,
    as a flame might burn up mountains,
so will you pursue them with your tempest,
    and with your wrath dismay them.
Fill their faces with dishonor,
    and they will seek your name, O Lord.
Let them be put to shame and be dismayed forever and ever,
    and let them be embarrassed and perish.

---

[13]Augustine, *Expositions on the Book of Psalms*; NPNF 1 8:262-63*.
[14]Cassiodorus, *Explanation of the Psalms*; ACW 52:83, 87.

And let them know that your name is the Lord;
  you alone are Most High over all the earth.

The sentiments expressed toward enemies in the psalm hardly seem to be those of Jesus. The psalm therefore posed an interpretive challenge for those using it as Christian prayer. The oldest commentary is transmitted in Latin under the name of Jerome, but has been identified as his translation of Origen. The exegesis is certainly typical of Origen. The author explains the opening of the psalm, "O God, who shall be likened to you?" as "Since no one is similar to you, we wish as a defender none other than you." Psalm 82:3 (83:2), "because, look, your enemies make a tumult," he says, can be explained "according to the tropological sense, in relation to the Church and to the heresies. But we can explain it, according to the literal sense, in relation to the Jewish people and the other nations, which from every side assaulted Judea."[15] Nevertheless, from what follows, it seems that the "people of God" in question is to be identified with the church. The phrase "and those who hate you raised their head" (Ps 82:3 [83:2]) elicits the comment: "Note what is said. It is clear that whoever raises the head, hates God. 'God opposes the proud, but gives grace to the humble'" (Jas 4:6; 1 Pet 5:5). There follows the admonition:

> If sometimes it happens that you are in conflict with someone, if then one of your brothers slanders you, and you remain humble for love of Christ, the other instead proud because of the devil, you imitate the one who said: "learn from me for I am gentle and humble of heart" (Mt 11:29). Whoever instead exalts himself, imitates the one who said: "I will ascend to heaven; above the stars of God; I will set my throne on high; I will be like the most high" (Isa 14:13-14).[16]

In Psalm 82:6-8 (83:5-7), which mention the various nations that made war against God's people, the names are said to contain "mysteries" and given etymological interpretations, that is, allegorical interpretations by

---

[15]CCL 78:90.

[16]Ibid. This collection of homilies on the Psalms has been transmitted in Latin under the name of Jerome. However, several scholars including V. Peri and H. Crouzel have identified them as translations from Origen by Jerome. For a discussion of the authorship, see Origen-Jerome, *74 omelie sul libro dei Salmi*, trans. G. Coppa (Milan: Edizioni paoline, 1993), pp. 11-32.

means of a supposed etymology. Further on he observes: "You see that these passages are very difficult; you see that they are obscure and we are obliged to spend time on the Hebrew words dense with mysteries."[17] It should be noted here that the word "mystery" already had the technical meaning in Hellenistic Jewish exegesis of "hidden meaning." The author continues: "If indeed we were not to explain as we have done, what use would it be to the churches of Christ to read the tents of the Idumeans, of the Ishmaelites, and the other names?"[18] As we have noted earlier, it was the common assumption in antiquity that sacred texts had hidden meanings. Finally this commentary manages to convert the imprecations of the psalm in Psalm 82:14-19 (83:13-18) into a prayer for the enemies instead of against them. Psalm 82:19 (83:18), "And let them know that your name is the Lord," is understood to be a prayer for their salvation.

Eusebius of Caesarea explains that Psalm 79 (80) had predicted the destruction of the vine and the fall of the nation of the Jews, with the burning and desolation of the place they honored and the two following psalms (Ps 80–81 [81–82]) teach why they suffered these things. This psalm, which is connected to those, makes a plea and a supplication for the people. After so many sadnesses it was necessary to offer a remedy. This is the meaning of the verse with which the psalm begins. Psalm 82:4-5 (83:3-4) speaks of annihilating the "name of Israel." This allows Eusebius to assimilate the church to the people of Israel.

> Those who combat God, then, do not wish that there should be among men a people of God; indeed, they try to cancel out even the name of Israel. But God, who has always been preparing a people of his own on the earth after the fall of the first one, has constituted the Church from among the gentiles, the new, young people set up on the whole earth with the election of the gentiles. Therefore the name of Israel is even more celebrated and the memory of all the men who are friends of God, while the beautiful works of piety shine forth.[19]

---

[17]CCL 78:91. The Latin word translated by "mysteries" is *sacramenta*, which in turn translates the Greek *musteria*.

[18]CCL 78:91.

[19]Eusebius, *Commentary on the Psalms*; PG 23:993-96.

Psalm 82:14-19 (83:13-18), in which it is said, "and they will seek your name, O Lord," is to be taken in a positive sense as a hope for conversion.

> He predicts that the death of the enemies of God will take place in two ways. One, to which he connects the best hopes for them, seeing that the knowledge of God, the comprehension of his name is a good, and that it is a good, for those who previously did not know God, to learn that he alone is "the Most High over all the earth." One can in fact hold that those, who have professed all this, have given up the memory of their previous polytheistic error and have abandoned the vain and false doctrine of the false gods.[20]

According to Theodoret of Cyrrhus, the psalm prophecies that, in the time after the return from Babylon, when the Jews were rebuilding the temple and the neighboring nations gathered together to make war on them, they would overcome the enemies with Zerubbabel in command and God lending assistance. Joel, Ezekiel, Micah and Zechariah had foretold this conflict. The psalm is "the inspired composition of the divine spirit" and "is expressed as a prayer to teach those under attack at that time how God must be placated."[21] Theodoret adopts a reading by Symmachus (another ancient Greek translator of the Old Testament) instead of the Septuagint, according to which Psalm 82:3 (83:2) reads: "They hatch a plot against your people, and scheme the downfall of your hidden one." Then he comments:

> In other words, since Christ the Lord would spring from them according to the flesh, and the nations were anxious to pull up by the roots the race of the Jews, the all-holy Spirit teaches them to offer this prayer: They employ malice and wiles not only against us but also against your hidden one concealed among us, who he prophesied would blossom from the tribe of Judah. After all, if the root were cut, how would the fruit grow?[22]

After invoking Isaiah 65:8-10 to supply a similar sense, he continues: "This is what they say in their prayer at this point. They presume to rage not

---

[20]PG 23:1000-1001.
[21]Theodoret, *Commentary on the Psalms*; FC 102:58.
[22]FC 102:58-59.

only against us but also against your hidden one. The cry 'Away with him! Away with him! Crucify him!' revealed them clearly as raging like dogs. What follows is also in harmony with this."[23] At the end, commenting on Psalm 82:18-19 (83:17-18), especially "And let them know that your name is the Lord" (Ps 82:19 [83:18]), he is able to find a positive meaning, indeed good will toward the enemies, even though it seems to be against the whole thrust of the text.

> They seek good things for the foes, even though under attack: they beg that they be enveloped in shame rather than audacity, and by means of the shame reap the benefit of divine knowledge, be rid of the error of the idols, and learn by experience that he alone is God and Lord, dwelling in the highest, having regard for lowly things, governing and controlling all creation, whose salvation he was concerned for, God from God, the Only-begotten Son after his incomprehensible incarnation.[24]

Augustine identifies the speaker of the psalm as the people of God, arriving at this identification through an etymology of the name Asaph. Then, interpreting the psalm as prophecy of the last days, he comments: "He seems to me to signify the last days, when these things that are now repressed by fear are to break forth into free utterance, but quite irrational."[25] Psalm 82:14 (83:13), "make them like a wheel,"

> is fitly taken as meaning that they should be constant in nothing that they think; but I think it may also be rightly explained, make them like unto a wheel, because a wheel is lifted up on the part of what is behind, is thrown down on the part of what is in front; and so it happens to all the enemies of the people of God. For this is not a wish, but a prophecy. He adds: "as the stubble in the face of the wind." By face he means presence; for what face has the wind, which has no bodily features, being only a motion, in that it is a kind of wave of air? But it is put for temptation, by which light and vain hearts are hurried away.[26]

---

[23]FC 102:59.
[24]FC 102:61.
[25]Augustine, *Expositions on the Psalms;* NPNF 1 8:397.
[26]NPNF 1 8:399.

Psalm 82:17 (83:16) ("Fill their faces with shame, and they shall seek your name, O Lord" in Augustine) is also taken as a reference to the last judgment, as is the following verse ("They shall blush and be vexed for ever and ever"). Augustine distinguishes two kinds of people: those who are put to shame and repent and those who are like stubble before the wind and who are "vexed forever."

> Good and desirable is this *which he prophesies for them*: and he would not prophesy thus, unless there were even in that company of the enemies of God's people, some men of such kind that this would be granted to them before the last judgment: for now they are mixed together, and this is the body of the enemies, in respect of the envy whereby they rival the people of God. And now, where they can, they make a noise and lift up their head: but severally, not universally as they will do *at the end of the world*, when the last judgment is about to fall. But it is the same body, even in those who out of this number shall believe and pass into another body (for the faces of these are filled with shame, that they may seek the name of the Lord), as well as in those others who persevere unto the end in the same wickedness, who are made as stubble before the wind, and are consumed like a wood and barren mountains. To these he again returns, saying, "They shall blush and be vexed for ever and ever" (v. 17). For those are not vexed for ever and ever who seek the name of the Lord, but having respect unto the shame of their sins, they are vexed for this purpose, that they may seek the name of the Lord, through which they may be no more vexed.[27]

Cassiodorus accepts the superscription of the psalm ascribing it to Asaph, as noted also by Augustine. According to Cassiodorus, Asaph conveys in Latin the sense of *congregatio* ("assembly"). He is not to be understood as the author of the psalm, but is inserted into the heading because of the meaning of his name. In earlier psalms he had made prophecies about the Lord's incarnation and now in the first section of this one speaks of his second coming.

> He asks that since at the end of the world the Lord's enemies will be exalted to the heights through Antichrist, His judgment may quickly take place, so that the lengthy license of the most oppressive enemy may not be able to

---

[27]NPNF 1 8:399.

ravage the entire Church. In the second section, he prays that vengeance may be exacted from them by citing the names of person similarly hostile, and he prays for their correction rather than seeks to curse them.[28]

With this general characterization of the psalm Cassiodorus can then interpret individual verses. The prayer in the first verse, that God not be silent, means: "Here the power of His future coming is already declared, for He who judges is not silent, and He who is revealed by the manifestation of His power does not restrain himself. Clearly at His first coming these attributes were not in evidence, *when he was led as a sheep to the slaughter.*"[29] For Psalm 82:3 (83:2), "those who hate you have raised their head," he offers: "The whole of this is more appropriately suited to the days of Antichrist, when the Lord's enemies will sound forth in noisy rebellions,"[30] for Psalm 82:5 (83:3), "let the name of Israel be remembered no more," refers to the persecution of Christians.

> That most savage persecution of Antichrist is to be carried out with the intention of utterly abolishing the Christian name from the earth as though it were some evil; they do not know that when they seek to kill Christ's servants they will augment the number of saints with their constant persecution. His mention of a nation in the singular indicates the Christian people; for though we are instructed that they are gathered from many nations, they are rightly called a single nation, for they are known to be sprung from the one origin of baptism.[31]

The reference to the "sanctuary of God" in Psalm 82:13 (83:12) is likewise to be understood in a Christian sense: "He next explains what this inheritance is: it is *the sanctuary of God,* the Christian people, of whom Paul says: *For the temple of God is holy, which you are*" (1 Cor 3:17). The mention of God's wrath in Psalm 82:16 (83:15) elicits the observation: "We have often said already that anger cannot be appropriate to the deity; the description is drawn from the behavior of men, who in judging wicked men are stirred

---

[28]Cassiodorus, *Explanation of the Psalms*; ACW 52:307.
[29]ACW 52:307-8.
[30]ACW 52:308.
[31]ACW 52:308-9.

by mental heat. Men are not disposed to find others guilty unless they are roused by the wicked deeds which they have committed."[32] In Psalm 82:17-18 (83:16-17) he finds grounds for a positive outcome: "now he turns to those who are to believe through the Lord's gift"; and "A rebuke often sets them right when they see that they incur general blame."[33] So interpreted the imprecations of the psalm on the literal level lose their force and the content of the psalm is understood so that

> all that concerns the Lord's incarnation is brought to pass, all that attests the belief of the Gentiles is made clear. There remains the time of the Judgment which we all undergo in common. But before that we must believe, so that at the Judgment the vengeance which is prophesied cannot condemn us in our wickedness.[34]

PSALM 108(109):1-16

> O God, do not pass over my praise in silence,
> because a sinner's mouth and a deceiver's mouth—it was opened against me;
>   they spoke against me with a deceitful tongue.
> And they surrounded me with words of hate
>   and made war on me without cause.
> In return for my love they would slander me,
>   but I, I would pray.
> And they rewarded me evil for good
>   and hatred for my love:
> "Appoint a sinner against him,
>   and let a slanderer stand on his right.
> When he is tried, may he come out condemned
>   and let his prayer be counted as sin.
> Let his days become few,
>   and may another seize his position.
> Let his sons become orphans
>   and his wife a widow.

---

[32]ACW 52:311.
[33]ACW 52:312.
[34]ACW 52:313.

As they totter, let his sons wander about and beg;
    let them be driven out of their homesteads.
Let a creditor scrutinize all that he has;
    let strangers plunder his toils.
Let there be no one to support him
    nor anyone to pity his orphans.
Let his children go to destruction;
    in one generation let his name be blotted out.
May the lawlessness of his fathers be remembered before the Lord,
    and may the sin of his mother not be blotted out.
Let them be before the Lord continually,
    and may their memory be destroyed from the earth,
since he did not remember to do mercy
    and pursued to death a person
    needy and poor and stunned in heart." (Ps 108[109]:1-16)

This lengthy psalm (thirty-one verses) more than most presented a challenge to the interpreter, for it offers an unrelieved catalog of curses against enemies, causing even John Chrysostom to exclaim: "Goodness me! How extreme his anger, when not even the untimeliness of orphanhood may meet with mercy."[35] How could this be reconciled with the teaching of Jesus to bless one's enemies and return evil with good? However, a clue to its interpretation had been provided in the New Testament, where it is cited by Peter in Acts 1:20 with reference to Judas Iscariot. This made it possible to interpret the psalm in a historical sense, that is, as prophecy already fulfilled. David had spoken as a prophet, but not always in his own name. In this case, many commentators saw the speaker as Jesus speaking then of things now already fulfilled. A number of commentators, beginning already with Origen,[36] have a tendency to see the Jews as well as Judas in the prophecy, which is seen then to refer to their ruin fulfilled in the destruction of Jerusalem.

Eusebius of Caesarea follows the lead of Origen and treats the psalm as referring to the person of Christ, and treating of his sufferings.

---

[35]Chrysostom, *Commentary on the Psalms*, 2:2.
[36]See Origen-Jerome, *74 omelie*, pp. 374-75.

This is attested by the book of Acts, where Peter, mentioning the ruin of the traitor Judas and exhorting that another be chosen to fill up the number of the twelve apostles, makes use of the prophetic testimony in this psalm: "Let his habitation become desolate, and let there be no one to live in it"; and "His office let another take." Thus, according to the teaching of Peter, this expression is to be referred to Judas, as well as the others which are found in the psalm. The Savior, then, begins by expressing himself in a human manner, with these words, since he became man, while remaining God as he was. That is, he beseeches the Father not to permit the adversaries to succeed in what they propose. As for him, his entire intention was to extinguish from the midst of men all idolatry and to establish on the earth the praise of the Father, something which he teaches also elsewhere saying: "I will announce your name to my brethren, in the midst of the assembly I will sing your praise" (Ps 21:23).[37]

Having established the principal reference of the psalm, Eusebius also tries to interpret other details. Psalm 108(109):14-16, which refer to the lawlessness of "his fathers" and "the sin of his mother" are seen to be references to the past history of the Jews: "He calls their fathers those who in the desert acted wickedly, those who in the time of the judges, of the kings and after the return from Babylon, lived in iniquity." The "mother" is taken to refer to Jerusalem, "in which it was shamefully dared to kill Christ the Sovereign."[38]

John Chrysostom notes that this psalm is very disturbing for many people because it is composed completely of cursing and reveals the speaker's anger, which not only is directed to wrongdoers but also extends to children and parents.

No single disaster suffices for him, but he piles trouble on trouble. I mean, notice how much cursing he invokes: Appoint a sinner against him, and let a slanderer stand at his right hand (v. 6), that is, let him fall foul of accusers, wicked people and schemers, and not prevail over them.... Now, from this point on they are still harsher by far than the preceding: he prays for or-

---

[37]Eusebius, *Commentary on the Psalms*; PG 23:1333.
[38]PG 23:1337.

phanhood and widowhood for the survivors. Admittedly, these things necessarily happen with him gone; all the same he lists them by way of a curse,
in the heat of his anger.... Goodness me! How extreme his anger, when not
even the untimeliness of orphanhood may meet with mercy—and not only
no mercy, but that he may be caught up in ultimate ruin.[39]

He then comments at considerable length in an effort to defuse the anger,
including redefining the meaning of the word "children."

> One point first: why was it, when one person sinned and the psalmist pro-
> tested, that his children were punished, and his wife and parents as well?
> Secondly, who is the object of the curses? Thirdly, how does the leader of
> the apostles show the psalm refers to Judas—or, rather, not the whole
> psalm but part of the psalm? Scripture says, remember, "It is written in the
> book of Psalms, Let his dwelling become desolate, and let there be no oc-
> cupant of his quarters" [Acts 1:20, citing Ps 69:25 and Ps 109:8].
>
> Now, what would you call this kind of expression: inspired composition
> or cursing? Inspired composition in the form of cursing. Elsewhere too, in
> fact, we shall find something similar; Jacob also had recourse to it. You see,
> since the listeners should benefit from what befalls others, they fashion
> many inspired compositions in such a manner that fear is heightened by the
> form of utterance as regards our way of life....
>
> So to whom does the psalm refer? Some things are in reference to Judas, the
> Spirit prophesying through David, the remainder about others. Again you see
> this in the manner of inspired composition. Often you will find it so composed
> that the opening refers to one person and the remainder to another....
>
> If, however, the psalmist asks for the children to be punished, do not be
> alarmed, dearly beloved: he calls children here those associated in their
> wickedness. Scripture, you see, is in the habit of calling children those con-
> nected by kinship and those linked by wickedness, even if not children by
> nature, as when it says, "You are children of the devil" (John 8:44
> paraphrase).[40]

Theodoret of Cyrrhus recognizes the seeming contradiction between the
cursing of the psalmist and the teaching of Jesus to bless our persecutors,

---

[39]Chrysostom, *Commentary on the Psalms*, 2:1-2.
[40]Ibid., 2:3-5.

and he also takes his lead from the citation in Acts 1:20 to interpret it in terms of prophecy fulfilled.

> This psalm prophesies the saving Passion, the Jews' madness and the betrayal of Judas. It leads us to this meaning, and the great Peter was speaking publicly [about it], both in charging Judas with betrayal and in giving a demonstration of the prophecy from it (Acts 1:20). Let no one who hears the Lord imposing the obligation to bless our persecutors consider the prophecy to be in opposition to the obligation: the inspired word in this case does not proceed by way of cursing but by foretelling the punishments coming both to Jews and to Judas. This prophecy is expressed as a prayer, as is very much the custom everywhere in the divine Scripture.[41]

Theodoret also tries to interpret individual verses in terms of historical fulfillment. With regard to Psalm 108(109):8, "Let his days become few, / and may another seize his position," Theodoret comments: "This prophecy had its fulfillment: he immediately suffered death by hanging, and instead of him Matthias took his place in the number of the apostles."[42]

Augustine follows the tradition in using the citation of the psalm in Acts as the starting point for his interpretation.

> Every one who faithfully reads the Acts of the Apostles, acknowledges that this Psalm contains a prophecy of Christ; for it evidently appears that what is here written, "let his days be few, and let another take his office," is prophesied of Judas, the betrayer of Christ. . . . For as some things are said which seem peculiarly to apply to the Apostle Peter, and yet are not clear in their meaning, unless when referred to the Church, whom he is acknowledged to have figuratively represented, on account of the primacy which he bore among the Disciples; as it is written, "I will give unto you the keys of the kingdom of heaven," and other passages of the like purport: so Judas represents those Jews who were enemies of Christ, who both then hated Christ, and now, in their line of succession, this species of

---

[41]Theodoret, *Commentary on the Psalms*; FC 102:200.
[42]FC 102:201.

wickedness continuing, hate Him. Of these men, and of this people, not only may what we read more openly discovered in this Psalm be conveniently understood, but also those things which are more expressly stated concerning Judas himself.[43]

Cassiodorus, also taking his cue from the citation in Acts, reads the first five verses of the psalm as a description of Jesus' own situation, and he explains the first verse as: "Our Lord and Savior in the role of servant which he deigned to assume asks the Father should not cause the praise of His resurrection to remain unspoken, for in the lowliness of the flesh He was to suffer grim insults from the Jews."[44] In the second section, beginning with Psalm 109(108):6, he speaks "first at length of Judas, who was capable of all evils."[45] Cassiodorus sought to interpret the references specifically. For example, the phrase "His prayer be turned to sin" was taken to be a reference to the Lord's prayer ("Our Father"),

> which Judas together with the rest of the apostles had undertaken to carry through, is seen to have become for him the most serious sin, for in it are contained the words: *And forgive us our debts, as we too forgive our debtors.* But what could he forgive his debtors for, when he betrayed the Author of all kindnesses? So it was right that His holy prayer should be turned into sin for Judas, because he sinned and set an execrable precedent.[46]

In the following verse (Ps 108[109]:8) the Greek version contained the word *episkopēn*, translated here as "position," but the word was also the word for "bishopric." That made it possible for Cassiodorus to comment:

> In the same way the days of Judas' tenure of apostleship became few, whereas others after him remained as apostles by observing the Lord's will. And so that the most sacred number of apostles should not be reduced by the death of Judas, already at that time another was foretold as supplanting him, so that the total of twelve should be preserved undiminished. The *bishopric* is the highest order of the Church. *Episcopus* means overseer, be-

---

[43]Augustine, *Expositions on the Psalms*; NPNF 1 8:536.
[44]Cassiodorus, *Explanation of the Psalms*; ACW 53:103.
[45]Ibid., p. 104.
[46]Ibid., p. 105.

cause with the help of divine grace he guards the Lord's flock from his high seat like a most careful shepherd.[47]

After additional reflections on the office of bishop, Cassiodorus states: "It is appropriate for us to remember what is most clearly stated in the Acts of the Apostles, that this verse was written about Judas," and he then cites Acts 1:16, 20, and concludes: "Thus no-one can doubt that this passage is to be wholly related to Judas, and we realize that this psalm is a prophecy about the Lord's passion, the words of the gospel and the witness of the apostle Peter."[48] When the texts are so specifically interpreted, they lose their general force.

Cassiodorus sought to do this for the entire psalm and even to see allusions to events after the time of Jesus. With reference to Psalm 108(109):20 ("This is the work of them who detract me before the Lord; and who speak evils against my soul"), he comments:

We must interpret this verse as directed against all unfaithful men, but He seems to attack two heresies in particular. The Arians disparage the Son's presence in God the Father by attesting that the Son is inferior to Him; they shamelessly label as inferior Him whom men in general confess as Creator of all. The Apollinarists likewise speak evils against the Lord's soul when they say that His divinity took on only human flesh and not a soul, and their infidelity does not give way though worsted by numerous proofs. So the words here are properly understood as uttered against these in particular, but also against all heretics in general; they will have no portion in the Lord's kingdom.[49]

With no small amount of ingenuity Cassiodorus manages to interpret the whole psalm in this manner, thus defusing its negative potential, and notes finally: "This is the fifth of the psalms which have discoursed at greater length on lines earlier laid down about the Lord's passion; the earlier ones are Psalms 21, 34, 54, 68. First, all begin with the person of the Lord Christ. Second, they are seen to speak in a prayer. Third, they related the events of the Lord's passion."[50]

---

[47]Ibid.
[48]Ibid., p. 106.
[49]Ibid., p. 110-11.
[50]Ibid., p. 115.

Psalm 109(110):5-6

The Lord at your right shattered kings on a day of his wrath.
He will judge among the nations,
  will make full with corpses;
  he will shatter heads on the land of many.

The first part of this psalm had already been interpreted in the New Testament as a messianic psalm with a christological sense (see Acts 2:34; Heb 1:3, 13; 8:1; 10:12). It was understood to refer to the triumphant resurrection of Jesus and his ascension to the right hand of the Father. The epistle to the Hebrews had further developed Psalm 109(110):4 ("You are a priest forever according to the order of Melchisedek") to show how Jesus in his person had replaced the institutions of the priesthood, the temple and the Old Testament sacrifices. The problem, to the extent that it was perceived, lay with the final verses, which seemed to speak of violence and retribution.

John Chrysostom is concerned as usual to counter the idea of anger on the part of God or the idea that God could actually swear like a human being. But he also allegorizes, without using the word, the words of the psalm to make them refer to "current rebels against the church." The verse is understood to be prophetic both in relation to the past and to the future.

> When swearing is mentioned, do not think in terms of swearing. I mean, as in the case of anger, there is no anger on God's part, only the exercise of retribution, no passion; likewise no swearing. God does not swear, you see; he merely says what will happen without fail. Consequently, after mentioning the glory of the holy ones, placing enemies under his feet, and the day of his power, he then mentions also present things. . . .
>
> What is the force of *The Lord is at your right hand*? Since he touched on the incarnation, he directs his attention to the flesh in receipt of assistance: it is seen to be struggling and sweating—and sweating to such a degree that blood flowed—and given strength (Luke 22:24). The nature of the flesh is like that, you see. *He will crush kings on the day of his wrath.* You would not be wide of the mark to say this refers to the current rebels against the church and about those accountable in the future for their sins and impieties.

He will pass judgment on the nations, he will fill them with corpses (v. 6).
What is the meaning of *He will pass judgment on the nations*? He will sentence, he means, he will condemn the demons. For proof that he has passed
judgment, listen to Christ's words, "Now is the judgment for this world,
now the ruler of this world will be cast out." And elsewhere, "And I, if I am
lifted up, shall draw all people to me" (Jn 12:31-32). Now, do not be put off
if the expression he employs is more materialistic: this is Scripture's way. *He
will crush heads in many people's land.* If you prefer to take this in a spiritual
sense, you would say that he is doing away with folly; if, on the other hand,
in a material sense, it refers to the fate of the Jews, whom he utterly ruined
with great ferocity.[51]

Cassiodorus, following Augustine, gives a "spiritual" reading of the verses.
After alluding to the messianic interpretation of the earlier part of the
psalm as something already accomplished, he seems to interpret the
"breaking of kings" in the same sense. In the next verse "he shall engineer
falls" is interpreted spiritually to mean "He engineers falls when He makes
sins fall headlong from human hearts and causes harmful faults to vanish
by most salutary improvement." "Crushing heads" also receives a spiritual
interpretation to refer to those "who do not have Christ as their head" and
endure correction.

> *He hath broken kings* denotes those of whom Psalm 2 says: *The kings of the
> earth stood up, and the princes met together against the Lord and against his
> Christ.* He broke them when He laid low their pride with the power of His
> omnipotence, for if they had not been broken they would have stuck fast in
> the harmful rigidity of their malice.
>
> Verse 6. *He shall judge among nations, he shall engineer falls, he shall crush
> many heads in a land of abundance.* Observe the peculiar senses of the words.
> In the previous verse he said that kings were to be *broken* because of their
> tyrannical pride; now he relates that nations are *judged* for their common
> sins. Both happily tumble from their purposes when they abandon their
> earlier ill-will through their righteous decision to be converted. Ponder too
> the statement here that He judges to engineer falls. He engineers falls when

---

[51]Chrysostom, *Commentary on the Psalms*, 2:28-29.

He makes sins fall headlong from human hearts and causes harmful faults to vanish by most salutary improvement. This can be understood from the exemplary passage in which he says: *Thou shalt destroy them, and thou shalt not build them up* (Ps 28[27]:5); for this would surely not have been said if certain persons were not being destroyed for a happier renewal. Next comes: *He shall crush many heads in a land of abundance.* These are none other than the heads of those who do not have Christ as their head, for those who follow the devil in sundry errors undoubtedly find their heads crushed when they endure correction. By *head* (*caput*) we mean the lofty, distinguished crown of the body which gets its name from *capere* (to take), because it takes in all our senses—sight, hearing, taste, smell, touch—and our members have none of these except touch. So we can rightly call our Head Him whom we decide to follow. He calls a *land of abundance* that which nurtures numerous sinners, a harvest and seedbed, so to say, of vices.[52]

PSALM 136(137):8-9

O daughter Babylon, you wretch!
  Happy shall he be who will requite you with the requital
  with which you requited us!
Happy shall he be who will grab your infants
  and dash them against the rock!

These verses posed a special challenge to Christian interpretation, since one could hardly imagine a more vindictive attitude evidently directed toward a whole people and indeed to be taken out so cruelly on infants. Such an attitude could scarcely be reconciled with the teaching of Jesus about forgiveness of enemies, not to mention his positive attitude toward children.

Origen interpreted the infants of Babylon to mean "confused thoughts caused by evil."

The infants of Babylon, which means confusion, are the confused thoughts caused by evil which have just been implanted and are growing up in the soul. The man who takes hold of them, so that he breaks their heads by the firmness and solidity of the word, is dashing the infants of Babylon against

---

[52]Cassiodorus, *Explanation of the Psalms*; ACW 53:122-23.

the rock; and on this account he becomes blessed. Supposing, then, that God does command men to kill the works of iniquity, children and all, and to slaughter their entire race, His teaching in no way contradicts the proclamation of Jesus.[53]

Origen is responding here to a series of objections by the philosopher Celsus. He allegorizes the various texts, which, he insists, are to be read "spiritually" rather than literally. Here the command to requite the Babylonians must be understood allegorically as a command to kill the "works of iniquity." Origen also makes use of a technique found earlier in Philo to derive allegorical meanings through the supposed etymologies of names, in this case of Babylon, interpreted to mean "confusion."

Another version of this interpretation is given by Origen in a homily on Joshua where the rock is interpreted to mean Christ (1 Cor 10:4). The context is a discussion of the wars of Joshua in the conquest of the land. These Origen has already interpreted to refer to the wars against "the vices in ourselves."[54] Origen interprets the phrase "nothing that draws breath may be left behind" (Josh 11:11)[55] to refer to impulses such as that of anger: "you must so act that not even the impulse of wrath retains a place within you."[56] The same holds true of the other vices. "The disciple of Jesus must live so that nothing at all of these draws a breath in his heart."[57] He then invokes the interpretation of Psalm 136 (137) in support of this teaching.

The Prophet also forewarns about this, looking forward in the Psalms and saying, "Blessed is the one who seizes your little ones and dashes them against the rock," who seizes, namely, the little ones of Babylon, which are understood to be nothing else but these "evil thoughts" (Mt 15:19) that confound and disturb our heart. For this is what Babylon means. While these thoughts are still small and are just beginning, they must be seized and dashed against that "rock" who is "Christ" (1 Cor 10:4), and, by his order, they must be slain, so that nothing in us "may remain to draw breath."

[53]Origen, CCels 7.22; trans. Henry Chadwick (London: Cambridge University Press, 1953), p. 413.
[54]See the treatment of this theme in the previous chapter.
[55]Origen, HomJos 15.3; FC 105:143.
[56]Ibid.
[57]Origen, HomJos 15.3; FC 105:144.

> Therefore, just as on that occasion it was a blessed thing to seize and dash the little ones of Babylon against the rock and to destroy evil thoughts immediately when they are first beginning, so also now it should be considered a blessed and perfect thing if "nothing is left behind" in us that "could draw breath" after the manner of the heathen.[58]

In order to arrive at this conclusion Origen has made use of several exegetical procedures: the use of etymology to discover a meaning and the rule of interpreting the Scriptures by means of the Scriptures.[59] He also assumes that the author of the book of Psalms is David, who is a prophet; that is, he is speaking about hidden or more profound matters.

A similar interpretation is found in the homilies on the Psalms transmitted in Latin under the name of Jerome, which may be his translation of Origen,[60] where the thoughts come to be identified with concupiscence.

> By little ones are indicated the thoughts. To give an example, I have gazed at a woman, I have desired her. If I do not cut away that concupiscence immediately, if I do not take it by the feet and dash it against the rock while the concupiscence is still small, then later when it has grown large, it cannot be cut out. Blessed then is he who grabs it at once and dashes it against the rock. And the rock is Christ (1 Cor 10:4).[61]

This solution to the problem was readily accepted by many of the commentators who followed Origen. In Eusebius's version of this interpretation the children become the "seeds of evil" and the "beginnings of confused errors." He first notes that it is better never to see Babylon or become involved in her vices, but then it is good to make prisoners of the Babylonians, understood as vices, and bring them back to the fear of God. Then it is even better not to let their little ones grow, but to tear them to pieces against the rock.

---

[58]Ibid.

[59]For an explanation of this principle, see Mark Sheridan, ed., *Genesis 12–50*, ACCS OT 2 (Downers Grove, IL: InterVarsity Press, 2002), pp. xxxiv-xxxvi.

[60]See ch. 7 above, note 16.

[61]CCL 78:298: "Paruuli dicuntur cogitationes. Verbi gratia, uidi mulierem, concupiui eam: statim si non abscidero concupiscentiam illam, et sicut pedem tennuero, et allisero ad petram donec parua est concupiscentia, non potest postea abscidi quando creuerit. Beatus ergo est qui statim abscidit, et allidit eam ad petram. Petra autem Xpistus est."

You are not mistaken if you say that the little ones of Babylon are the seeds of evil, the beginnings of whatever sin into which it is possible to fall. For this reason it is well said that he is happy who hastens to eliminate them with the word of the Savior ("the rock, in fact, was Christ" 1 Cor 10:4), so that they cannot grow and become destructive.[62]

For Hilary of Poitiers, who was certainly following Origen, the children become "the tender vices of the body."[63] And finally we have two versions of Evagrius of Pontus's comment on the psalm verse. In his *Scholia on Psalms*, the children are base or "bad thoughts." In the *Ad monachos* they are "evil thoughts."[64] In this exegetical tradition, what were known in the philosophical tradition as the "beginnings of passion" (*propatheiai*), now identified with thoughts, become in effect incipient passion "related to its mature form as child to adult."[65]

In the West the same interpretation was adopted also by Augustine.

Babylon then has persecuted us when little, but God has given us when grown up knowledge of ourselves, that we should not follow the errors of our parents. . . . How shall they repay her? As she hath served us. Let her little ones be choked in turn: yes let her little ones in turn be dashed, and die. What are the little ones of Babylon? Evil desires at their birth. For there are [those], who have to fight with inveterate lusts. When lust is born, before evil habit gives it strength against you, when lust is little, by no means let it gain the strength of evil habit; when it is little, dash it. But you fear, lest though dashed it die not; "Dash it against the Rock; and that Rock is Christ."[66]

Cassiodorus, at the beginning of his commentary on the psalm, notes that it refers to the exile after the capture of Jerusalem by Nebuchadnezzar, as also "the prophet Jeremiah records," but he cautions: "we must interpret

---

[62]Eusebius, *Commentary on the Psalms*; PG 23:37.

[63]CSEL 22:734: "in quem beatus est, qui filiae Babylonis paruuolos, id est tenera adhuc corporis uitia allidet et conteret."

[64]H. Gressmann, *Nonnenspiegel und Mönchsspiegel des Evagrios Pontikos*, TU 39.4 (Leipzig: Hinrichs, 1913), pp. 153-65.

[65]Richard A. Layton, *Didymus the Blind and His Circle in Late-Antique Alexandria: Virtue and Narrative in Biblical Scholarship* (Urbana: University of Illinois Press, 2004), p. 131.

[66]Augustine, *Expositions on the Book of Psalms*; NPNF 1 8:632.

these events spiritually, for as Paul says: *All these things happened to them in figure*" (1 Cor 10:11). On Psalm 136(137):9 he writes:

> They are still addressing the flesh, stating that the person who takes hold of his little ones, meaning his harmful vices, is blessed, because he has already made progress towards controlling them; for when we hold something we take it in our power, and it ceases to be free since it has begun to be enslaved by us. . . . We do well to analyse their phrase: *Thy little ones*, meaning sins of the flesh born of a wretched mother. While small they are easily grasped and effectively dashed against the heavenly Rock; but once they begin to mature and reach a most vigorous manhood, sterner struggle is commenced with them, and they are not easily overcome by our weakness.[67]

The same interpretation as a reference to the beginnings of evil thoughts is found in reference to the spirit of fornication in the works of John Cassian (d. 435).

> It behooves us as well to destroy the sinners in our land—namely, our fleshly feelings—on the morning of their birth, as they emerge, and, while they are still young, to dash the children of Babylon against the rock. Unless they are killed at a very tender age they will, with our acquiescence, rise up to our harm as stronger adults, and they will certainly not be overcome without great pain and effort.[68]

With this interpretation by the principal Western monastic writer, the psalm came to be recited by innumerable communities of monks and nuns throughout the Middle Ages and beyond until the modern period. A clear allusion to the same interpretation is found in the *Rule of St. Benedict*: "While these temptations were still *young, he caught hold of them and dashed them against* Christ" (prol. 28).[69]

Not all commentators adopted Origen's interpretation. Those in the Antiochene tradition generally did not follow the allegorical interpreta-

---

[67]Cassiodorus, *Explanation of the Psalms*; ACW 53:364.

[68]John Cassian, *Inst.* 6.13; ACW 58:159.

[69]Timothy Fry et al., eds., *RB 1980: The Rule of St. Benedict in Latin and English with Notes* (Collegeville, MN: Liturgical Press, 1981), p. 163.

tions of the Alexandrian school. In his comment on the psalm John Chrysostom notes:

> The inspired authors, after all, say many things not on their own account but to describe the feelings of others and bring them to the fore. I mean, if you are looking for his attitude, listen to him saying, "If I have meted out evil for evil" (Ps 7:4), where he goes beyond the due response allowed him by the Law. But when he tells of the sufferings of others, he depicts their anger, their pain, which is what he did in this case, bringing to the fore the desire of the Jews, who let their rage extend even to such a young age.[70]

This is the technique of "prosopological" interpretation, that is, determining the person (*prosōpon*) who is speaking in the text. It creates a distance between the text and the reader by suggesting that the sentiment expressed is not necessarily that of the author. But in this case, Chrysostom could not leave it at that and felt constrained to add: "The teaching of the New Testament is not like that, however: we are bidden to give food and drink to our enemies, to pray for those who abuse us."[71]

Summary: Many difficult passages in the Old Testament Scriptures could be ignored and omitted from Christian worship, but the book of Psalms became a Christian prayer book. It therefore required special attention. The ancient Christian commentators on the Psalms applied a variety of rules and strategies to render acceptable and give a Christian meaning to the problematic parts of the Psalter. These included identifying the speaker in the Psalms, reading them as prophecy and interpreting them allegorically.

---

[70]Chrysostom, *Commentary on the Psalms*, 2:244-45.
[71]Ibid., 2:245.

Ancient and Modern Ways of
Dealing with the Problematic Texts

These words, however, are for those who are friends of the letter
and do not think that the Law is spiritual and is to be understood
spiritually. But we, who have learned that all things which are written are
written not to relate ancient history, but for our discipline and use, understand
that these things which are said also happen now not only in this world,
which is figuratively called Egypt, but in each one of us also.

ORIGEN, *HOMILIES ON EXODUS* 2.1

ALTHOUGH MANY OF THE PRESUPPOSITIONS of ancient interpretation
are no longer tenable in the light of our historical knowledge and many of
the rules used by ancient Christian interpreters may no longer be viable,
their theological interpretation of the texts still has value for us today.
Finding a Christian meaning for the Scriptures today is still a challenge.
This chapter seeks to compare how ancient and modern interpreters meet
this challenge, especially with reference to texts already examined in
chapters six and seven. The different sets of texts present different kinds of
problems. In chapter six, the ancient Christian interpretation of three sets
of texts was presented: Genesis 1–4, Genesis 16 and the texts relating to the
conquest of the land in Deuteronomy and Joshua.

Genesis 1–4: The Story of the Creation and Fall

The situation facing the ancient interpreters of Genesis was quite different from that with which many modern exegetes are concerned. Many modern writers, on the one hand, tend to be interested in placing the texts in their ancient literary setting, that is, in the history of the development of ancient Near Eastern religious literature, and comparing it with other creation narratives such as the Egyptian or Mesopotamian ones. In this context the biblical narratives are often seen to reflect a favorable theological development. Some contemporary interpreters, on the other hand, may be interested in using the biblical narrative against modern historical-critical studies or against the theory of evolution, insisting on the "special" creation of humanity. More recently we have witnessed the development of various forms of "creationism" in which the biblical narrative is presented as an alternative to modern scientific theories of the origin of the universe and human beings. Both types of concerns were completely outside the intellectual world of the ancient Christian writers. The ancient texts were never intended to present alternatives to such modern questions, nor were they so interpreted in antiquity.

The ancient writers had a different problem. They had to defend the Bible against charges of *mythos,* that it presented a mythological version of human origins. Such is evident already in the assertion of the author of the *Letter of Aristeas* (see chap. 3) that "no ordinances have been made in scripture without purpose or fancifully [*mythōdōs*]."[1] And at the end of his work explaining how the law of Moses should be read, he says to his reader: "These matters I think delight you more than the books of the mythologists, for your inclination lies in the direction of concern for things that benefit the mind, and to them you devote the greater time."[2] A hundred and fifty years later Philo also found it necessary to defend the biblical accounts from the charge that they were mythological in character.

---

[1]*Letter of Aristeas* 168, in R. J. H. Shutt, trans., "Letter of Aristeas," in *The Old Testament Pseudepigrapha,* ed. James H. Charlesworth, *Expansions of the "Old Testament" and Legends, Wisdom and Philosophical Literature, Prayers, Psalms and Odes, Fragments of Lost Judeo-Hellenistic Works* (Peabody, MA: Hendrickson, 2010), 2:24.

[2]*Letter of Aristeas* 322 (in ibid., p. 34).

As already noted in chapter six, he says in regard to the idea of God planting a garden: "Let not such fables [*mythopoiia* = "myth-making"] even enter our mind. For not even the whole world would be a place fit for God to make His abode, since God is His own place, and He is filled by Himself, and sufficient for Himself, filling and containing all other things in their destitution and barrenness and emptiness, but Himself contained by nothing else, seeing that He is Himself One and the Whole."[3] Philo frequently defends the biblical text against such a "mythical" understanding. Such frequent defenses makes it clear that in fact the texts were considered by many to be mythical in character. The alternative for Philo was not to insist on a literal reading, but on a theological interpretation.

By the time of Philo, the Greek word "myth" had already long had a negative connotation as something "false" or "unreal." The late fifth-century-B.C. historian Thucydides had contrasted myth with his idea of history: "Assuredly they will not be disturbed either by the lays of a poet displaying the exaggeration of his craft, or by the compositions of the chroniclers that are attractive at truth's expense; the subjects they treat of being out of the reach of evidence, and time having robbed most of them of historical value [literally "credibility" = *apistōs*] by enthroning them in the region of legend [*mythōdes*]."[4] Myth had also come to be recognized as one of the building blocks, or *progymnasmata*, of rhetoric, and the manuals of rhetorical studies described how it could be used.[5]

However, as already described in chapter two, the negative connotation of "myth" was due in large part to the efforts of Plato to substitute philosophical discourse for mythical discourse. The defenders of Homer had then insisted that "no stain of abominable myth disfigures his poems."[6] In defending Homer, Heraclitus contrasts myth with philosophy: "He emphatically does not give us any pretentious myth about

---

[3]Philo, *Leg.* 1.43-44; LCL 226:175.
[4]Thucydides, *Histories* 1.21; *The Peloponnesian War*, trans. Richard Crawley (London: J. M. Dent; New York: E. P. Dutton, 1910), p. 14.
[5]See, e.g., George A. Kennedy, *Progymnasmata: Greek Textbooks of Prose Composition and Rhetoric* (Atlanta: Society of Biblical Literature, 2003), pp. 23, 74.
[6]Donald A. Russell and David Konstan, *Heraclitus: Homeric Problems*, Writings from the Greco-Roman World (Atlanta: Society of Biblical Literature, 2005), p. 3.

talking arrows; on the contrary, there is a philosophical doctrine in the line."[7] The early Christian authors had to defend the biblical narratives from the same negative charge that they were "mythical." Origen reports that Celsus regarded the writings of Moses as "myths": saying the philosopher held that "but if Moses wrote for a whole nation and left them histories and laws, his words are considered to be empty myths not even capable of being interpreted allegorically."[8] Defending the Christian interpretation of Moses, Origen writes: "but they [the Christians] accord it greater honor by showing what a depth of wise and mysterious doctrines is contained by those writings. The Jews, on the other hand, have not looked deeply into them, but read them superficially and only as stories [*mythikōteron*]."[9] Later in the same work Origen defends the Jews against Celsus, noting that Moses had taught basic truths such as the immortality of the soul and the reward for the good: "These truths were proclaimed still under the form of a story [*mythikōteron*] because they were children and only had the understanding of children; but now to those who seek for the meaning and wish to advance in it, what hitherto were myths, if I may use the word, have been transformed into the inner truth which had been hidden from them."[10]

For Origen and many others, the alternative to accepting these biblical stories as myth was not to insist on a literal meaning but to seek a theological meaning, as has already been noted in chapter six. Even one of the few ancient Christian authors who could be called a literalist, Epiphanius (late fourth century A.D.), shrank from accepting many details literally. Explicitly reacting against Origen, whose allegorical explanations he rejected, calling them "mythological," he insisted on taking many details literally such as the garden, the trees of knowledge and of good and evil, and even the tunics of skin (Gen 3:20). But in regard to the creation of humanity "in the image" of God, he warned: "Do not investigate indiscreetly the gifts

---

[7]Ibid., p. 23. The reference to Homer is *Iliad* l.46.
[8]Origen, *CCels* 1.20; trans. Henry Chadwick (London: Cambridge University Press, 1953), p. 21. All further quotations from *CCels* are from this translation.
[9]Ibid., 2.4.
[10]Ibid., 5.42.

that God has given to man through grace. For us it is enough not to deny that every man is in the image of God, but we are not curious to know how we are in the image of God."[11] Further on in the same passage, he says that only God knows what it means. Epiphanius, however, was quick to defend himself from the charge of anthropomorphism, stating that "we are not ignorant that God is invisible and incomprehensible, and therefore we cannot think that the 'image' refers to the body."[12] Then, considering Genesis 2:7, which states of God that he "breathed into his nostrils the breath of life," Epiphanius remarks, "The Scripture says 'blew,' but we cannot say that the soul is a particle of God, nor affirm that it is extraneous to that breath. How that can be more precisely understood, only God knows."[13] Theodoret of Cyrrhus, who also tried to interpret the garden literally, was more theologically forceful regarding the interpretation of Genesis 2:7. In answer to the question: "If the soul is derived from the breath of God, must it not be a part of God's being?" he replies:

> Such an idea is a piece of the worst irreligion and blasphemy. Holy Scripture used this expression to bring out the ease of the creation. Moreover, it darkly suggests[14] the nature of the soul: that it is a created spirit, invisible and spiritual, free of the materiality of bodies. You should also understand that this idea would require us first to imagine lungs, muscles to squeeze and contract them, a windpipe attached to the lungs, a palate, and last of all a mouth to breathe in air. But, if the divinity is incorporeal, surely his breath should also be thought of in a manner befitting God [*theoprepōs*].[15]

From these texts it should be clear that the ancient Christian writers were guided by theological considerations in their interpretations of the primeval history in Genesis. They recognized that the text appeared to have a mythical character and that it required a proper understanding of

---

[11]Epiphanius, *Ancoratus* 55; GCS 25.

[12]Ibid.

[13]Ibid.

[14]The word used here is *ainittetai* which, as explained in chap. 2, is one of the earliest words used to introduce a nonliteral interpretation.

[15]Theodoret, *The Questions on the Octateuch*, trans. Robert Charles Hill (Washington, DC: Catholic University of America Press, 2007), 1:59-61.

the nature of God to interpret it correctly. It would be very anachronistic
to read modern preoccupations into their interpretations.[16]

GENESIS 16–21: THE STORY OF SARAH AND HAGAR

The story of Sarah and Hagar, as we have seen in chapters three and six,
posed a challenge to Jewish and Christian interpreters. The problem was
that it presents "holy persons"[17] engaging in behavior that appear to be
scandalous. By the standards of the time of Philo and Paul, it was a case of
adultery proposed by Sarah and accepted by Abraham the patriarch and
future father of a great nation, whether from the Jewish perspective or
from the universalist reinterpretation offered by Paul. But these persons
were thought to be models for behavior. The ancient solution was to
assume that the text had to have a hidden or allegorical significance. Since
that is not a viable option for modern commentators, such conduct must
either be excused or condemned. We find both in modern commentary.

A note to Genesis 16:2 in the New American Bible reads: "The custom
of an infertile wife providing her husband with a concubine to produce
children is widely attested in ancient Near Eastern law; e.g., an Old As-
syrian marriage contract states that the wife must provide her husband
with a concubine if she does not bear children within two years." The *New
Jerome Bible Commentary* offers a similar observation: "A Nuzi text of the
15th cent. is an example of a Hurrian legal custom similar to that invoked
by Sarah: 'If Gilimminu bears children, Shennima shall not take another
wife. But if Gilimminu fails to bear children, Gilimminu shall get for
Shennima a woman from the Lullu country (i.e., a slave girl) as a concubine. In that case Gilimminu herself shall have authority over the
offspring."[18] It is not stated, but seems to be understood that this infor-

---

[16]As Andrew Louth remarks: "The Fathers read the first chapters of the Bible as unfolding a theological
understanding of the human condition." He contrasts such an approach "to what much modern scholarship regards as ancient legends of limited theological value." See Andrew Louth, ed., *Genesis 1–11*, ACCS
OT 1 (Downers Grove, IL: InterVarsity Press, 2001), p. lii.

[17]See chap. 5 for Augustine's assertion that such things that appear to be shameful are "wholly figurative."

[18]Raymond Edward Brown, Joseph A Fitzmyer and Roland E Murphy, *The New Jerome Biblical Commentary*
(Englewood Cliffs, NJ: Prentice-Hall, 1990), pp. 21-22. There it is noted that the information is taken
from E. A. Speiser, *Genesis* (Garden City, NY: Doubleday, 1964), p. 120.

mation is offered to show that the patriarch and his wife were not doing anything unusual by the standards of their time. Implicit is the idea that their behavior is thus understandable and not to be condemned. Implicit also may be the idea that such behavior is no longer acceptable. Actually Ambrose, without knowing anything of such ancient documents, had offered a similar view: "But we should consider first of all that Abraham lived prior to the law of Moses and before the gospel; adultery, it seems, was not yet prohibited at this time. The penalty for the crime goes back only to the time of the law, which made adultery a crime. So there is no condemnation for the offense that precedes the law but only one based on the law. Abraham then cannot be said to have violated the law since he came before the law."[19]

Many modern readers may not be convinced by this reasoning. From the other end of the theological spectrum we find a firm condemnation of both Sarah and Abraham.

> Too often we time-conscious earthlings resent His long delays and take matters into our own hands, usually to our great distress. If we could learn to keep trusting Him when our situation looks the bleakest, we would save ourselves much grief. This impulsive sin had its effect on the relationship between Abraham and Sarah. Hagar got pregnant and eventually became proud and unmanageable. Sarah blamed Abraham for the whole problem when it was actually her own idea. Then she dealt harshly with Hagar, and her unkindness exposed the bitterness and resentment in her soul. Meanwhile, Abraham shirked his duty. He should have said "No" to Sarah's sinful scheme in the first place. But now he told her to handle the problem herself, to do whatever she wanted to do, but to stop badgering him about it (Gen 16:6).[20]

This condemnation is no doubt motivated by a legitimate concern that unwary readers might be misled by the biblical story. In the first case we have an explanation from a historical-critical perspective which suggests that there has been development in the history of manners and morals.

---

[19]Ambrose, *On Abraham* 1.4.23; CSEL 32.1:517-18.
[20]The comment is found on www.bible.org (June 27, 2013), self-defined as a "broadly evangelical" website: Richard L. Strauss, "Yes, My Lord—The Story of Abraham and Sarah," *Bible.org*, June 28, 2004. https://bible.org/seriespage/yes-my-lord—-ithe-story-abraham-and-sarahi.

However, this development seems to make the texts irrelevant or no longer normative. In the second case the texts are considered to be still relevant, and therefore behavior that is not acceptable must be clearly condemned. Both points of view are quite different from the ancient one that assumed the texts must have a meaning useful for us, which is to be sought beneath the letter of the text.

WIPING OUT THE NATIONS: DEUTERONOMY AND JOSHUA

The modern approach to the problem posed by these texts for Christians has often been quite different from the ancient Christian reaction. This may be due in part, but only in part, to the different orientation of modern interpreters, who are generally seeking to discover the original meaning of texts as opposed to finding spiritual nourishment in them that is suited "for us" (1 Cor 9:10). In his famous book *From the Stone Age to Christianity*, published in 1957, the noted biblical scholar and archaeologist William F. Albright wrote:

> From the impartial standpoint of a philosopher of history, it often seems necessary that a people of markedly inferior type should vanish before a people of superior potentialities, since there is a point beyond which racial mixture cannot go without disaster. When such a process takes place—as at present in Australia—there is generally little that can be done by the humanitarian—though every deed of brutality and injustice is infallibly visited upon the aggressor.[21]

From Albright's point of view, "it was fortunate for the future of monotheism that the Israelites of the Conquest were a wild folk, endowed with primitive energy and ruthless will to exist, since the resulting decimation of the Canaanites prevented the complete fusion of the two kindred folk which would almost inevitably have depressed Yahwistic standards to a point where recovery was impossible."[22] As Albright saw it, the conquest served to replace an inferior people with a superior one: "Israel, with its

---

[21]William Foxwell Albright, *From the Stone Age to Christianity: Monotheism and the Historical Process* (Baltimore: Johns Hopkins Press, 1957), p. 280.
[22]Ibid., pp. 280-81.

pastoral simplicity and purity of life, its lofty monotheism, and its severe code of ethics."[23]

This point of view has been severely criticized on the one hand, but on the other hand, various milder versions of the same historically oriented, nontheological view have been proposed. Keith Whitelam has characterized Albright's view as "an outpouring of undisguised racism which is staggering."[24] He observes:

> Albright's characterization of the sensuous, immoral Canaanite stands in a long line of Orientalist representations of the Other as the opposite of the Western, rational intellectual. It is a characterization which dehumanizes, allowing the extermination of native populations, as in the case of Native Americans where it was regrettable but "probably inevitable"; the claim is couched in terms of the progress that colonial or imperial rule will bring.[25]

Albright claimed to be writing from the "impartial standpoint of a philosopher of history." It was certainly not a theological point of view. He never pauses to ask whether such a view is compatible with the teaching of Jesus Christ as the early Christian writers do.

In an important work dealing with the question of violence in the Bible, Regina M. Schwartz (*The Curse of Cain*, 1997) notes that in trying to reconstruct the history of the conquest "Germans have tended to favor a theory of gradual settlement, maintaining that immigration and assimilation of Hebrews with Canaanites occurred because the seasonal migration of semi-nomads entailed agreements between herders and farmers," whereas in the United States the dominant school of thought produced "theories of invasion of the indigenous population in a massive conquest by outsiders—here, the destruction of key cities in the late thirteenth century offers archeological proof despite our not knowing who or what forces led to that destruction."[26] All of these versions of the con-

---

[23]Ibid., p. 281.

[24]Keith W. Whitelam, *The Invention of Ancient Israel: The Silencing of Palestinian History* (New York: Routledge, 1995), p. 84.

[25]Ibid.

[26]Regina M. Schwartz, *The Curse of Cain: The Violent Legacy of Monotheism* (Chicago: University of Chicago Press, 1997), p. 61.

quest, she observes, "turn out to be less violent, less oppressive, and less morally repugnant than the version in the biblical narrative: 'and when the Lord your God gives them over to you, and you defeat them, then you must utterly destroy them; you shall make no covenant with them, and show no mercy to them' (Deut 7:2)."[27] But she also observes critically that "replacing this aggression with a more congenial version of the conquest certainly makes the Bible more palatable, but the historian's sleight of hand begs a question of ethical accountability."[28] The people who continue to read these texts do not read them as archaeologists who seek to minimize the violent aspects of the text.

Schwartz's observation, although it does introduce the ethical question into the discourse, is not yet on the theological level. Reducing the violence to a minimum does not solve the theological problem, the question about the nature of God. If God orders the destruction of even one innocent child instead of a whole nation or seven nations, we still have a major theological problem. What kind of a god could do such a thing? The principal question concerns the nature of God, the concept of God. For the early Christian writers this was determined by the teaching of Jesus Christ, not by a reading of Old Testament texts apart from their fulfillment in the New Testament.

Some recent authors admit that "probably the most difficult Old Testament ethical issue is the divine command to kill the Canaanites"[29] and "Perhaps the Old Testament texts that potentially make Yahweh appear the most racist are the one that describe divinely mandated slaughters of foreigners, specifically the Canaanites."[30] It may be instructive to see how they deal with the issue. Paul Copan quotes Deuteronomy 20:16: "you shall not leave alive anything that breathes" (NASB). Neither women nor children nor the aged are excepted from this command. Copan an-

[27]Ibid.
[28]Ibid.
[29]Paul Copan, *Is God a Moral Monster? Making Sense of the Old Testament God* (Grand Rapids: Baker Books, 2011), p. 158.
[30]David T. Lamb, *God Behaving Badly: Is the God of the Old Testament Angry, Sexist and Racist?* (Downers Grove, IL: IVP Books, 2011), p. 76.

nounces that he will devote four chapters to this difficult question and begins by asking if the Canaanites really were that wicked. With a citation from William F. Albright describing the bloody Canaanite rites, Copan concludes that "it's no wonder God didn't want the Israelites to associate with the Canaanites and be led astray from obedience to the one true God."[31] Moreover, the Canaanites were not singled out alone for punishment: "Yahweh frequently threatened many nations with judgment when they crossed a certain moral threshold."[32] Copan wisely avoids the terminology of race and speaks instead of culture: "What guidelines do we have to determine when a culture is irredeemable, beyond the point of no moral and spiritual return?"[33] The answer is that a special revelation is needed before any such undertaking, but that was present in the case of the Canaanites: "without such clear divine guidance, Israel wouldn't have been justified in attacking the Canaanite strongholds."[34] He mounts a vigorous defense against the charge of genocide (anachronistic in any case) by the Israelites and insists that "God was concerned with *sin*, not *ethnicity*."[35] But he does not address the question of collective punishment, whether of Israel or of other nations. Next Copan argues on the plane of cosmic warfare: "God's commands to Israel to wipe out Canaan's idols and false, immoral worship illustrate the cosmic warfare between Yahweh and the dark powers opposed to his rule."[36] These wars "represent a clash of two world orders: the one rooted in reality and justice, the other in reality-denial and brute power."[37] Then Copan offers additional arguments to ameliorate the force of the text in Deuteronomy: "Moses's language is also an example of ancient Near Eastern exaggeration. He did not intend a literal, all-encompassing extermination of the Canaanites" and this is supported by the archeological evidence as well as the biblical text, which "point to minimal observable

---

[31]Copan, *Is God a Moral Monster?*, p. 160.
[32]Ibid.
[33]Ibid., p. 161.
[34]Ibid.
[35]Ibid., p. 165 (author's emphasis).
[36]Ibid., p. 167.
[37]Ibid.

material destruction in Canaan as well as Israel's gradual infiltration, as-similation, and eventual dominance there."[38]

Copan offers additional argumentation in the same vein, which space does not permit to be reported here, basically in defense of a very anthro-pomorphic and anthropopathic God, who often seems to reason in the language of a modern politician. At the end, to be sure, he does arrive at the New Testament: "to glimpse God more clearly, as revealed in Jesus."[39] He seems unsatisfied with his own defense of God and suggests that the Christian can reply to the critics of the Old Testament text: "While I can't tidily solve the problem of the Canaanites, I can trust a God who has proven his willingness to go to such excruciating lengths—and depths—to offer rebellious humans reconciliation and friendship [through the incarnation]."[40] He notes further: "However we're to interpret and re-spond to some of the baffling questions raised by the Old Testament, we shouldn't stop with the Old Testament if we want a clearer revelation of the heart and character of God."[41] But Copan never addresses the real theological question: the nature of God. Early Christian writers on the whole did not have such hesitations. They were concerned not with de-fending an anthropomorphic and anthropopathic God, but with inter-preting the text in the light of the nature of God as revealed by Jesus Christ. They were also seeking spiritual nourishment for their readers and were operating with a different concept of the nature of Scripture than that in-troduced in modern times.

David Lamb, already quoted above, speaks of "this most troubling aspect of the Old Testament," but seeks to deal with it first by minimizing it. He describes the texts in Joshua as hyperbolic and notes that other texts in Joshua and Judges suggest that the Israelites did not kill all the Canaanites. He then concludes that "to reconcile these two diverse perspectives on Is-rael's conquest, a nonliteral reading of the texts that speak of 'all' people

---

[38]Ibid., p. 185.
[39]Ibid., p. 196.
[40]Ibid., p. 197.
[41]Ibid.

being destroyed is required."[42] He then compares Joshua's victory over the Canaanites with the conquests of Ashurnasirpal and Mesha and, having previously eliminated the word "all," is able to arrive at the conclusion that there is "no mention of women or children, and no descriptions of brutality or mutilation."[43] Finally, he asserts that, unlike Assyria and Moab, who were pursuing an expansionist policy, "Israel was simply attempting to gain a homeland." Furthermore, "they were repossessing land that had belonged to their family," and "they had a legitimate right to be reestablished in the land of their ancestors."[44] Lamb too defends Yahweh from the charge of racism by noting that he punished evil nations including the Israelites with death and exile. However, in the end, like Copan, he also seems unsatisfied with his defense of God and admits: "The Canaanite conquest is probably the most problematic topic in the Old Testament, and it will, therefore, be impossible to 'solve it' in a few pages."[45] This is certainly to his credit, but the further statement is not reassuring regarding his concept of God: "I must resort to taking it on faith that even though God commanded his people to kill the Canaanites, he still loves the nations and ultimately wants to bless them."[46] The author is unable in the end to let go of his literal reading of the text. His concept of "Scripture" seems to require that he accept things in the Scriptures that cannot be reconciled with a theologically more developed concept of God. Maintaining the transcendence of God, his difference from human beings and their ways of behaving, was more important for the ancient Christian interpreters.

THE PROBLEM OF THE PSALMS

In chapter seven I focused on the problem posed by the use of the Psalter as a Christian prayer book and how the ancient commentators dealt with the passages that cursed enemies, whether collective or individual. These are also known as the imprecatory or cursing psalms. Of course there are

---

[42]Lamb, *God Behaving Badly*, p. 77.
[43]Ibid.
[44]Ibid., p. 78.
[45]Ibid., p. 81.
[46]Ibid.

many other beautiful passages of thanksgiving and praise in the Psalms, which offer no problem to Christians. On the contrary they can easily be used as Christian prayers. There are also many psalms that had received at least a hint for their interpretation through their use or citation in the New Testament writings. Nevertheless, in this most heterogeneous collection of prayers, there are many passages that present a theological problem for Christian usage. How can Christians pray such passages? What should they be thinking when uttering such words? We have seen the various techniques used by the early Christian writers to deal with this problem.

Modern commentators in the historical-critical tradition often ignore the problem. They are not interested in such theological questions, but rather in establishing the original meaning and the original usage of these poems. They are interested in dating the psalms to various periods in temple worship or in private settings and determining the various literary genres. A good example of such a commentary is that of Mitchell Dahood in the Anchor Bible. Dahood was a Ugaritic scholar and very much interested in establishing the meanings of words through parallels in Ugaritic texts. He makes many interesting suggestions, but his interest is primarily historical, and theological only in a historical sense, that is, in describing the theology to be found in the Psalms.[47]

There are exceptions to this rule, however. An early example is the commentary by Charles Augustus Briggs and Emilie Grace Briggs in the International Critical Commentary series published over a hundred years ago, which contains a wealth of philological and historical material, but also much about the history of the interpretation of the Psalms.[48] Briggs was well aware of the allegorical interpretation practiced in the patristic period, but he does not focus on particular interpretations. In the introduction, however, he does take up the question of the imprecatory psalms and defends them against what he regards as modern objections.

The only objections to the canonicity of the Psalter seriously entertained

---

[47]Mitchell J. Dahood, *Psalms*, 2 vols., AB 16-17 (Garden City, NY: Doubleday, 1966-1974).

[48]Charles A. Briggs and Emilie Grace Briggs, *A Critical and Exegetical Commentary on the Book of Psalms*, 2 vols., ICC (Edinburgh: T & T Clark, 1907).

are based on a number of imprecations upon enemies and protestations of righteousness on the part of suffering servants of God. These objections are invalid because they fail to apprehend that these imprecations and protestations belong necessarily to earlier stages of religion and to certain historic situations where they have their essential propriety.[49]

Citing the example of Jesus in the Gospels and other New Testament texts such as Revelation, Briggs insists that there is a legitimate sense in which imprecation can be understood by Christians, a sense that involves the justice and righteousness of God, but he repeats his conviction that the forms found in the Psalms belong "to earlier stages of religion."

> There is a place, therefore, for imprecation in the highest forms of Christianity, only it is more discriminating than in the OT religion and much more refined. In substance, the imprecations of the Psalter are normal and valid; in their external form and modes of expression they belong to an age of religion which has been displaced by Christianity.[50]

Then in an allusion to particularly offensive passages that must include Psalm 137:9 (dashing the heads of the infants against the rock) he comments:

> It is the form and general character of these imprecations which are most obnoxious to the modern mind, especially the physical sufferings that are invoked, the dishonoring of wives and daughters, and the slaughter of babes, even of the unborn. This is from the point of view of the solidarity of interest in the family, tribe, and nation; and especially from the ancient principle of the duty of revenge which was inherited by sons and kinsmen; so that the only way to avoid future peril of revenge was the extermination of all who would be likely in the future to undertake it.[51]

One cannot help but wonder if it is really just the "modern mind" that finds difficulty with such passages. This is to underestimate the sensibility of ancient writers. Indeed, based on the interpretations set out in chapter seven, one could argue that the latter often seem more humanly and theologically sensitive than modern writers. The invocation of "solidarity of

---

[49]Ibid., p. xcvii.
[50]Ibid., p. c.
[51]Ibid., p. ci.

interest in the family, tribe, and nation" to explain the "extermination of all"
in order to avoid the "future peril of revenge" seems intended to extenuate
the horrible wish of the psalmist. A note found in the New American Bible
for this verse offers a similar observation: "the children represent the
future generations, and so must be destroyed if the enemy is truly to be
eradicated."[52] That may explain the logic of the psalm's author, but it does
not deal adequately with the question of how Christians today can pronounce such words and express a wish for something to be done that
would surely be considered a "crime against humanity" in the International
Criminal Court. No doubt crimes against humanity have been committed
throughout human history, but that does not lessen their horror. At least
Briggs recognizes that these words "belong to an age of religion which has
been displaced by Christianity." As I have noted also in chapter seven, John
Chrysostom expresses the Christian point of view even more clearly: "The
teaching of the New Testament is not like that, however; we are bidden to
give food and drink to our enemies, to pray for those who abuse us."[53]

Briggs wrote shortly before the genocidal horrors of the twentieth
century began. In a commentary published originally in German shortly
after the Second World War, Artur Weiser insisted that the "reason why the
psalmist calls down God's punishment on the enemy is in order to show
with whom the final decision rests, whether with men who blaspheme in
their arrogant mockery or with God who is not mocked."[54] However, he
admits that this concern "is obscured and suppressed by his subsequent
words of blind hate and vulgar rage."[55] He observes also that the psalmist,
contemplating the sufferings of his people, "has no longer either the
strength or the will-power to curb his mounting rage. In a frightfully cruel
outcry he wishes for the complete extermination of Babylon."[56] Weiser
offers the concluding reflection:

[52]The New Jerome Biblical Commentary simply notes that this verse represents an "extreme example of the
law of talion" without offering any theological interpretation. Presumably that excludes it as a legitimate
sentiment for Christians. See p. 550.
[53]Chrysostom, Commentary on the Psalms, 2:245.
[54]Artur Weiser, The Psalms: A Commentary (Philadelphia: Westminster Press, 1962), p. 796.
[55]Ibid.
[56]Ibid.

We shall not be able to contemplate here, without being ourselves deeply affected, how the poet plunges into the abyss of human passion. We must, however, neither generalize this humanly understandable outburst of hate, with which we are also confronted in Isa. 13:16, and regard it as the Old Testament's exclusive attitude towards Babylon (cf. Jer. 29:7), nor must we forget because of it how earnestly and bravely the poet has previously striven for the assurance of his continued relationship with God and for God's honour before he was overcome by human passion.[57]

Here the sentiment of the psalmist is correctly described as "blind hate and vulgar rage." It is clearly not to be recommended, nor to be thought of as typical of the Old Testament. However, no indication is given as to how the Christian can use such words, nor is it contrasted with the sentiments expressed in the New Testament.

In another more recent commentary by Leslie Allen, the questionable assertion is made regarding the interpretation of this verse that "perhaps the citizen of a European country who has experienced its invasion and destruction would be the best exegete of such a psalm."[58] The commentator observes: "The passion that throbs in every line is the fruit of suffering. Is it ignoble? Certainly not if one takes seriously the religious framework of the psalmist."[59] After stressing the various concepts of "a chosen nation," "a territory possessed by divine right," "holy war" and others needed to understand the psalmist's context, he nevertheless concludes: "The Christian faith teaches a new way, the pursuit of forgiveness and a call to love. Both its intrinsic non-nationalism and its facility to fall back upon an eschatological final reckoning, the Last Judgment, aid such a course."[60] But it seems that the psalmist's sentiments can be understood in terms of the last judgment, for he asserts that Psalm 137:9 forms part of the "OT backdrop to the new Babylon of Rev 17–18."[61] The final word on the verse is that "the meaning of Jerusalem to him [the psalmist], its sacra-

---

[57]Ibid., p. 797.
[58]Leslie C. Allen, *Psalms 101–150*, WBC (Waco: Word, 1983), p. 242.
[59]Ibid.
[60]Ibid.
[61]Ibid., pp. 242-43.

mental role in God's revealed purposes as reflection of the divine, could permit no lesser retribution. It is his love for God that makes him curse: his God is not mocked."[62] Perhaps one may be permitted to ask: but is his God the Father of Jesus Christ?

From yet another part of the contemporary theological spectrum comes a different kind of attempt at justifying the words of the psalmist in Psalm 137:9. The author appeals to the concept of God's justice and tries to put the verse in the context of other passages that stress God's justice and punishment of sinners. He concludes: "When the psalmist prays for Babylon to have its infants dashed against the rocks, he is asking that the law of retribution be carried out through God's prescribed means (a warring nation) to punish Babylon with the same evil Babylon had inflicted on Israel. He is invoking God for the judicial punishment of the wicked."[63] Apparently, understood in this way, the psalm verse becomes an acceptable prayer for Christians. This is highly questionable, and many Christians would not agree. First of all, it is not clear that this is what the psalmist is wishing for. Is he really "invoking God for the judicial punishment of the wicked"? Is this not reading a more abstract theological idea into a verse that expresses a genocidal wish? Second, is the "law of retribution" (*lex talionis*) really compatible with Christian teaching? Does God really use a "warring nation" to carry out his punishments? Undoubtedly there are those who would answer positively. Many others would not. We have in this psalm a problem similar to that posed by the annihilation of the nations in Deuteronomy and Joshua already treated earlier. Can we imagine that God engages in collective punishment, even of infants? I prefer the answer of John Chrysostom: "The teaching of the New Testament is not like that."[64]

Before leaving the problem of the imprecatory psalms, another modern

---

[62]Ibid., p. 243.

[63]Steven J. Cole, "Psalm 137: Difficult Words, but True," *Bible.org.* https://bible.org/book/export/html/21989.

[64]One suspects that the inability to let go of such a problematic verse may be due to presuppositions about the nature of the biblical text or differing biblical "theologies," a subject I cannot explore here. However, one may usefully consult Justin S. Holcomb, *Christian Theologies of Scripture: A Comparative Introduction* (New York: New York University Press, 2006).

work on the subject of the Psalms is worth considering.[65] Twenty years ago William Holladay published a work on the use and interpretation of the Psalms throughout history that offers a wealth of information. He also attempts to deal with the problem of the cursing psalms. Although he is well versed in the early Christian commentaries on the Psalms, he does not seem fully aware of the presuppositions and rules followed by Origen and many others. In his summary of Origen's work, he praises him for his awareness of form-critical and rhetorical shifts in the text, his ability to find Christian meaning in the text and scriptural parallels, but his final comment is: "But he also quickly finds opportunity for the kind of philosophical reflection that is more an expression of his Neoplatonic culture than of the mind-set of the Old Testament."[66] This would seem to suggest that the "mind-set of the Old Testament" is the norm for interpretation. However, his discussion considered as a whole is more nuanced than that, and he does investigate in detail the interpretation of the Psalms in the early Christian writings. In a later chapter titled "Censored Texts" he takes up the question of the cursing psalms and asks "whether it is appropriate to omit psalms, or portions of psalms, from our worship."[67] He reviews the various problematic psalms or portions of psalms, noting in regard to Psalm 137:9 that "these words are particularly harsh as an ending for the psalm."[68] His review of texts omitted in the Roman Catholic Liturgy of the Hours leads to the conclusion that all of the omissions refer to the psalmist's enemies, and this in turn leads to a more lengthy consideration of the attitude Christians should have toward their enemies. Among his considerations are that "Jesus taught Christians to love their enemies," "that Christians are warned in many ways against self-righteousness" and "that it is not legitimate for Christians to wish death on their enemies."[69] This leads to the conclusion that expressions "such as are found in Pss 55:16;

---

[65]William L. Holladay, *The Psalms Through Three Thousand Years: Prayerbook of a Cloud of Witnesses* (Minneapolis: Fortress, 1993).

[66]Ibid., p. 171.

[67]Ibid., p. 304.

[68]Ibid., p. 307.

[69]Ibid., p. 312.

58:11; or 137:9 are excluded for Christians" and the further conclusion "that in Christian worship we are occasionally justified in omitting certain sequences in the Psalms."[70] Holladay finds similar omissions in the Common Lectionary (Protestant) and notes the "constant tendency the church has to bypass material with a negative import."[71]

However, Holladay is not really happy with this solution and in a later chapter expresses the dilemma of either reading and reciting the full Psalter "and risk more than one shudder at the savage wishes expressed there toward personal and national enemies" or reading and reciting "a bowdlerized Psalter as it comes to us sanitized by some lectionary or hymnal committee and risk missing the grittiness of the biblical faith."[72] He poses the question in terms of an opposition between the canonical principle reflected in 1 Timothy 3:16, that "all scripture is inspired by God and is useful" versus "wondering what is useful about celebrating the bashing of Babylonian babies' brains."[73] His solution is to propose a "christological" reading of the Psalms, "to do in our day what the church fathers and the Reformers did less systematically in their day."[74] Although he offers many examples of such interpretation, he does not offer such a reading in regard to Psalm 137:9.

Here we must part company with him and suggest that in fact many of the church fathers did much more systematically and coherently what he is proposing. Naturally he does not call what he is proposing an "allegorical" interpretation, but it is certainly not a literal one. The text says one thing and he proposes to read it as saying another. This is what the fathers of the church were doing. Their rules were more complicated and it certainly takes more work to dig out their explanations today, but they gave the Psalms a sense consistent with Christian belief. This required a work of preparation and instruction in the tradition of interpretation so that at the time of prayer the person reciting Psalm 137:9 would not think of real

---

[70]Ibid., p. 313.
[71]Ibid., p. 314.
[72]Ibid., p. 346.
[73]Ibid.
[74]Ibid.

babies' heads but rather of smashing his or her aggressive and destructive thoughts on the rock, which is Christ, as explained in chapter seven.

Summary: In comparing the interpretation offered by ancient and modern writers of several texts or sets of texts, we have seen that in some cases (Gen 1–4) the problematic surrounding ancient and modern interpretations is different. Ancient and modern interpreters are responding to different concerns. In other cases (the annihilation of the nations in Joshua and the cursing psalms), different ideas about the nature or concept of "Scripture" seem to be operative, which prevent some modern commentators from letting go of a literal meaning that ancient authors had no difficulty rejecting on "theological" grounds. The imprecatory passages in the book of Psalms offer a particular challenge when used as Christian prayer.

CONCLUDING REFLECTIONS

In recent centuries, because of a growing historical consciousness, the presuppositions and rules of ancient interpretation have been rendered inoperable. For example, authors beginning with Philo and then followed by Origen, Eusebius, Didymus, Jerome and many others eagerly sought out supposed etymologies of Hebrew names, because they thought these provided clues to the deeper or hidden meaning of texts. We know now (at least since the late eighteenth century) that Hebrew was not the original language of the human race and that the etymologies of the Hebrew names used in order to discover hidden meanings do not in fact correspond to the real meanings of the words. Because of modern linguistic and philological studies, we know now that human languages developed like a genealogical tree and we have reached the conclusion that there is not and never was a hidden meaning in these names. We are no longer able to accept the ancient idea that sacred texts in general have a hidden meaning, and this removes the theoretical basis of the search for an allegorical meaning. Thus we cannot share Origen's conviction that Christ can be found throughout and beneath the text of the Old Testament.[75] Modern interpretative methods aim at establishing, not the hidden meaning suited to us, but the original historical meaning. Thus the ancient solution of finding a hidden acceptable meaning in order to neutralize or displace the unacceptable literal meaning is excluded.

However, the theological difficulty with these texts remains, for it is a perennial problem, or at least a problem that will remain as long as the texts are read and used to guide, regulate and inspire human behavior. "God is not like a man," but in these ancient texts God is portrayed as a man (*anthrōpomorphos*) and with human passions (*anthrōpopathos*). It is necessary to distinguish also between the true theological problem, that is, how to understand the nature of God, and the practical problem, which is relevant, that the concept of God is used to justify human behavior that is destructive. Those who have "false opinions and make impious or ignorant assertions about God," to use the words of Origen, justify their behavior with their conception of God. The "letter kills," according to Origen, literally and spiritually.[76] "False" opinions about God include not only relatively innocent notions such as that God has eyes, a mouth and speaks literally, but also that he is angry, vindictive, punishes to the third and fourth generation innocent people, conducts wars and even annihilates entire peoples, today more commonly called genocide. It is not difficult for the "simple" (today more commonly called literalists) to find inspiration and justification for these ideas in the Bible. Both Plato and

---

[75]For a more complete exposition of this idea, see my articles, "Old Testament" and "Scripture," in *The Westminster Handbook to Origen*, ed. John Anthony McGuckin (Louisville, KY: Westminster John Knox, 2004), pp. 159-62 and 197-201.

[76]The phrase comes from 2 Cor 3:6. Origen makes reference to the phrase many times. In his homily 11 on Numbers, referring to the wise scribe of the kingdom mentioned in Mt 13:52, he says: "Now it will be [the task] of a wise scribe, and of one who is 'instructed about the kingdom of God, who knows how to bring forth new and old things from these treasures,' to know how in each passage of Scripture either to reject completely the 'letter that kills' and to seek 'the spirit that gives life,' or to confirm it in every way and prove the teaching of the letter to be useful and necessary, or to fittingly and properly introduce a mystical meaning, even while the historical sense remains." Origen, *Homilies on Numbers*, trans. Thomas P. Scheck, ed. Christopher A. Hall, ACT (Downers Grove, IL: IVP Academic, 2009), pp. 51-52. Gregory of Nyssa also, in his vigorous defense of figurative interpretation, insists that "one ought not in every instance to remain with the letter (since the obvious sense of the words often does us harm when it comes to the virtuous life). . . . This moreover is why he says, 'The letter kills, but the spirit gives life'" (2 Cor 3:6). Gregory of Nyssa, *Homilies on the Song of Songs*, trans. Richard A. Norris Jr. (Atlanta: Society of Biblical Literature, 2012), p. 5.

Origen were right to be concerned about the influence of texts on human behavior. However, their solutions were different. Origen and other early Christian authors sought not to ban the texts but to interpret them in a way fitting to God and consistent with belief that the Word of God in the fullest sense is Jesus Christ. In him alone do we find the fullness of revelation, and all the earlier writings must be evaluated in the light of this revelation of the divine philanthropy, the love of God for the human race.

A theological interpretation of the Scriptures is no less relevant today than it was in the early centuries of the church. The original historical meaning of the these texts is not sufficient, especially in an era of increasing literalist readings.[77] Indeed, the original historical meaning is often quite elusive because of the inner-scriptural interpretative process involved in the historical development of the texts that came to be included in both Testaments. In any case there is no reason why the "real" and permanently valid meaning for Christians should be identified with the "original" meaning of the Old Testament texts. Many were reinterpreted already in the New Testament. We must always ask how these texts can be understood by Christians, and this question involves theology, the discourse about the nature of God. The literal, isolated text is not normative, but rather theology, not in the broad, all-inclusive sense in which it is often used now nor in the confessional sense of "Lutheran," "Calvinist" or "Catholic" theology, but in the original sense of the word, the discussion about the nature of God. In this sense the theological question should be primary in the interpretation of Scripture today. Perhaps the most enduring and fitting solution remains that of Philo, Origen and John Chrysostom with which we began: God spoke then like a father to his children. That should not be confused with the way he really is in himself. God does not behave like humans.

---

[77]I hesitate to use the word *fundamentalist* to describe these readings because the word has come to be used recently very differently from its original sense a hundred years ago. Now it seems to be used often simply to express disapproval or disdain.

Appendix

Ancient Christian Hermeneutics

THE PRESUPPOSITIONS, THE CRITERIA
AND THE RULES EMPLOYED[1]

PASSING REFERENCES HAVE BEEN MADE in this book to various rules and procedures employed by ancient Christian writers in interpreting the Scriptures. Many of these are quite different from those used today by contemporary interpreters. Therefore it seems useful to gather some of the more important ones together in this appendix. These have been divided into presuppositions about the nature of the text, criteria for establishing the meaning and some rules to be used in finding the meaning. These divisions are for the sake of organizing the material. Others might prefer to call some things "rules" that I have called "criteria." In what follows Origen of Alexandria (died ca. 254) is cited often because he is the first Christian writer to have attempted to codify the procedures for interpreting the Scriptures and his influence on later writers is immeasurable.

1. PRESUPPOSITIONS ABOUT THE NATURE OF THE
TEXT OF THE SCRIPTURES

To understand the rules and procedures employed by ancient Christian interpreters in their search for the meaning of the Scriptures, it is nec-

---

[1]This appendix draws on material previously published in various essays collected in Mark Sheridan, *From the Nile to the Rhone and Beyond: Studies in Early Monastic Literature and Scriptural Interpretation* (Rome: Pontificio Ateneo Sant'Anselmo, 2012), and from the introduction to Mark Sheridan, ed., *Genesis 12–50*, ACCS OT 2 (Downers Grove, IL: InterVarsity Press, 2002).

essary above all to appreciate the presuppositions about the nature of the Scriptures with which they approached their task. The understanding of or the concept of "Sacred Scripture" has not been a constant in Jewish and Christian history.[2] Even in antiquity one can perceive development of the concept.

a. The Scriptures contain hidden meaning. Of the Hellenistic Jewish interpreters who exerted a direct influence on the development of Christian interpretation, Philo of Alexandria was by far the most important. In his work *On the Contemplative Life*, describing the way of life of the Jewish community known as the Therapeutae, Philo observes: "For to these people the whole law book seems to resemble a living creature with the literal ordinances for its body and for its soul the invisible mind laid up in its wording."[3] The word "mind" (*nous*) used here can also be translated as "meaning." This invisible meaning, Philo explains, is conveyed by allegory. The content made available through allegorical interpretation was often teaching about morals (ethics) and nature (physics) drawn from the philosophical tradition. This was justified in Hellenistic Jewish exegesis (and also later in Christian interpretation) on the grounds that the philosophers had borrowed from Moses, who had lived earlier than all the philosophers.

Origen, inspired by the anthropology found in 1 Thessalonians 5:23,[4] expanded this idea of the body and soul of Scripture to include the "spirit" of Scripture as well: "For just as man consists of body, soul and spirit, so in the same way does the scripture, which has been prepared by God to be given for man's salvation."[5] Origen connected this with the saying of Proverbs 22:20: "Now then, copy them for yourselves three times over" (NETS), which he interpreted as three senses or levels of meaning to be found in the Scriptures. He also related these three senses to three different

---

[2]For a survey of various "theologies" of Scripture see Justin S. Holcomb, *Christian Theologies of Scripture: A Comparative Introduction* (New York: New York University Press, 2006).
[3]Philo, LCL 363:161.
[4]1 Thess 5:23: "and may your spirit and soul and body be kept sound and blameless at the coming of our Lord Jesus Christ" (RSV).
[5]Origen, *PArch* 4.2.4; G. W. Butterworth, trans., *On First Principles* (London: SPCK, 1936), p. 276.

stages of initiation in the spiritual life of the Christian: beginners, those who had progressed and the advanced or "perfect," a distinction inspired by 1 Corinthians 2–3.

The designation of Jesus in John's Gospel as the "Word" (*logos*) made it possible for Origen to identify the Scriptures understood as the "Word of God" with Jesus, the eternal Word of God become flesh. The same eternal Word is present in both, and thus the real subject of the Old Testament Scriptures is also Jesus. He is the key to interpreting the Scriptures correctly. According to Paul, the face of Moses was covered by a veil (2 Cor 3:7-18), a reference to Exodus 34:33-34. "Moses" here means the Law, or the first five books of the Bible. When the veil is taken away, however, Christ is revealed as already present in the entire Old Testament. For example, commenting on the verse of the Canticle in which the bridegroom is pictured "leaping upon the mountains, / bounding over the hills" (Song 2:8), he observes: "when the veil is removed for the Bride, that is, for the Church that has turned to God, she suddenly sees Him leaping upon those mountains—that is, the books of the Law; and on the hills of the prophetical writings. . . . Turning the pages of the prophets one by one, for instance, she finds Christ springing forth from them."[6] The "veil" as interpreted by Origen is often simply the literal historical account or the "letter."[7] In order to remove this veil, however, the coming of Christ was indispensable. The light contained in the Law of Moses, covered by a veil, shown forth at the coming of Christ, when the veil was removed and it became possible to have "knowledge of the goods of which the literal expression contained the shadow."[8] For Origen it is the divine Word of God incarnate who ties all together, the ancient Scriptures understood largely as prophecy and the fullness of revelation in the person of Jesus.[9]

---

[6]Origen, *ComCt* 3 (2:8).

[7]For other examples of the use of this text, see Origen, *HomGn* 2.3; 7.1; 12.1; *HomLev* 1.1; *HomNum* 26.3.

[8]Ibid., *PArch* 4.1.6.

[9]However, the idea that the Scriptures contain hidden or secret meanings was not limited to Hellenistic Jewish or Christian interpreters. James Kugel has noted "the assumption that all ancient interpreters seem to share is that the Bible is a fundamentally cryptic document." Kugel argues that the roots of the assumption go back to the Bible itself. James L. Kugel, *The Bible As It Was* (Cambridge, MA: Harvard University Press, 1997), pp. 2, 18.

Later writers developed the idea of multiple senses of the Scriptures even further. Although the terminology is found first in Gregory of Nyssa, the first clear explanation of the fourfold sense to become so popular in the Latin Middle Ages is found in the fourteenth *Conference* of John Cassian. In fact Cassian distinguishes between the literal sense and three spiritual ones. He offers the city of Jerusalem as the primary example. In its literal sense, it is the historical city often mentioned in the Scriptures and still in existence. On the "tropological" level (moral explanation), it represents the human soul often addressed by God as "daughter Sion." On the "allegorical" level, it represents the church or the economy of salvation. And on the "anagogical" level it is the Jerusalem above, the future city of the blessed waiting to be revealed.[10] Many other passages and figures in the Scriptures can be understood to have multiple levels of meaning.

The fundamental understanding of the Scriptures as a book containing hidden meaning, having a body and a soul, or body, soul and spirit, can be illustrated in several other ways. Already before Origen, Clement of Alexandria had developed an extensive theoretical approach to the nature of the Scriptures. For Clement, the Scriptures, like all sacred texts, are by their nature enigmatic.[11] The Word of God is not in the first place the written Scriptures, but the divine Logos. It is he who by becoming himself the gospel "breaks the mystic silence of the prophetic enigmas."[12] Thus Christ, the Word of God, is the hermeneutical key for all of the written Scriptures. The Logos acts in fact as hierophant (one who shows the holy), who initiates his own into the truly sacred mysteries of the Father, an exegetical activity, since the divine mysteries are hidden in the Scriptures.[13]

This belief in the hidden or nonliteral meaning of the Scriptures is revealed also in the early Christian writers' use of a common terminology to indicate such a meaning, stemming from the Greek word *ainittetai*, which

---

[10]John Cassian, *The Conferences*, 14.8.3.
[11]Clement of Alexandria, *Strom.* 5.4-10.
[12]Ibid., *Prot.* 1.10.1; trans. from S. Keough, "Exegesis Worthy of God: The Development of Biblical Interpretation in Alexandria" (PhD diss., University of St. Michael's College, Toronto, 2007), pp. 139-40.
[13]Clement of Alexandria, *Prot.* 12.120.1.

means "to hint or to indicate obscurely." Its root is the same as the word "enigma" (*aenigma*), defined by some in antiquity as particularly obscure allegory. The word was employed first in Homeric exegesis, precisely to indicate a nonliteral meaning. In a manual of interpretation from the first century, the writer states: "Homer, we discover is much the same in both epics, not telling disreputable tales of the gods, but giving enigmatic hints [*ainittomenōn*] by means of the technique we have been studying."[14] The "hints" are generally to philosophical allegories. The same terminology can be found in Philo; Clement of Alexandria; Origen; Eusebius; Didymus; Cyril of Alexandria; and the Antiochenes, Diodore, Chrysostom, Theodore and Theodoret. Thus, in commenting on Psalm 2:2, "The kings of the earth presented themselves, and the rulers came together in concert," Diodore has no difficulty in saying that the text is hinting at Herod and Pilate.[15] Similarly, in explaining Psalm 30:8 (29:9 LXX): "I shall cry to you, Lord, and make my petition to my God," Diodore says that David is hinting at the Father and the Son.[16] Commenting on the phrase "Let them have control over the fishes of the sea" in Genesis 1:26, John Chrysostom writes: "Evidently he is already revealing to us at this point some mystery lying hidden. Who are to have control? Quite clearly he has spoken this way to hint at the formation of woman. Do you see how there is nothing in Sacred Scripture which is contained there idly or to no purpose? Instead, even the chance word has treasure stored up in it."[17] Notwithstanding differences over the use of the word "allegory," the difference in basic assumptions about the nature of Scripture between Origen and Chrysostom is not great.

Another indication of the ancient concept of Scripture can be seen in the various phrases used to designate or describe the Scriptures in antiquity. Among the many terms used to designate the Scriptures are the phrases the "sacred oracles" or "divine oracles," which translate a variety of

---

[14]Donald A. Russell and David Konstan, *Heraclitus: Homeric Problems*, Writings from the Greco-Roman World (Atlanta: Society of Biblical Literature, 2005), p. 9; see also pp. 69-71.

[15]Diodore of Tarsus, *Commentary on Psalms 1–51*, trans. Robert C. Hill, Writings from the Greco-Roman World (Atlanta: Society of Biblical Literature, 2005), p. 7.

[16]Ibid., pp. 90-91.

[17]John Chrysostom, *Homilies on Genesis* 10.7; FC 74:132.

Greek expressions. The expressions are first used of the Jewish Scriptures by Philo. Philo often uses the term "oracle" (*chrēsmos*) to indicate a particular text or to cite a text from the Pentateuch, but he also employs the term in the plural (*chrēsmoi*) to describe the contents of the Pentateuch or to refer to it as a whole. In the second book of the *Life of Moses* he states: "Now I am fully aware that all things written in the sacred books [*ieroi biblio*] are oracles [*chrēsmoi*] delivered through Moses."[18] The term "oracles" (*chrēsmoi*) is placed in parallel with the "sacred books" (*ieroi bibloi*) in another text where Genesis 24:1 is cited.[19] Philo uses both expressions for "oracle" (*chrēsmoi* and *logia*) many times with the plural definite article to indicate the Scriptures as a whole. Sometimes these expressions are qualified as sacred (*ieroi*) or divine (*theia*). This usage suggests that the Scriptures are a collection of oracles, since the terms in the singular refer to specific utterances of oracles.[20]

This terminology, which had its origin in the oracles of Greek popular religion, is also found in the Greek translation of the Old Testament, the Septuagint. One example in the New Testament is of particular interest. In Romans 3:1 Paul asks rhetorically: "Then what advantage has the Jew? Or what is the value of circumcision?" He answers in Romans 3:2: "Much in every way. For in the first place the Jews were entrusted with the oracles [*logia*] of God." Origen comments that even though the divine oracles are now entrusted to the Gentiles, nevertheless, according to Paul, they were entrusted first to the Jews. Then he continues: "I ask myself, however, what are those oracles of God of which it is said, 'which were entrusted to them as the first': whether Paul says that referring to the letters and to the books of the law, or to the meaning and to the interpretation of it? We see in fact that very many of the Jews, who are always studying, from infancy to old age, but do not ever arrive at the knowledge of the truth."[21] The problem from Origen's point of view is that the Jews received only the letter of the

---

[18]Philo, *Mos.* 2.188; LCL 289:543.

[19]Philo, *Sobr.* 17.

[20]See H. Burkhardt, *Die Inspiration heiliger schriften bei Philon von Alexandrien* (Giessen/Basel: Brunnen, 1992), pp. 112-25, for a detailed analysis of the numerous passages where Philo employs these terms.

[21]Origen, *ComRm* 2.14 (915B-916B).

oracles and not the true meaning. It is the very nature of oracles to be obscure and require interpretation. This is what the Jews were unable to do because they clung to the letter.

Many other Christian writers after Origen used this terminology to refer to the Scriptures. Eusebius, for example, refers to the Scriptures saying: "the divine oracles teach" and "the oracles of the Hebrews preserve the memory."[22] In another case he cites Psalm 33:16-19 saying how "very trustworthy and true are the divine oracles."[23]

b. God is the author of the text: "Divine writings" and "inspiration." One of the most important presuppositions about their nature of the Scriptures is that the text of Scripture is "divine writing," not human. Through an examination of the fulfillment of the "oracles" of Christ (Mt 7:22; 24:14) and of other prophetic utterances in the Scriptures (Gen 49:10; Hos 3:4), Origen demonstrates the divine nature of the Scriptures or, as he says, that they are "divine writings."[24] Origen accepts the common doctrine that the Holy Spirit inspired all the authors of Scripture, whether Moses or the apostles, to such an extent that the Holy Spirit is to be considered the true author of the sacred texts.[25] The corollary of this is that "the words which are believed by us to be from God are not the compositions of men,"[26] a conclusion that has important consequences for the concept of "Scripture" and its interpretation. The same idea is restated further on: "the sacred books are not the works of men, but . . . they were composed and have come down to us as a result of the inspiration of the Holy Spirit by the will of the Father of the universe through Jesus Christ."[27]

One consequence of the idea of the divine, not human, composition of Scripture is that God is the author of the text even in (what a modern writer might consider) its most insignificant details. Commenting on Genesis 22:1, where God calls out "Abraham, Abraham," Origen exhorts

---

[22]Eusebius, *Praep evang.* 1.1.8; 2.6.12.

[23]Eusebius, *Hist. eccl.* 9.9.7.

[24]Origen, *PArch* 4.1.2-3.

[25]Ibid., *PArch* 1, praef. 4; 1.3.1; 4.2.7; 4.3.14; *CCels* 3.3; 5.60; *ComMt* 14.4; *HomGn* 7.1; *HomEx* 2.1; *HomNum* 1.1; 2.1; *HomJos* 8.6; *Hom 1R(1S)* 5.4.

[26]Origen, *PArch* 4.1.6; Butterworth, p. 265.

[27]Ibid., 4.2.2; Butterworth, p. 272.

his congregation, "Observe each detail which has been written. For, if one knows how to dig into the depth, he will find a treasure in the details, and perhaps also, the precious jewels of the mysteries lie hidden where they are not esteemed."[28] The phrase "a treasure in the details" could be taken as emblematic for a certain understanding of the nature of the biblical text itself. In this particular case Origen goes on to explain that nowhere had God ever called Abraham by the name Abram nor had he ever said "Abram, Abram." The reason why God never called Abraham by the name Abram is that he could not call him by a name that was to be abolished, but only by the name that he himself gave, the name that means "I have made you a father of many nations" (Gen 17:5). Similar details such as "the high land" (Gen 22:2 LXX) and "the third day" (Gen 22:3) serve as a springboard for spiritual or christological interpretations.[29] Thus details are given a high significance that they did not have in the original context of the narrative of the sacrifice of Isaac. This procedure may even run counter to the normal rules of rhetoric, as in the case of Origen's interpretation of "the hand of Moses and Aaron" (Num 33:1 LXX) to represent two aspects of the spiritual life, the practical and the contemplative, inseparably united (one hand) even though this is a clear case of synecdoche (use of singular for plural), a well-known figure of speech.[30] Such procedures are possible because of the basic conception of the text as an oracular, encoded text with an esoteric meaning, even if the text itself is public and widely diffused. John Chrysostom follows a similar procedure with his emphasis on the "exactness of the text" (*akribeia*).

2. CRITERIA FOR A CORRECT INTERPRETATION

a. It must be "worthy of God." An important criterion of interpretation, which flows from the presuppositions about the nature of the text, is that its real meaning must be "worthy of the divine majesty."[31] In this phrase we can perceive an ancient idea that had been used as a hermeneutical tool

---

[28]Origen, *HomGn* 8.1.
[29]Ibid., 8.3-4.
[30]Origen, *HomNum* 27.6.
[31]Origen, *HomLev* 7.5.

in the interpretation of Homer and then later by Philo in the interpretation of the Law of Moses, where its most characteristic expressions are found in the word *theoprepēs*, meaning "fitting" or "appropriate" to God and "worthy of God" (*axios tou theou*). The concept is formulated by Origen also in the context of the controversial principle of the missing literal sense (*defectus litterae*). He explains that certain stumbling blocks and impossibilities have been inserted in the Law and the History "in order that we may not be completely drawn away by the sheer attractiveness of the language, and so either reject the true doctrines absolutely, on the ground that we learn from the scriptures nothing worthy of God, or else by never moving away from the letter fail to learn anything of the more divine element."[32] The more skilful and inquiring readers may thus "gain a sound conviction of the necessity of seeking in such instances a meaning worthy of God."[33] This principle as well as the accompanying ideas of illogical (*alogon*) and impossible (*adynaton*) things inserted into the text by the divine author in order to incite the reader to seek a suitable meaning are already used extensively by Philo of Alexandria.

These presuppositions produce a paradoxical situation: the text on the literal level may not be worthy of God, but when it is given a spiritual interpretation it can be seen to be divine and, viewed as a divine composition, it is superior to all other human texts. Origen remarks: "And he who approaches the prophetic words with care and attention will feel from his very reading a trace of their divine inspiration [*to entheon*] and will be convinced by his own feelings that the words which are believed by us to be from God are not the compositions of men."[34] The reader is able to perceive the inspired nature (*to entheon*) of the Scripture through a kind of mystical transport or "enthusiasm" (*enthysiasmos*). It may be possible to perceive this even on the level of the literal text, but certainly not in the literal level of many or most texts of the Old Testament, for Origen says explicitly that it was not possible before the advent of Christ. What is per-

---

[32]Origen, *PArch*, 4.2.9; Butterworth, p. 285.
[33]Ibid., 4.2.9; Butterworth, p. 287.
[34]Ibid., 4.1.6; Butterworth, p. 265.

ceived then is not the literal text but the "spiritual nature" or the "light" contained within the Law of Moses.[35]

b. The Scriptures are "for us" and therefore must be "useful." Origen often cites 1 Corinthians 10, especially 1 Corinthians 10:6, 11,[36] to emphasize that the Scriptures were written "for us," and reach their fulfillment in the present time (the time of the church), which is also understood as the end of the ages. The text is often cited as an introduction to moral exhortation, which is indeed the original Pauline context of 1 Corinthians 10:1-11. Thus, in commenting on the expression "by mud and bricks" (Exod 1:14) Origen states: "These words were not written to instruct us in history, nor must we think that the divine books narrate the acts of the Egyptians. What has been written 'has been written for our instruction' and admonition."[37] There follows a moral exhortation in which the king of Egypt "who knew not Joseph" is interpreted as the devil.

Similarly, in dealing with the command of the king of Egypt to the midwives to kill the male children of the Israelites, Origen states: "But we, who have learned that all things which are written are written not to relate ancient history, but for our discipline and use, understand that these things which are said also happen now not only in this world, which is figuratively called Egypt, but in each one of us also."[38] He then continues the allegorical interpretation, explaining that the passions of the flesh are symbolized by the females but the male represents the rational sense and the intellectual spirit. It is this that the devil (the king of Egypt) wishes to destroy.[39]

The notion of the actuality of the scriptures seems to be the presupposition for allegorizing. Indeed, the idea of the actuality of Scripture is virtually a corollary of the notion of Scripture itself and the result of the canonization of the texts in the society. The notion that the Scriptures were

---

[35]Origen, *PArch* 4.1.6; see also *ComJn* 1.30 (33.205); *CCels* 6.5.

[36]1 Cor 10:6: "Now these things occurred as examples for us, so that we might not desire evil as they did"; 1 Cor 10:11: "Now these things happened to them as a warning, but they were written down for our instruction, upon whom the end of the ages has come."

[37]Origen, *HomEx* 1.5.

[38]Ibid., 2.1.

[39]Among the other texts where Origen cites 1 Cor 10:6, 11, may be mentioned *HomEx* 7.4; *HomJos* 5.2; *HomJr* 12.3; 19.15; *HomJd* 2.3; *HomEz* 12.2.

written "for us," that they are therefore to be interpreted in reference to us and our situation, is hardly original with Paul or Origen. It can be detected already in Deuteronomy in the emphasis on "today" (Deut 4:1-3), which is no longer the time of the events being related but the time when Moses recounted the events once again before the entrance into the Promised Land ("Deuteronomy" means the second giving of the law). In fact, the Deuteronomist had in mind his own time many centuries after Moses.[40] The author of the *Letter of Aristeas* (second century B.C.) shows a similar concern for the actuality of the text, which he achieves through allegory.[41] To this general idea of the actuality of the Scriptures Paul has added the concept of the two ages (1 Cor 10:11), which considerably facilitates the possibility of allegorical comparisons between the two ages, then and now, such as is found in 1 Corinthians 10:1-11 and Galatians 4:21-24. While the notion of the two ages helps to specify the content of the allegory, it is not essential to the idea of the actuality of the Scriptures or to the allegorical procedure itself.

Since the text is "for us," it must also have a meaning that is "useful" to us, a criterion of interpretation that had already been developed by Philo and was suggested also by the affirmation that all Scripture is useful (2 Tim 3:16). "Useful" generally means that which is helpful for moral or spiritual nourishment.[42] The presence of this criterion has been noted in a number of authors beginning with Origen and including Didymus, Gregory of Nyssa, Diodore, Theodore of Mopsuestia, Cyril and Hesychius.[43] Origen, speaking

---

[40]The notion of the actuality of the Scriptures can be found in Deuteronomy also in the insistent phrase "which I command you this day" (e.g., Deut 4:40) and in the statement "not with our fathers did the LORD make this covenant, but with us, who are all of us here alive this day" (Deut 5:3).

[41]"All the rules which he has laid down with what is permitted in the case of these birds and other animals, he has enacted with the object of teaching us a moral lesson. For the division of the hoof and the separation of the claws are intended to teach us that we must discriminate between our individual actions with a view to the practice of virtue." *The Letter of Aristeas* 150–51, R. H. Charles, ed., *The Apocrypha and Pseudepigrapha of the Old Testament* (Oxford: Clarendon, 1913), 1:108.

[42]See Mark Sheridan, "The Concept of the 'Useful' as an Exegetical Tool in Patristic Exegesis," *Studia Patristica* 39, ed. F. Young, M. Edwards and P. Parvis, papers presented at the Fourteenth International Conference on Patristic Studies, Oxford, 2003 (Leuven: Peeters, 2006), pp. 253-57.

[43]Manlio Simonetti, *Lettera e/o Allegoria: Un contributo alla storia dell'esegesi patristica* (Rome: Institutum Patristicum "Augustinianum," 1985), p. 79, notes that one of Origen's fundamental exegetical principles is practical, so that all the Scriptures, in which every word has its precise reason for being there, must result in what is spiritually useful to the interpreter.

in one of his homilies on Joshua about the obscurity of the Scriptures and the difficulty of understanding them, cites it directly and concludes, "Thus if it is 'inspired by divine influence and is useful,' we ought to believe that it is useful even if we do not discern the usefulness."[44] He compares the Scriptures to food or drink prescribed by a physician, whose usefulness we do not immediately perceive but which works its effects with time, and concludes, "we should also believe this about Holy Scripture, that it is useful and benefits the soul even if our perception at the present does not understand why."[45] He insists that "there is a certain strength in Holy Scripture that may avail the reader, even without explanation."[46] However, the real usefulness of Scripture does not lie on this level, but in "the explanation of hidden and secret things," as he hints even in this passage.

Commenting on the story of Deborah in the book of Judges (Judg 4:4-6), after quoting 2 Timothy 3:16 explicitly, Origen asks what profit it is to us if we hear that Deborah was the wife of Lappidoth and was sitting under a palm tree.[47] The only way to make the text useful is to give it an allegorical interpretation. Likewise, interpreting the Canticle where the bridegroom invites the bride to show her face (Song 2:13-14), Origen remarks: "But these things seem to me to afford no profit to the readers as far as the story goes; nor do they maintain any continuous narrative such as we find in other Scripture stories. It is necessary, therefore, rather to give them all a spiritual meaning."[48] That spiritual meaning refers of course to the moral life of the individual soul, the hermeneutical key that Origen applies along with that of the church throughout his interpretation of the Canticle.[49] The criterion of usefulness is applied not only to historical narrative but to the mass of legislation as well. Thus Origen writes: "A similar method can be discerned also in the law, where it is often possible to find a precept that is useful for its own sake, and suitable to the time when the law was given.

[44]Origen, HomJos 20.2; FC 105:177.
[45]Ibid.
[46]Origen, HomJos 20.2; FC 105: 178.
[47]Origen, HomJd 5.1.
[48]Origen, ComCt 4.15; ACW 26:247.
[49]See ComCt 1.1.

Sometimes, however, the precept does not appear to be useful."[50] That means that it must be interpreted spiritually, since all Scripture is useful.

3. Some Rules of Interpretation

a. Interpreting the Scriptures by means of the Scriptures. The phrase "spiritual things with spiritual things" (1 Cor 2:13)[51] denotes a hermeneutical procedure that permeates the exegetical work of Origen as well as that of many other ancient exegetes. In his homily on the ark in Genesis, Origen remarks toward the end: "To be sure, if someone can, at leisure, bring together Scripture with Scripture, and compare divine Scripture and fit together 'spiritual things with spiritual' we are not unmindful that he will discover in this passage many secrets of a profound and hidden mystery."[52] For the patristic exegete it is axiomatic that one should seek the explanation of a term or a figure in other texts where the same word is used. To the modern interpreter, conditioned as he is to literary genres and different historical contexts, it seems almost capricious to explain a passage in one book by means of a passage having only a slight verbal similarity from another book of a different literary genre written in a different epoch. To the patristic exegete (or at least the Alexandrian exegete), such a procedure was necessary and absolutely consistent with the basic premise of the unified authorship of Scripture.

Origen invokes this procedure explaining how to discover the meaning of passages that, taken literally, are impossible.

> Accordingly he who reads in an exact manner must, in obedience to the Saviour's precept which says, "Search the scriptures," carefully investigate how far the literal meaning is true and how far it is impossible, and to the utmost of his power must trace out from the use of similar expressions the meaning scattered everywhere through the scriptures of that which when taken literally is impossible.[53]

---

[50]Origen, *PArch* 4.2.9; Butterworth, p. 286.

[51]Origen's translation. He read the Greek terms *pneumatikois* and *pneumatika* as neuters and as synonyms for "words of Scripture." See F. Cocchini, *Il Paolo di Origene*, Verba Seniorum (Roma: Edizioni Studium, 1992), pp. 118-19.

[52]Origen, *HomGn* 2.6.

[53]Origen, *PArch* 4.3.5; Butterworth, p. 296.

Elsewhere Origen relates a simile that he heard from a rabbi in which the Scriptures are compared to a house with a large number of locked rooms. Each room has a key, but the keys have been mixed up and dispersed throughout the house. The key then to one passage of Scripture is to be found in other passages. We are able to understand obscure passages of Scripture when we take as a point of departure a similar passage from another portion of Scripture, because "the principle of interpretation has been dispersed among them."[54] Origen puts this principle into practice in his commentary on the Canticle, where in order to explain Song 2:9, in which the beloved is compared to a gazelle or young stag, he assembles all references to these animals in other books of Scripture.[55]

This procedure of explaining Scripture by Scripture is based on the fundamental premise that the Holy Spirit is the true author of the whole Bible.[56]

A similar if not identical procedure can be found already in the New Testament in the writings of Paul. In Galatians 3:16 Paul constructs an exegetical chain using the word for "seed" found in Genesis 13:15 (Gen 17:8; 22:18; 24:7) and 2 Samuel 7:12-14. In Romans 4:1-8 he brings together Genesis 15:6 and Psalm 32:1-2 because of the hook word "reckon."[57] This exegetical principle was known later in rabbinic literature as *gezera shava*. However, in justifying his constant use of this procedure, Origen does not appeal so much to the example of Paul as to the principle itself, which he finds stated in 1 Corinthians 2:13 ("comparing spiritual things to spiritual").[58] Origen seems in fact to be the first to interpret this phrase as an exegetical principle.[59] The Jewish schools related texts on the basis of verbal simi-

---

[54]Origen, *Philoc* 2.3. For the most recent edition of this text, see Origène, *Philocalie*, ed. M. Harl and N. de Lange, SCh 302 (Paris: Editions du Cerf, 1983), pp. 244-43.

[55]Origen, *ComCt* 3.

[56]This is stated quite explicitly in *HomEz* 1.4, where Origen says that everything that has been written are words of the same God.

[57]See Richard B. Hays, *Echoes of Scripture in the Letters of Paul* (New Haven: Yale University Press, 1989), pp. 13, 55, 85. Carol Kern Stockhausen, *Moses' Veil and the Glory of the New Covenant*, Analecta Biblica 116 (Rome: Editrice Pontificio Istituto Biblico, 1989), pp. 26-27, 56-59, finds extensive use of this procedure in 2 Cor 3:1-6.

[58]The passages in which Origen appeals to this text are numerous. Among them may be mentioned *HomGn* 2.6; 6.3; 7.4; *HomEx* 1.2; *HomNum* 16.9; *HomEz* 1.2; 1.4; 6.4; *ComCt* 3; *ComJn* 13.361; *CCels* 4.71; 7.11.

[59]Francesca Cocchini, *Il Paolo di Origene*, Verba Seniorum (Rome: Edizioni Studium, 1992), p. 119.

larities, beginning with the school of Hillel at the end of the first century.[60] Origen could hardly have been ignorant of the fact that this method was employed in the Jewish and pagan schools, but he consistently appeals to Paul as his authority for the method. Thus, for Origen, Paul provided the rule and the example that bound the ancient Scriptures inextricably to the new revelation. Indeed, Origen often understands the phrase "spiritual things with spiritual things" to mean precisely the comparison of passages of the Old and New Testaments respectively.[61]

In keeping with the context of 1 Corinthians 2:13, Origen also insists that only one who is "spiritual" or "perfect" is capable of comparing "spiritual things with spiritual things."[62] The person who is still spiritually a "child" (1 Cor 3:1-2), who is nourished "with milk" and "is unskillful in the word of justice" nor is he able to receive the "solid food" of the divine wisdom and knowledge of the law (cf. Heb 5:13-14), cannot "compare spiritual things with spiritual." Those, on the other hand, who do not follow "the letter which kills" but the "spirit which quickens," receive the spirit of adoption, which allows them to penetrate beneath the letter of the law. Applying this same rule further to the story of Hagar and Ishmael, Origen dwells on the fact that Ishmael was given a bottle of water in contrast to a well of living water (Gen 21:14). Bringing together the texts of Genesis 21:14; 26:14-17; Galatians 4:28; and Proverbs 5:15-16 on this basis, Origen concludes:

> The bottle of the Law is the letter, from which that carnal people drinks, and thence receives understanding. This letter frequently fails them. It cannot extricate itself; for the historical understanding is defective in many things. But the Church drinks from the evangelic and apostolic fountains which never fail, but "run in its streets" (Prov 5:16), because they

---

[60]Saul Lieberman, "Rabbinic Interpretation of Scripture," in *Hellenism in Jewish Palestine: Studies in the Literary Transmission, Beliefs and Manners of Palestine in the I Century B.C.E.—IV Century C.E.*, 2nd ed. (New York: JTS, 1962), p. 60n104.

[61]See, e.g., Origen, *HomEx* 1.2; FC 71:228: "Anyone, therefore, can perhaps, 'by comparing spiritual things with spiritual things' and putting old things together with new and new with old, perceive the mystery of Egypt and the descent of the patriarchs into it, if he can investigate those words spiritually and follow the thought of the Apostle."

[62]Origen, *HomGn* 7.4.

always abound and flow in the breadth of spiritual interpretation. The Church drinks also "from wells" when it draws and examines certain deeper things from the Law.[63]

This method indicated by the phrase "comparing spiritual things with spiritual things" was also combined by Origen with the use of etymologies. An etymology employed in one place to explain a text can be used wherever the same name occurs to introduce the same meaning into the text, even though the texts themselves may be unrelated. Thus Origen interprets Genesis 45:27-28, in which both the names Jacob and Israel occur, in such a way that the name Israel represents spiritual intelligence, "he who sees in his mind the true life which is Christ, the true God."[64] He also says that the two names, Jacob and Israel, can be interpreted this way wherever they occur in Scripture and gives a long list of such occurrences.[65]

b. The use of etymology to generate meanings. The special fascination with the meaning of names should be seen as part of the more general Alexandrian conviction that the literal sense of Scripture covered a deeper meaning, which it was the task of the exegete to uncover.[66] The use of etymologies to generate interpretations of scriptural texts was hardly new with Origen. Although Paul does not make use of this procedure, it was well established in his time. Both Jewish and Greek authors exploited this possibility. Philo seems to have been the first to develop systematically the Old Testament etymologies, but he had predecessors.[67] Although a certain interest in etymology may be detected already in some of the Old Testament accounts of origins, Jewish authors may have been influenced by the use of this procedure in the Hellenistic world, particularly in the interpretation of the Homeric epics. Stoic authors employed this technique and sought to give it philosophical and linguistic justification. Ety-

---

[63]Origen, *HomGn* 7.5.

[64]Ibid., 15.3. This meaning is of course based on the story in Gen 32:28-30. Philo had already interpreted the name Israel to mean "he who sees God" (*Somn.* 2.173).

[65]Ibid., 15.4.

[66]See Franz Wutz, *Onomastica sacra; Untersuchungen zum Liber interpretationis nominum hebraicorum des Hl. Hieronymus* (Leipzig: J. C. Hinrichs, 1914), p. 352.

[67]See Lester L. Grabbe, *Etymology in Early Jewish Interpretation: The Hebrew Names in Philo* (Atlanta: Scholars Press, 1988).

mology and allegorical interpretation tended to go hand in hand.[68] Christian authors, above all Origen, used the work of Philo and added to the tradition material for the New Testament names.[69] By the third century alphabetical lists of names with these etymologies probably existed as well as lists that followed the order of the biblical books. Most authors under Alexandrian influence made use of the etymologies to generate allegorical or spiritual interpretations of the text.

c. Allegory: With and without the literal sense. The term "allegory" is often understood to be a "method" of interpretation, in distinction to the modern "historical-critical" method. In fact this ancient practice or procedure means merely that the text says one thing and the/a meaning is something else.[70] When Origen arrives at Genesis 21:9-10 in his homilies on Genesis, he says that he defers explicit commentary because the apostle has already indicated how these things are to be understood, and he quotes Galatians 4:21-24. He then notes that, despite the distinction made by Paul between the flesh and the promise, Isaac was in fact born according to the flesh. Sarah did in fact give birth, and Isaac was circumcised in the flesh.

---

[68]See especially the work by David Dawson, *Allegorical Readers and Cultural Revision in Ancient Alexandria* (Berkeley: University of California Press, 1992). Dawson points out that "in general, it seems that etymology was part of the Stoic theory of nominal meaning. Nominal meaning was a physical relationship between single names (nomina) and the objects they represented. In a process of primordial naming or dubbing by wise nomenclators, the 'essence' or 'content' of an object became the 'meaning' of the word used to name it" (p. 31).

[69]For the complex development up to the time of Jerome, see Wutz, *Onomastica sacra*, pp. 13-51; and R. P. C. Hanson, "Interpretations of Hebrew Names in Origen," *Vigiliae Christianae* 10 (1956): 103-23. Jerome, in the preface to his own work on the Hebrew names, seems to regard Origen as the author of the New Testament material. See *Liber interpretationis hebraicorum nominum*, ed. P. Antin, CCL 72 (Turnhout, Belgium: Brepols, 1959), p. 59. Wutz argues against the authorship of a New Testament *Onomasticon* by Origen (*Onomastica sacra*, pp. 38, 42) and attributes it rather to an unknown Alexandrian scholar working in the years 260-270 (p. 36).

[70]The word means literally "to say another thing" (from *allegorein*). It is the rhetorical procedure by which one thing is said and another intended. The verb *allegorein* is found first in Philo and Josephus and the substantive *allegoria* in Cicero. Plutarch says that what in his day was called *allegoria* was earlier called *hyponoia* (the underlying sense). See F. Büchsel, "allegoreo" *Theologisches Wörterbuch zum Neuen Testament*, ed. G. Kittel and G. Friedrich (Stuttgart: Kohlhammer, 1932), 1:260. Quintilian describes allegory as the continuous use of analogy, *metaphora continuata*, see H. N. Bate, "Some Technical Terms of Greek Exegesis," *JTS* 24 (1922–1923): 60. Both the noun and the verb were used also to describe allegorical interpretation. This practice already had a long history in the Greek-speaking world, particularly in the interpretation of Homer, before Philo used it systematically to interpret the Hebrew Scriptures (see especially Jean Pépin, *Mythe et Allégorie: Les origines grecques et les contestations judéo-chrétiennes*, nouvelle édition, revue et augmentée (Paris: Etudes Augustiniennes, 1976).

Paul's interpretation is remarkable because he says that these things, which undoubtedly occurred according to the flesh, are to be understood allegorically. Paul teaches in this way, says Origen, so that we may learn how to behave with regard to other things, above all with regard to those passages where the historical narrative does not seem to indicate anything worthy of the divine law.[71] Origen, who is often accused of neglecting or denying the literal level of the text, is here insisting on its reality. As he sees it, the interpretation that Paul has offered, and that is to serve as a model for others, does not obliterate the literal meaning of the historical narrative but is superimposed on it and presupposes it.

Origen makes reference to this text elsewhere, especially when he wishes to emphasize the possibility or need of an allegorical interpretation that does not invalidate the literal meaning of the text.[72] He cites it in the context of a lengthy discussion about the need to distinguish between those texts or prescriptions of the law that are not to be observed in any case according to the letter, those that are not to be completely changed by allegory but are to be observed as formulated in the Scriptures, and those that can stand according to the letter but for which one must also seek an allegorical interpretation.[73] An example of the latter is Genesis 2:24, in which it is stated that a man shall leave his father and mother and be united with his wife and the two will become one flesh. Paul has shown that this is to be interpreted allegorically (Eph 5:32), but the teaching of Jesus (Mt 19:5-6) makes it equally clear that it is to be observed according to the letter. Paul's interpretation of Genesis 21:9-10 in Galatians 4:21-24 is to be understood in the same way. The narrative can be understood literally, but it should also be understood allegorically as referring to the two testaments.

However, Origen also uses the term "allegory" to indicate a meaning that replaces the literal sense. To do this he often invokes the Pauline phrase "understanding the law spiritually," a reference to Romans 7:14, one of the Pauline texts most frequently cited by Origen. In attempting to

---

[71]Origen, HomGn 7.2.
[72]See Origen, ComJn 22.67-74; HomGn 13.3; ComRm 2.13 (907BC); HomJos 9.8; HomGn 6.1.
[73]Origen, HomNum 11.1.

explain the scandalous story in Genesis in which Abraham gives his wife to Abimelech, saying that she is his sister, Origen tells his listeners, somewhat polemically, that if anyone wants to understand these words literally, he should gather with the Jews rather than with the Christians. The passage that follows is worth citing at length for the juxtaposition of texts and the insight that it gives into Origen's understanding of the task of interpretation.

> But if he [the hearer] wishes to be a Christian and a disciple of Paul, let him hear Paul saying that "the Law is spiritual" [Rom 7:14], declaring that these words are "allegorical" [see Gal 4:22-24] when the law speaks of Abraham and his wife and sons. And although no one of us can easily discover what kind of allegories these words should contain, nevertheless one ought to pray that "the veil might be removed" from his heart, "if there is anyone who tries to turn to the Lord" [2 Cor 3:16]—"for the Lord is the Spirit" [2 Cor 3:17]—that the Lord might remove the veil of the letter and uncover the light of the Spirit and we might be able to say that "beholding the glory of the Lord with open face we are transformed into the same image from glory to glory, as by the Spirit of the Lord" [2 Cor 3:18].[74]

This passage is of particular interest because it gives us in condensed form almost the entire exegetical program of Origen. For him "spiritual" understanding of the law or of the Scriptures in general is equivalent to allegorical understanding. Origen uses the term "allegory" in the same sense as Paul to denote a text in which one thing is said but another is intended. The text taken literally does have meaning, but there is also another meaning, which is generally the more important one. This discovery of the allegorical meaning can also be described as removing the veil, for which interior conversion and possession of the Spirit of the Lord are required. In this case, by means of an etymology that ascribes the meaning of "virtue" to Sara, Origen is able to transpose the whole story onto the moral plane and to explain away the scandalous aspects of the story.[75]

---

[74]*HomGn* 6.1; FC 71:120-121.

[75]Origen, *HomGn* 6.1-2. He says that Sarah means "prince" or "ruler" and that this represents "virtue." Philo, *Abr.* 99 refers to some natural philosophers who said that Abraham's wife was "virtue," her Chaldean name "Sarra" meaning "ruler" (*archousa*) in Greek, because nothing is fitter for ruling or more capable of com-

In a similar situation in his homilies on Numbers, Origen remarks that if passages from Leviticus or Numbers are read without giving an adequate explanation, this can make the hearers critical of Moses. They begin to ask why such passages having to do with the Jewish ritual, the observance of the Sabbath and so on are read in church since they have nothing to do with the hearers. To avoid such scandals, says Origen, it is necessary to explain that "the Law is spiritual."[76] Here again Origen cites 2 Corinthians 3:16 as an exhortation to be converted to the Lord so that he will take away the veil and Moses will appear to us not as deformed but glorious and splendid.[77]

In the twentieth century it became popular to distinguish allegory and typology, but there is no justification for this distinction in antiquity before the time of Diodore of Tarsus, as has already been mentioned earlier (see chap. 5).[78]

---

manding than virtue. Origen concludes this homily with a defense of this kind of interpretation that is worth quoting for the outlook it reveals: "Let the Church of God, therefore, in this way understand the births, in this way receive the procreations, in this way uphold the deeds of the fathers with a fitting and honorable interpretation, in this way not disgrace the words of the Holy Spirit with foolish and Jewish fables, but reckon them to be full of honor, full of virtue and usefulness. Otherwise, what edification will we receive when we read that Abraham, such a great patriarch, not only lied to king Abimelech, but also surrendered his wife's chastity to him? In what way does the wife of so great a patriarch edify us if she is supposed to have been exposed to defilements through marital indulgence? These things are what the Jews suppose, along with those who are friends of the letter, not of the spirit."

[76]Origen, HomNum 7.2; Scheck, Numbers, p. 27.

[77]Origen, HomNum 7.2.

[78]For a survey of views on the subject, see my essay "The Concept 'Critical': What Would a Critical History of Theology Be Like?" in From the Nile to the Rhone and Beyond, pp. 479-96, especially pp. 487-90.

Biographical Sketches
of Early Christian Writers and
Other Significant Authors

Ambrose of Milan (c. 333–397; fl. 374–397) was bishop of Milan and teacher of Augustine who defended the divinity of the Holy Spirit and the perpetual virginity of Mary. He used the writings of Philo and Origen in composing his own homilies on Scriptural subjects.

Ambrosiaster (fl. c. 366–384) was the name given by Erasmus to the author of a work once thought to have been composed by Ambrose.

Athanasius of Alexandria (c. 295–373; fl. 325–373) was bishop of Alexandria from 328, though often in exile. He wrote his classic polemics against the Arians and in defense of Nicaea while most of the eastern bishops were against him.

Augustine of Hippo (354–430) was bishop of Hippo and a voluminous writer on philosophical, exegetical, theological and ecclesiological topics. He formulated the Western doctrines of predestination and original sin in his writings against the Pelagians.

Basil the Great (b. c. 330; fl. 357–379) was one of the Cappadocian fathers, bishop of Caesarea and champion of the teaching propounded at Nicaea in 325. His numerous writings include commentaries on the early chapters of Genesis and the Psalms as well as the Moral and Monastic Rules.

Benedict of Nursia (c. 480–547) is considered the most important figure in the history of Western monasticism. Benedict founded several monasteries, the most notable of which was at Montecassino, but his lasting influence lay in his famous Rule. The Rule outlines the theological and inspirational foundation of the monastic ideal while also legislating the shape and organization of the cenobitic life.

Caesarius of Arles (c. 470–543) was the bishop of Arles, renowned for his attention to his pastoral duties. Of his surviving works the most important is a collection of some 238 sermons that display an ability to preach Christian doctrine to a variety of audiences.

Cassian, John (360–432) was author of the *Institutes* and the *Conferences,* works purporting to relay the teachings of the Egyptian monastic fathers on the nature of the spiritual life, which were highly influential in the development of Western monasticism and recommended in the *Rule of St. Benedict.* He is the only western spiritual writer translated into Greek and venerated throughout the Eastern Churches as a saint.

Cassiodorus (c. 485–c. 580) was founder of the monastery of Vivarium, Calabria, where monks transcribed classic sacred and profane texts, Greek and Latin, preserving them for the Western tradition. He authored an extensive commentary on the psalms, making use of the earlier tradition.

Chromatius (fl. 400) was bishop of Aquileia, friend of Rufinus and Jerome and author of Scriptural commentaries and sermons.

Clement of Alexandria (c. 150–215) was a highly educated Christian convert from paganism, head of the catechetical school in Alexandria and pioneer of Christian scholarship. His major works, *Protrepticus, Paedagogus* and the *Stromata,* bring Christian doctrine face to face with the ideas and achievements of his time.

Cyprian of Carthage (fl. 248–258)was the martyred bishop of Carthage who maintained that those baptized by schismatics and heretics had no share in the blessings of the church.

Cyril of Alexandria (375–444; fl. 412–444) was Patriarch of Alexandria whose extensive exegesis, characterized especially by a strong espousal of the unity of Christ, led to the condemnation of Nestorius in 431.

Cyril of Jerusalem (c. 315–386; fl. c. 348) was bishop of Jerusalem after 350 and author of *Catechetical Homilies.*

Didache (c. 140). Of unknown authorship, this text intertwines Jewish ethics with Christian liturgical practice to form a whole discourse on the "way of life." It exerted an enormous amount of influence in the patristic period and was especially used in the training of catechumen.

Didymus the Blind (c. 313–398) was an Alexandrian exegete much influenced by Origen and admired by Jerome.

Diodore of Tarsus (d. c. 394) was bishop of Tarsus and an Antiochene theologian. He authored a great number of exegetical, doctrinal and apologetic works, which come to us mostly in fragments because of his later condemnation as the predecessor of Nestorianism. Diodore was a teacher of John Chrysostom and Theodore of Mopsuestia.

Ephrem the Syrian (b. c. 306; fl. 363–373) was a Syrian writer of commentaries and devotional hymns which are sometimes regarded as the greatest specimens of Christian poetry prior to Dante.

Epiphanius of Salamis (c. 315–403) was bishop of Salamis in Cyprus, author of the *Ancoratus* and a refutation of eighty heresies (the *Panarion*). Epiphanius was instrumental in the condemnation of Origen at the end of the fourth century.

Eusebius of Caesarea (c. 260/263–340) was bishop of Caesarea, partisan of the Emperor Constantine and first historian of the Christian church. He argued that the truth of the gospel had been foreshadowed in pagan writings but had to defend his own doctrine against suspicion of Arian sympathies.

Evagrius of Pontus (c. 345–399) was a disciple and teacher of ascetic life who astutely absorbed and creatively transmitted the spirituality of the Egyptian and Palestinian monasticism of the late fourth century. Although Origenist elements of his writings were formally condemned by the Fifth Ecumenical Council (Constantinople II, A.D. 553), his literary corpus continued to influence the tradition of the church.

Gennadius of Constantinople (d. 471) was Patriarch of Constantinople, author of numerous commentaries and an opponent of the Christology of Cyril of Alexandria.

Gnostic is the name now given generally to followers of Basilides, Valentinus, and even Marcion, Mani and others. The name derives from the Greek word for knowledge and is applied to writings that purport to communicate a secret knowledge. A characteristic belief is that matter is a prison made for the spirit by an evil or ignorant creator, and that redemption depends on fate, not on free will. The category is controversial.

Gregory of Nazianzus (b. 329/330; fl. 372–389) was a Cappadocian father, bishop of Constantinople, friend of Basil the Great and Gregory of Nyssa, and author of theological orations, sermons and poetry.

Gregory of Nyssa (c. 335–394) was bishop of Nyssa and younger brother of Basil the Great. A Cappadocian father and author of extensive works including the *Life of Moses*, catechetical orations and commentaries, he was a philosophical theologian of great originality.

Hesychius of Jerusalem (fl. 412–450) was a presbyter and exegete, thought to have commented on the whole of Scripture.

Hilary of Poitiers (c. 315–368) was bishop of Poitiers and called the "Athanasius of the West" because of his defense (against the Arians) of the common nature of Father and Son. His writings include commentaries on Matthew and the Psalms as well as theological and historical works. He was strongly influenced by Origen and Athanasius.

Ignatius of Antioch (c. 35–107/112) was a bishop of Antioch who wrote several letters to local churches while being taken from Antioch to Rome to be martyred. In the letters, which warn against heresy, he stresses orthodox Christology, the centrality of the Eucharist and unique role of the bishop in preserving the unity of the church.

Irenaeus of Lyons (c. 135–c. 202) was a bishop of Lyons who published the most famous and influential refutation of Gnostic thought, appealing to the "tradition" of the Church.

Jerome (c. 347–420) was a gifted exegete and exponent of a classical Latin style, now best known as the translator of the Latin Vulgate. He defended the perpetual virginity of Mary, attacked Origen and Pelagius and defended the growing ascetic movement.

John Chrysostom (344/354–407; fl. 386–407) was a bishop of Constantinople noted for his orthodoxy, his eloquence and his attacks on Christian laxity in high places. His literary production was enormous, including numerous homilies on Genesis and the Psalms.

Josephus, Flavius (c. 37–c. 101) was a Jewish historian from a distinguished priestly family. Acquainted with the Essenes and Sadducees, he himself became a Pharisee. He joined the great Jewish revolt that broke out in 66 and was chosen by the Sanhedrin at Jerusalem to be commander-in-chief in Galilee. Showing great shrewdness to ingratiate himself with Vespasian by foretelling his elevation and that of his son Titus to imperial dignity, Josephus was restored his liberty after 69 when Vespasian became emperor.

Justin Martyr (c. 100/110–165; fl. c. 148–161) was a Palestinian philosopher who was converted to Christianity, "the only sure and worthy philosophy." He traveled to Rome where he wrote several apologies against both pagans and Jews, combining Greek philosophy and Christian theology. He was eventually martyred.

Marcion (fl. 144) was a heretic of the mid-second century who rejected the Old Testament and much of the New Testament, claiming that the Father of Jesus Christ was other than the Old Testament God (*see* Gnostics).

Maximus of Turin (d. 408/423) was a bishop of Turin. Over one hundred of his sermons survive on Christian festivals, saints and martyrs.

Origen of Alexandria (b. 185; fl. c. 200–254) was an influential exegete and systematic theologian. He was condemned (perhaps unfairly) for maintaining the preexistence of souls while purportedly denying the resurrection of the body. His extensive works of exegesis focus on the spiritual meaning of the text. He was the first Christian writer to comment on most of the biblical books and his influence on later interpreters is incalculable.

Philo of Alexandria (c. 20 B.C.–c. A.D. 50) was a Jewish-born exegete who greatly influenced Christian patristic interpretation of the Old Testament. Born to a rich family in Alexandria, Philo was a contemporary of Jesus and lived an ascetic and contemplative life that makes some believe he was a rabbi. His interpretation of Scripture based the spiritual sense on the literal. Although influenced by Hellenism, Philo's theology remains thoroughly Jewish.

Rufinus of Aquileia (c. 345–411) was an Orthodox Christian thinker and historian who translated into Latin and thus preserved many of the works of Origen. Rufinus defended Origen against the strictures of Jerome and Epiphanius. He lived the ascetic life in Rome, Egypt and Jerusalem (the Mount of Olives).

Second Letter of Clement (c. 150). The so-called *Second Letter of Clement* is an early Christian sermon probably written by a Corinthian author, though some scholars have assigned it to a Roman or Alexandrian author.

Tertullian of Carthage (c. 155/160–225/250; fl. c. 197–222) was a brilliant Carthaginian apologist and polemicist who laid the foundations of Christology and trinitarian orthodoxy in the West, though he himself was later estranged from the catholic tradition due to what he considered its laxity, and became attached to the Montanist movement..

Theodore of Mopsuestia (c. 350–428) was bishop of Mopsuestia and founder of the Antiochene, or literalistic, school of exegesis. A great man in his day, he was later condemned as a precursor of Nestorius.

Theodoret of Cyr (c. 393–466) was bishop of Cyr (Cyrrhus) and an opponent of
Cyril of Alexandria who commented extensively on Old Testament texts as a
lucid exponent of Antiochene exegesis.

Select Bibliography

Ambrose. *Hexameron, Paradise, and Cain and Abel*. Translated by John J. Savage. FC 42. Washington, D.C.: The Catholic University of America Press, 1961.

———. "The Mysteries." In *Theological and Dogmatic Works*. Translated by Roy J. Deferrari. FC 44. Washington: Catholic University of America Press, 1963.

Aristotle. *Metaphysics, Books X-XIV*. Translated by Hugh Tredennick. LCL 287. Cambridge, MA; London: Harvard University Press; Heinemann, 1947.

Augustine. "On Christian Doctrine (*Doctr. chr.*)." In *St. Augustine's City of God and Christian Doctrine*. Translated by J. F. Shaw. NPNF 2. Series 1. Edited by Philip Schaff and Henry Wace. 14 vols. 1886-1900. Reprint, Peabody, MA: Hendrickson, 1994.

———. *The City of God, Books XVII-XXII*. Translated by Gerald G. Walsh. FC 24. Washington, D.C.: Catholic University of America Press, 2008.

———. "Expositions on the Book of Psalms (*Enarrat.*)." NPNF 8. Series 1. Edited by Philip Schaff and Henry Wace. 14 vols. 1886-1900. Reprint, Peabody, MA: Hendrickson, 1994.

———. *On Genesis: Two Books on Genesis Against the Manichees; On the Literal Interpretation of Genesis, An Unfinished Book*. Translated by Roland J. Teske. FC 84. Washington, D.C.: Catholic University of America Press, 1990.

———. *The Trinity*. Translated by Stephen McKenna. FC 45. Washington, D.C.: Catholic University of America Press, 2002.

Basil of Caesarea. "Homily on Psalm 48." In *Exegetic Homilies*. Translated by Agnes Clare Way. FC 46. Washington, D.C.: The Catholic University of America Press, 1963.

Caesarius of Arles. *Sermons, Volume II*. Translated by Mary Magdeleine Mueller. FC 47. Washington, D.C.: Catholic University of America Press, 1964.

Cassiodorus. *Explanation of the Psalms*. Translated by P. G. Walsh. ACW 51, 52, 53.

New York: Paulist Press, 1990/1991. 3 vols.

Cicero, Marcus Tullius. *De Officiis*. Translated by Walter Miller. LCL 30. Cambridge, MA: Harvard University Press, 1913.

———. "On Divination." *De Senectute; De Amicitia; De Divinatione*. Translated by William Armistead Falconer. LCL 154. London: William Heinemann, 1923.

———. "On the Nature of the Gods (*De natura deorum*)." In *De Natura Deorum; Academica*. Translated by H. Rackham. LCL 268. Cambridge, MA: Harvard University Press, 1933.

———. *Tusculan Disputations*. Translated by J. E. King. LCL 141. London; New York: W. Heinemann; G. P. Putnam's Sons, 1927.

Clement of Alexandria. "Christ the Educator (*Paed.*)." In *Fathers of the Second Century: Hermas, Tatian, Athenagoras, Theophilus, and Clement of Alexandria*. Translated by F. Crombie et al. ANF 2. Edited by Alexander Roberts and James Donaldson. 10 vols. 1885-1887. Reprint, Peabody, MA: Hendrickson, 1994.

———. "The Exhortation to the Greeks." In *Exhortation to the Greeks; The Rich Man's Salvation; To the Newly Baptized*. Translated by G. W. Butterworth. LCL 92. Cambridge, MA: Harvard University Press, 1919.

———. *Stromateis*. In *Fathers of the Second Century: Hermas, Tatian, Athenagoras, Theophilus, and Clement of Alexandria*. Translated by F. Crombie et al. ANF 2. Edited by Alexander Roberts and James Donaldson. 10 vols. 1885-1887. Reprint, Peabody, MA: Hendrickson, 1994.

Cyril of Alexandria. *Letters 1-50*. Translated by John I. McEnerney. FC 76. Washington, D.C.: The Catholic University of America Press, 1987.

Eusebius of Caesarea. *Praeparatio Evangelica*. Translated by E. H. Gifford. Grand Rapids: Baker Book House, 1981.

———. *The Proof of the Gospel, Being the Demonstratio Evangelica of Eusebius of Caesarea*. Translated by W. J. Ferrar. London; New York: SPCK; Macmillan, 1920.

Gregory of Nyssa. *Ascetical Works*. Translated by Virginia Woods Callahan. FC 58. Washington, D.C.: The Catholic University of America Press, 1967.

———. *Homilies on the Song of Songs*. Translated by Richard A. Norris Jr. Atlanta: Society of Biblical Literature, 2012.

———. "On the Making of Man." In *Gregory of Nyssa: Dogmatic Treatises, etc.* Translated by William Moore. NPNF 5. Series 2. Edited by Philip Schaff and Henry Wace. 14 vols. 1886-1900. Reprint, Peabody, MA: Hendrickson, 1994.

———. "On the Soul and Resurrection." In *Dogmatic Treatises, etc.* Translated by William Moore. NPNF 5 Series 2. Edited by Philip Schaff and Henry Wace. 14 vols. 1886-1900. Reprint, Peabody, MA: Hendrickson, 1994.

Jerome. "Homily 66 on Psalm 88 (89)." In *The Homilies of Saint Jerome*, Volume 2. Translated by Marie Liguori Ewald. FC 57. Washington, D.C.: Catholic University of America Press, 2005.

John Cassian. *The Conferences.* Translated by Boniface Ramsey. ACW 57. New York: Paulist Press, 1997.

———. *The Institutes.* Translated by Boniface Ramsey. ACW 58. New York: The Newman Press, 2000.

John Chrysostom. *Commentary on the Psalms.* 2 vols. Translated by Robert C. Hill. Brookline, MA: Holy Cross Orthodox Press, 1998.

———. *Homilies on Genesis 1-17.* Translated by Robert C. Hill. FC 74. Washington, DC: The Catholic University of America Press, 1986.

———. *Homilies on Genesis 18-45.* Translated by Robert C. Hill. FC 82. Washington, D.C.: The Catholic University of America Press, 1990.

———. "Homilies on the Epistles of Paul to the Corinthians." In *Saint Chrysostom: Homilies on the Epistles of Paul to the Corinthians.* Translated by Talbot W. Chambers. NPNF 12. Series 1. Edited by Philip Schaff and Henry Wace. 14 vols. 1886-1900. Reprint, Peabody, MA: Hendrickson, 1994.

———. "Homilies on the Gospel of Matthew." In *Saint Chrysostom: Homilies on the Gospel of Saint Matthew.* Translated by George Prevost. NPNF 10. Series 1. Edited by Philip Schaff and Henry Wace. 14 vols. 1886-1900. Reprint, Peabody, MA: Hendrickson, 1994.

———. "On the Epistle to the Hebrews." In *Saint Chrysostom: Homilies on the Gospel of St. John and the Epistle to the Hebrews.* Translated by Frederic Gardiner. NPNF 14. Series 1. Edited by Philip Schaff and Henry Wace. 14 vols. 1886-1900. Reprint, Peabody, MA: Hendrickson, 1994.

Maximus of Turin. *The Sermons of St. Maximus of Turin.* Translated by Boniface Ramsey. ACW 50. New York: Newman Press, 1989.

Origen. "Commentary on John." In *Origen: Commentary on the Gospel According to John, Books 13-32.* Translated by Ronald E. Heine. FC 89. Washington, D.C.: The Catholic University of America Press, 1993.

———. "Commentary on the Gospel of Matthew (*ComMt*)." In *The Gospel of Peter; The Diatessaron of Tatian; The Apocalypse of Peter; The Vision of Paul; The Apoc-*

alypses of the Virgin and Sedrach; The Testament of Abraham; The Acts of Xanthippe and Polyxena; The Narrative of Zosimus; The Apology of Aristides; The Epistles of Clement (complete text); Origen's Commentary on John, Books 1-10; and *Commentary on Matthew, Books 1, 2, and 10-14.* Translated by John Patrick. ANF 9. Edited by Alexander Roberts and James Donaldson. 10 vols. 1885-1887. Reprint, Peabody, MA: Hendrickson, 1994.

———. *Contra Celsum.* Translated by Henry Chadwick. London: Cambridge University Press, 1953.

———. *On First Principles.* Translated by G. W. Butterworth. New York: Harper & Row, 1966.

———. "Homilies on Genesis." In *Origen: Homilies on Genesis and Exodus.* Translated by Ronald E. Heine. FC 71. Washington, D.C.: The Catholic University of America Press, 1982.

———. *Homilies on Jeremiah; Homily on 1 Kings 28.* Translated by John Clark Smith. FC 97. Washington, D.C.: Catholic University of America Press, 1998.

———. *Homilies on Joshua.* Translated by Barbara J. Bruce. FC 105. Washington, D.C.: The Catholic University of America Press, 2002.

———. *Homilies on Leviticus 1-16.* Translated by Gary Wayne Barkley. FC 83. Washington, D.C.: The Catholic University of America Press, 1990.

———. *Homilies on Luke, Fragments on Luke,* pp. 5-162. Translated by Joseph T. Lienhard. FC 94. Washington, D.C.: The Catholic University of America Press, 1996.

———. *Homilies on Numbers.* Translated by Thomas P. Scheck. Downers Grove, IL: IVP Academic, 2009.

———. *The Song of Songs: Commentary and Homilies.* Translated by R. P Lawson. ACW 26. New York: Newman Press, 1956.

Philo. "Allegorical Interpretation of Genesis 2 and 3 (*Leg.*)." In *Philo: In Ten Volumes (and Two Supplementary Volumes).* Translated by F. H. Colson and G. H. Whitaker. LCL 226. Cambridge, MA; London: Harvard University Press; W. Heinemann, 1929.

———. "Concerning Noah's Work as a Planter (*Plant.*)." In *Philo: In Ten Volumes (and Two Supplementary Volumes).* Translated by F. H. Colson and G. H. Whitaker. LCL 247. Cambridge, MA; London: Harvard University Press; W. Heinemann, 1930.

———. "On the Creation (*Opif.*)." In *Philo: In Ten Volumes (and Two Supplementary Volumes).* Translated by F. H. Colson and G. H. Whitaker. LCL 226.

Cambridge, MA; London: Harvard University Press; W. Heinemann, 1929.

———. "On Dreams (*Somn.*)." In *Philo: In Ten Volumes (and Two Supplementary Volumes)*. Translated by F. H. Colson and G. H. Whitaker. LCL 275. Cambridge, MA; London: Harvard University Press; W. Heinemann, 1934.

———. "On Mating with the Preliminary Studies (*Congr.*)." In *Philo: In Ten Volumes (and Two Supplementary Volumes)*. Translated by F. H. Colson and G. H. Whitaker. LCL 261. Cambridge, MA; London: Harvard University Press; W. Heinemann, 1932.

———. "On Moses (*Mos.*)." In *Philo: In Ten Volumes (and Two Supplementary Volumes)*. Translated by F. H. Colson. LCL 289. Cambridge, MA; London: Harvard University Press; W. Heinemann, 1935.

———. *Philo: Supplement I. Questions and Answers on Genesis.* Translated by Ralph Marcus. LCL 380. Cambridge, MA: Harvard University Press, 1953.

———. "On the Posterity and Exile of Cain (*Post.*)." In *Philo: In Ten Volumes (and Two Supplementary Volumes)*. Translated by F. H. Colson and G. H. Whitaker. LCL 227. Cambridge, MA; London: Harvard University Press; W. Heinemann, 1929.

———. "The Sacrifices of Cain and Abel (*Sacr.*)." In *Philo: In Ten Volumes (and Two Supplementary Volumes)*. Translated by F. H. Colson and G. H. Whitaker. LCL 227. Cambridge, MA; London: Harvard University Press; W. Heinemann, 1929.

———. "On the Unchangeableness of God (*Deus*)." In *Philo: In Ten Volumes (and Two Supplementary Volumes)*. Translated by F. H. Colson and G. H. Whitaker. LCL 247. Cambridge, MA; London: Harvard University Press; W. Heinemann, 1930.

Plutarch. "How the Young Man Should Study Poetry (*De aud. poet.*)." In *Moralia*. Vol. 1. Translated by Frank Cole Babbitt. LCL 197. Cambridge, MA: Harvard University Press, 1927.

Seneca, Lucius Annaeus. "On Anger (*De ira*)." In *Moral Essays*. Translated by John W. Basore. LCL 214. London; New York: W. Heinemann; G. P. Putnam's Sons, 1928.

Tertullian. "Anti-Marcion (*Marc.*)." In *Latin Christianity: Its Founder, Tertullian*. Translated by S. Thelwall et al. ANF 3. Edited by Alexander Roberts and James Donaldson. 10 vols. 1885-1887. Reprint, Peabody, MA: Hendrickson, 1994.

Theodoret of Cyrrhus. *Commentary on the Letters of St. Paul.* Translated by Robert

C. Hill. Brookline, MA: Holy Cross Orthodox Press, 2001.

———. *Commentary on the Psalms*. Translated by Robert C. Hill. FC 101, 102. Washington, D.C.: The Catholic University of America Press, 2000.

Thucydides. *The Peloponnesian War*. Translated by Richard Crawley. London; New York: J. M. Dent; E. P. Dutton, 1910.

Name and Author Index

Abraham, 25, 65, 72-74, 86, 88, 106, 142-45, 148-49, 162, 198-99, 223-24, 235-36
Albright, William F., 200-201, 203
Alexandria, Alexandrians, 24, 37, 40, 61-62, 65, 77, 89, 108, 115, 117, 190-92, 229, 232-33
Allen, Leslie C., 209
Ambrose, 25, 65, 77, 97-98, 122, 133-34, 148, 164, 199
Ambrosiaster, 91, 93, 96, 98
Antioch, Antiochene, 40-41, 46, 61, 89-90, 116-17, 191, 221
Aphrodite, 54
Aristeas, 18, 22, 62, 76, 88, 107, 194, 227
Aristobulus, 18, 63-64
Aristotle, 55, 58
Augustine, 25, 97-98, 108, 122-23, 129, 133, 136-37, 139-42, 164-67, 170, 175-76, 182, 190, 198
Basil (the Great), 29, 55, 116, 136-37
Briggs, Charles A., 206-8
Cassian. See John Cassian
Cassiodorus, 164, 166, 168, 171, 176-77, 183-84, 186, 190
Celsus, 21, 28, 34-35, 37, 92, 188, 196
Chromatius (of Aquileia), 82
Chrysostom. See John Chrysostom
Cicero, 25, 45-46, 55-58, 90, 122, 233
Clement (of Alexandria), 18, 22-24, 40, 47, 55, 63, 65, 77, 108-10, 130, 220-21
Cole, Stephen J., 210
Copan, Paul, 202-5
Cyprian (of Carthage), 96
Cyril of Alexandria, 40, 84-85, 102, 116, 221, 227
Cyril of Jerusalem, 96
Dahood, Mitchell J., 206
David (king), 25, 84, 87, 163, 165, 169, 171, 179, 181, 189, 221
Didymus ("the blind" of Alexandria), 24, 40, 55, 65, 77, 115-16, 144-46, 148, 164, 213, 221, 227
Diodore (of Tarsus), 40, 90, 116-17, 221, 227, 236

Empedocles, 52, 54
Ephrem, 87, 98
Epiphanius, 196-97
Eusebius (of Caesarea), 24, 28-29, 40, 63, 77, 86-87, 110, 114, 164, 166, 169, 173, 179-80, 189, 213, 221, 223
Gregory (of Nazianzen), 29, 55
Gregory (of Nyssa), 29, 92, 97-98, 116, 135, 141, 214, 220, 227
Hagar, 25, 72-74, 89, 91, 142-46, 198-99, 231
Hays, Richard B., 230
Hera, 48, 51-52
Heraclitus (Pseudo-), 22, 50-54, 195, 221
Hesiod, 45, 47-48, 53
Hilary (of Poitiers), 25, 122, 190
Holcomb, Justin S., 210, 218
Holladay, William L., 211-12
Homer, 21-22, 45-55, 57, 59, 109, 114, 117, 195-96, 221, 225, 232-33
Ignatius (of Antioch), 105, 110
Irenaeus, 38, 77, 105-6, 110
Israel (Jacob), 74, 232
Jacob (patriarch), 72, 74, 181, 232
Jaeger, Werner, 17-18, 22, 46-47
Jerome, 25, 90-91, 101, 108, 111, 115, 122, 172, 179, 189, 213, 233
Jesus (of Nazareth), 20, 23, 25, 28, 36, 38-39, 50-51, 61, 65, 79-84, 86-87, 93, 96, 104-5, 109, 130, 142, 144, 149, 155-56, 158-63, 168, 170, 172, 179, 181, 183-85, 187-88, 201-2, 204, 207, 210-11, 215, 218-19, 223, 234
John Cassian, 19, 91-92, 107, 123-25, 135, 152-53, 155, 191, 220
John Chrysostom, 21, 24, 30, 40-43, 46, 82, 84, 87, 90, 93, 99, 102, 104, 107, 117-18, 129, 132-33, 136-41, 163-65, 179-81, 185-86, 192, 208, 210, 215, 221, 224
Jonah, 84-85
Josephus, Flavius, 65, 233
Joshua (book of), 25, 105, 149, 151-52, 155-61, 188, 193, 200, 204-5, 210, 213, 228
Julian (the Apostate), 117, 123
Justin Martyr, 106, 110
Keough, Sean, 220

Kronos, 48
Kugel, James L., 219
Lamb, David T., 202, 204
Marcion, 21, 23-24, 36-40, 81, 105, 118-20, 122
Maximus (of Turin), 96
Moses, 18, 20, 22-23, 51, 61-65, 67, 69-70, 75, 80-82, 84-88, 92-93, 96-97, 100-105, 109, 127, 130-31, 137, 141, 148, 152-53, 155-56, 194, 196, 199, 203, 218-19, 222-27, 230, 236
Origen, 18, 21, 24, 27-41, 43-44, 55, 59, 65, 77, 79, 81, 83-84, 86, 88-90, 92-95, 99-101, 103, 105-6, 110-15, 117, 127, 131-32, 140-41, 144, 147, 155-64, 172, 179, 187-91, 193, 196, 211, 213-15, 217-36
Paul (of Tarsus = St. Paul), 18-19, 23-24, 35, 37-39, 65, 79, 81, 87-91, 93-100, 102-6, 108-9, 111-12, 117, 134, 142-47, 169, 177, 191, 198, 219, 222, 226-27, 230-35
Philo (of Alexandria), 18, 20-24, 36-37, 40-41, 44, 55, 61, 65-77, 94-95, 110, 112, 115, 127-28, 130, 136, 138, 142-47, 188, 194-95, 198, 213, 215, 218, 221-22, 225, 227, 232-33, 235
Plato, 22, 47-49, 51, 53-55, 59, 128, 195, 215
Plotinus, 59, 233
Plutarch, 49
Plutarch (Pseudo-), 22, 50, 53-54
Ptolemy (Letter of), 21
Ptolemy (king), 62, 63
Sarah, 25, 72-74, 89, 142-46, 148, 162, 198-99, 233
Schwartz, Regina M., 201
Seneca, 57-58
Serapion, 135, 153-54
Sextus Empiricus, 59
Sheridan, Mark, 20, 74, 81, 88, 95, 111, 189, 217, 227
Simonetti, Manlio, 117, 227
Stoics, 22, 49, 55-58, 120, 232-33
Strauss, Richard L., 199
Tertullian, 24-25, 38, 118-22
Thales, 52
Theodore (of Mopsuestia), 90, 97-98, 117, 221, 227

SUBJECT INDEX

ainigma, 33, 46
ainitesthai (and related forms), 46,
    117, 197, 220-21
allegory (*allegoria*), 26, 40, 46,
    49-52, 59, 70, 72-74, 89-91, 97,
    106, 116-17, 143-45, 152-53, 162,
    164, 218, 221, 227, 233-36
alogia, 63
anger, 19, 24-25, 32-36, 42-43,
    57-59, 67, 69-70, 76-77, 107, 110,
    112, 120, 122-25, 150, 154,
    165-66, 177, 179-81, 185, 188,
    192
anoikeion, 44, 66-68, 71
anthropomorphism, 64, 66, 125,
    197
anthropopathism
    (*anthrōpopathos*), 35, 37, 44, 58,
    66-67, 72, 75-77, 108, 114-16,
    118, 125, 204, 214
apatheia, 57, 76, 121
atopia (folly), 22, 66
axios tou theou (worthy of God), 17,
    19, 22-24, 29, 32-33, 43-44, 49-50,

    55-56, 63, 65, 67-68, 77, 87-89,
    107-8, 112-14, 116, 119-25, 220,
    224-26, 234
defectus litterae (missing literal
    sense), 113, 225
dignus (and related forms), 24-25,
    33, 56, 112-13, 119-21, 123
ethics, 51-52, 54, 201, 218
etymology, 31, 75, 94-95, 173, 175,
    189, 232-33, 235
hyponoia, 49, 59, 233
literal (letter), 40-44, 51, 53,
    63-64, 70, 77, 88-90, 94, 101,
    107, 111-13, 118, 120, 123-24,
    128-29, 136, 139, 144-45,
    154-55, 159, 166, 172, 178, 188,
    195-97, 203, 205, 212-15,
    218-20, 225-26, 229, 232-35
logia, 40, 232
Logos, 34-35, 109, 131, 220
mythos (myth, mythical), 48-55,
    57, 59, 63, 69, 109, 114, 128,
    194-97, 233
oikonomia, 21, 27-28, 30

oracles, 40, 61, 76, 221-23
pathē, 32
philanthrōpia, 20, 25, 215
physics, 51, 54, 218
prosopon, prosopologia, 192
Septuagint, 27, 30-31, 68, 107, 164,
    174, 222
synkatabasis, 21, 30, 32, 41, 115,
    118, 137, 141
theologos (theologian), 20, 23
theology (*theologia*), 20-21, 27-29,
    44, 47
theoprepōs (and related forms), 41,
    43-44, 50, 66, 68, 70, 77, 114,
    116-18, 129, 137-39, 141, 165,
    197, 225
Torah, 80
tropophorein, 30-31
type, 117
typology, 90-91, 117, 236
useful (a criterion of
    interpretation), 19-20, 24, 29,
    32, 44, 85, 95, 113, 127, 144-45,
    155, 200, 212, 214, 226-29, 236

SCRIPTURE INDEX

John
1:21, *86*
6:49-58, *97*
12:31-32, *186*

Acts
1:16, *184*
1:20, *181-83*
1:29, *79*
2:34, *163, 185*
3:22-25, *85*
7:48, *75*
17:22, *37*

Romans
1:17, *167*
2:4-5, *35*
2:28-29, *160*
4:1-8, *230*
7:14, *235*
7:22, *131*

1 Corinthians
2:13, *229-31*
3:1, *30*
3:1-2, *231*
3:17, *177*

6:17, *169*
9:8-10, *88*
9:9-10, *88*
9:10, *19, 127, 200*
10:1-11, *97*
10:4, *188-90*
10:6, *153*
10:11, *191, 226-27*
13:12, *103*

2 Corinthians
3:1-6, *230*
3:6, *214*
3:7-18, *100, 219*
3:14, *100*
3:16, *100, 235*
3:17-18, *219*
3:18, *134*
5:4, *131*
5:16, *103*

Galatians
1:12-11, *38*
3, *109*
3:3, *147*
3:16, *230*
3:24, *144*

4:1, *144, 145*
4:8-9, *147*
4:21-24, *89, 233*
4:22-24, *235*
4:22-26, *88*
4:22–5:1, *143*
4:28, *231*

Ephesians
2:3, *35*
2:14, *84*
3:14-21, *131*
4:31, *154*
5:3-4, *155*
5:32, *234*
6:17, *161*

Philippians
3:20, *134*

Colossians
2:14-15, *155*
3:1, *157*
3:8, *35*

1 Thessalonians
5:23, *218*

1 Timothy
2:7, *79*
6:16, *124*

2 Timothy
3:16, *20, 95, 212, 227-28*

Hebrews
1:5, *137*
1:3, *163, 185*
1:13, *163, 185*
2:13, *30*
3:3-6, *87*
5:13-14, *231*
8:1, *163, 185*
10:1, *146*
10:12, *163, 185*

James
4:6, *172*

1 Peter
5:5, *172*

Revelation
17–18, *209*

Finding the Textbook You Need

The IVP Academic Textbook Selector
is an online tool for instantly finding the IVP books
suitable for over 250 courses across 24 disciplines.

ivpacademic.com